OUT EAST
— IN THE—
MALAY
PENINSULA

THE AUTHOR

G.E.D. Lewis, B.Sc., Ph.D., Dip. Ed., FRGS
Malayan Education Service 1938 – 1963

OUT EAST
— IN THE —
MALAY
PENINSULA

G. E. D. Lewis

PETALING JAYA
PENERBIT FAJAR BAKTI SDN. BHD.
1991

Penerbit Fajar Bakti Sdn. Bhd.
3, Jalan 13/3, 46200 Petaling Jaya
Selangor Darul Ehsan
© Penerbit Fajar Bakti Sdn. Bhd. 1991

ISBN 967 65 1594 9

Printed in Malaysia by
Percetakan Mun Sun Sdn. Bhd., Selangor Darul Ehsan

FOREWORD

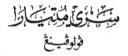 𝔖eri 𝔐utiara
Pulau Pinang

D r G.E.D. Lewis has asked me to write a foreword for this book which will be published soon. I am very delighted to do so as I have known him as one of the most respected education officers and educationists in Malaysia. This book will tell the story of a man who started work at Penang Free School, Malaysia, in 1938 to teach, to guide and to train thousands of young people to become good citizens of the country. Dr Lewis has been to every nook and cranny of the Malay Peninsula, and has served with distinction in several states of the Federation. He is known and respected by the ministers, the leaders of all communities, and particularly by thousands of friends, who have been members of the staff and pupils in several famous Malaysian educational institutions.

As I have served as the Malaysian Director-General of Education for quite some time, after Malaysia had gained her independence, I am aware that Dr Lewis is always held in high respect and great esteem even after he had long left the country. I consider it a great privilege to have gained his confidence and friendship, as well as that of his elder brother, another renowned educationist, the late Mr T.P.M. Lewis. I have no doubt that the services they have rendered will long be remembered by the former pupils, parents and well-wishers of the whole nation throughout this country.

I find this book very interesting, informative and most

valuable as it is full of witty remarks, and it is very well-substantiated with facts and figures. It is very fortunate indeed that Dr Lewis has been able to record his notes, anecdotes and experiences since, before, during, and after the Second World War in Malaysia with such vividness. Very few autobiographies can be as complete and as substantial as this one in describing such a long series of events and incidents for more than half of a century.

In conclusion, I wish to thank and congratulate most sincerely Dr G.E.D. Lewis on having written his personal memoirs in an interesting way to capture the reader's interest and concentration from the beginning to the end. The book will serve as an outstanding record of contemporary history during a very important period of Malaysian educational development.

Hamdan Jahir

TUN TAN SRI DATUK (DR) HAJI HAMDAN BIN SHEIKH
TAHIR

8th May, 1991.

PREFACE

his is a book about myself written mainly for my former students who are approaching old age, and some of whom may now have time to read it. It is also written for anybody else who may be interested to know what went on in the last days of British colonial administration in Malaysia.

I am grateful to Datuk Noordin bin Keling, Datuk Idris Babjee, Dr Ng Siew Kee and Datuk Mustafa Ali for some help in the writing of this book, and to the publishers for inviting me to do it.

G. E. D. Lewis

CONTENTS

Chapter 1

MY ROOTS IN WILD WALES

The Welsh people are light and agile. They are fierce rather than strong, and totally devoted to the practice of arms. Not only the leaders but the entire nation are trained in war. Sound the trumpet for battle and the peasant will rush from his plough to pick up his weapons....

Giraldus Cambrensis: Journey through Wales.
12th Century.

In the twelfth century, the Welsh went to war against the English to preserve their land and especially their language. They have more or less succeeded in doing that, and so the Welsh and the English are at peace today. Indeed, many of the Queen's Ministers and Judges are Welsh; when I was a boy, the Prime Minister was a Welshman. My father too was a supporter of the establishment, for he was a Detective Inspector at New Scotland Yard, London.

He was, of course, born in Wales in 1867 on a farm called Felinrhos, near the village of Llanycrwys. He was brought up first on a small farm called Abermangoed and then on a much bigger farm called Brynteg both in the Upper Cothi river valley, a most beautiful mountainous forested and fox-ridden part of Wales near Pumsaint in Carmarthenshire. Here lies the aptly named tiny village of Cwrt y Cadno which translated into English means the meeting point of foxes.

He was the eldest of three brothers and four sisters, and as Brynteg could not support such a large family he was no doubt compelled to leave and seek his fortune elsewhere. This he did by joining the Metropolitan Police, in London in 1889.

One of his earliest postings was as a Police Constable in Vine Street Police Station, off Piccadilly. Here he gained some notoriety for stopping runaway horses, a dangerous act which only a physically fit young man, familiar with horses, such as my father was coming from a mountain farm in rural Wales, could perform.

My father must have been ambitious to get on, for he studied French and other subjects at King's College, University of London, while he was still only a Police Constable, which I imagine was rather unusual in those days. So it is not surprising that he soon managed to gain promotion into the C.I.D. New Scotland Yard in 1892, reaching the rank of Detective Inspector in 1909.

As a detective in Scotland Yard he made many journeys overseas, which he described in his diary as 'on business'. Thus in 1905 he had to escort a senior colonial civil servant back to Lagos to face charges, for the misappropriation of government funds. Of course, there were no aeroplanes in those days, and he had to escort the culprit back to Nigeria in a ship and share a cabin with him.

As the prisoner was apparently a well-educated and charming person, my father decided to give him some freedom and allowed him to mix with the other passengers. Soon his prisoner was one of the most popular persons on board the ship. Indeed he became so popular that the other passengers made the man who had 'stolen the cash box' the Treasurer of the ship's sports committee, a most unfortunate development, to say the least.

Unfortunately this visit to Lagos led indirectly to my father's death, for while waiting for the trial to take place at Lagos he contracted dysentery, a disease which apparently was a contributory cause of his death many years later in 1912, at the early age of 45, in fact only a few weeks before I was born.

My father had married my mother in 1903. She came from a farm called Birds Hill near Llandeilo in South Wales, about 32 kilometres from my father's birthplace. So when he died in 1912, she returned to Birds Hill (where her brother and sister still lived) with my two brothers Tommy (TPM), John (JSA) and myself (GED).

And so I came to spend the earliest years of my life in Wales, and in a thoroughly Welsh part of Wales where I learnt to speak Welsh at home and in chapel, and English at school. Welsh was, therefore, my mother tongue and English a 'foreign' language.

My early years at Birds Hill were very happy. My two older brothers Tommy and John were good companions, though Tommy, as he was the eldest, always seemed to be going away somewhere. He was the first to go to school in England, the first to go to a university and play rugby, and the first to go out East. He was the pioneer who showed us the way, so he was my idol for many years.

But being the youngest of the three had some disadvantages as well as advantages. For example, I always had to wear my brothers' clothes, read their books, and so on. However, I did eventually get a suit that was especially made for me. It was a knickerbocker kind of suit with many pockets. I well remember the first day I went to school wearing that suit.

One of the most persistent memories I have of my early days in Wales is of going to school. I recall very little of the actual school work. This is probably because my 3-kilometre walk to school was full of interest. First, there was the bit down the drive from our farm to the white gates at the entrance to Birds Hill. Then the walk down the short hill known in Welsh as Rhiw yr adar (the hill of birds) with its hedges covered with violets, and across the steep hump of the Roman bridge (for this section of my route was along an old Roman road) over a small torrent of a stream. On the other side of the bridge the route went past the house of a farmer called John Gwyn (whose dog bit me on the leg one morning), then up a steep hill past two thatched cottages, in one of which there was a weaver, and alongside a thick dark forest.

Beyond the dark forest, the road climbed up another hill, and past several birds' nests hidden in the hedge. One of them I treasured very much, for the bird which lived there was a 'yellow hammer', a beautiful yellow bird quite rare as far as I was concerned. Finally, on reaching the top of the hill, past a broken-down cottage which had some juicy gooseberries in its derelict garden, the road sloped gently down towards Llangathen and the school.

The schoolmaster at Llangathen School in my time was a certain W. W. P. Lewis, a very kind and tolerant man, who could easily be persuaded to our way of thinking when the occasion arose. Thus when one day, during a one o'clock break we spied a fox being chased by the hounds across the

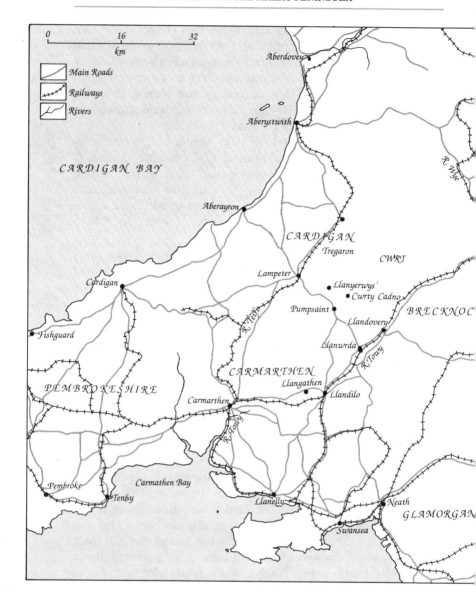

WEST WALES, 1912

During my early days in Wales (1912 – 1922), the railway was the most important method of travelling 'long' distances, for example from Llandeilo to Swansea.

adjacent field, we did not hesitate to join in the excitement. As the chase continued and time went by, most of the children dropped out and returned to school, but Alfred my classmate and I were in at the death in a nearby wood, and managed to acquire some of the foxes' fur in the process as well, we returned about one hour late, and handed the foxes' fur to the delighted W. W. P. Lewis. There was no reprimand, only 'better ask me for permission next time boys'.

But the greatest excitement of all which took place during the First World War, was when I was at school at Llangathen one day, and I was having lunch at a nearby cottage. There were no school meals in those days, and my mother had arranged for me to have lunch at a nearby cottage, where Sarah and Mary, two elderly sisters, lived.

I was half-way through my lunch, which consisted of cocoa and sandwiches (the former provided by Sarah and Mary, the latter by my mother), and the gramophone with its enormous speaker was going full blast for my entertainment. Suddenly Sarah rushed in through the cottage door and in great excitement summoned her sister in Welsh, to come out of the cottage immediately for she said, 'There is a great animal coming up the valley.'

I was out like a shot and there in the valley directly in front of us was a huge airship with a cross on it. It was a German Zeppelin! We were thunderstruck. A British airship would have been a surprise, but an enemy German Zeppelin slowly going past us up the valley was unbelievable. Fortunately, it dropped no bombs and fired no bullets. I never did discover what happened to it, where it had come from and where it went. Presumably it was on a daring reconnaissance, but of course all it saw at Llangathen was a tranquil rural scene.

Apart from such excitements as fox hunting and the confrontation with the Zeppelin, we children also had other interesting and sometimes dangerous pastimes. For example, one 'forbidden' pastime was to hire a bicycle which had no brakes, from Jim Ost the postman's son at Llangathen and free-wheel it down the hill from the school across the main road to Aberglasne Mansion. There were only very occasional motor cars on this road in those days, but there was some slight risk that we might collide with one some day and probably get killed—hence its attraction!

Another pastime was to go down to Aberglasne Mansion during the lunch break and wave at the German prisoners of war who were kept there behind bars. Of course we thought they were highly dangerous criminals and felt very brave doing this.

Bird nesting was also very popular and I had a collection of birds' eggs. On one occasion one of the 'naughty' girls at Llangathen School, Olive Haines, instigated me to try and rob an owl's nest of its eggs. I tried and the owl, to our great surprise, flew straight at us and put us to flight in no time.

There was, I regret, some dishonesty and vandalism too. The main dishonest thing we did was to steal some of the weights used for weighing out groceries from the small sweet shop next door to the school, and then tell the shopkeeper that we had found them outside, for which service he would reward us with some sweets. I suspect the shopkeeper knew what we were up to and tolerated us.

Vandalism was a rare phenomenon. But there was one occasion when Alfred my classmate and I, for no reason that I can now think of, spent half an hour on our way home from school, breaking the slates of the chapel roof. I suppose to damage such a holy roof provided us with some excitement.

Bullying was a rare event. There was, however, a period lasting about a year when I was given a hiding pretty well every night on the way home from school. The bully would force me to fight another boy about my age, then if I showed signs of overcoming him, was set upon by the bully. I could not of course cope with two boys and so always got the worst of it, that is until the bully boy left school. Then I regret to say I paid back with interest all the indignities I had suffered for a year—but not for long, just a couple of weeks.

My class at Llangathen consisted of three: Phyllis Lewis the schoolmaster's daughter, Arianwen Rees the daughter of the owner of the sawmills at Broad Oak, and Alfred the son of the tailor at Cilsane—all living within walking distance of Llangathen. Our education at Llangathen was relaxed, but it obviously did us no harm; perhaps it did us a lot of good, for three out of the four of us went on to universities.

Although we all came from Welsh-speaking homes, Welsh was not taught; indeed we were forbidden to speak it at school. Imagine my surprise many years later to discover that my teacher Miss Evans who throughout my early school days only spoke to us in English at school was in fact a fluent Welsh speaker.

My attitude to the English was of course affected by these facts. As a Welsh-speaking boy I was proud of being Welsh, for after all were not the Welsh and the other Celts the first people to inhabit the British Isles, whereas the English came much later. So why was our Welsh language, the language of the original inhabitants, forbidden at school? Presumably because Wales was a small country, and there were more English than Welsh, and so the English could do what they liked. This seemed to me to be very unfair and so I did not like the English very much, at least for a while.

This did not of course make me disloyal to our country, or even a Welsh nationalist. In those days we were at war with Germany, and after all Lloyd George, a Welshman, was Prime Minister and my mother's hero. So, consequently I decided I would have to tolerate the English and their stuck-up ideas about the Welsh language.

The denigration of the Welsh language by the English upset me quite a lot; but what upset me even more was when young Welsh people went to London for a few weeks and came back saying they had forgotten how to speak it! Of course I didn't believe them; in fact I despised them for it.

I loved the life at Birds Hill. Although it was only a small farm I was able to pursue various outdoor pursuits such as riding, rabbitting, nesting and catching butterflies.

Riding my Welsh Cob 'Dick' was my favourite pastime. I did this without the aid of a saddle, just as the Red Indians did. Of course I had no saddle because I could not afford one, though I don't think I realized the reason for it at that time. Consequently, I frequently fell off Dick, especially when I had him in a gallop—but put this down to inexperience and bad horsemanship.

So when one day I went to stay with relatives in the Brecon area, it came as a great surprise to me to find them riding on saddles. My Brecon relatives also appeared to prefer to speak English to Welsh. Indeed I put down such sophistication as riding with saddles as being something to do with the English, and left it at that.

I was an expert at catching rabbits and also moles. I was of course too young to handle a shotgun, and so had no alternative but to use snares. Traps I thought too cruel, but apparently snares were all right. Rabbits sometimes provided pocket money, for a rabbit could be sold for a shilling.

Collecting birds' eggs was a popular pastime with all country boys. There also seemed to be plenty of birds. But I never collected the eggs of the yellow hammer, for it was my favourite bird, and I wanted it to breed.

As for butterflies, I must have run miles and miles chasing them. Butterflies such as the Peacock and Red Admiral were quite common, but there was one butterfly I had great trouble catching. It was called the 'Little Blue'. The Little Blue was a very elusive little butterfly. It would suddenly appear and fly at great speed along a hedge and then just as suddenly disappear over the hedge as one was about to cover it with a net.

I also had experience with many other animals. For example, once as I was walking across a field, a rabbit ran up to me. I picked it up and it appeared to be shivering with fright; then suddenly I saw a stoat coming straight for me. I took off immediately for home with the rabbit, scared stiff and convinced that the stoat was after both of us.

Summer was of course the best time of the year, and hay-making the busiest and most interesting time. But the methods used were labour intensive and back-breaking. For me the most exciting part of it was the cutting of the hay. This was done with a machine pulled by two horses. The excitement was to chase any wildlife hiding in the long grass, especially towards the end, when a small plot of standing grass was left in the middle of the field providing protection for who knew what. Perhaps a fox, a rabbit, a bird, or a hedgehog?

The back-breaking bit was getting the hay dry. This meant turning the rows of hay by hand with the aid of a hand rake, not only once but two or three times. And if there was rain, turning it over again so that the green or damp underside got the sun.

One of the great advantages of being brought up in the country is that one is close to the earth and the sky. Moreover, it so happened that Birds Hill and its area had much interesting geology and archaeology.

Thus one day while sweeping the farmyard, I decided to remove a small rock which projected out of the ground. It was not a very hard rock, and when I eventually got it out of the ground it disintegrated into thick layers or 'flags' of soft stone. When I examined it, I discovered on its flat surface the clear impression of a fishlike animal. I just couldn't imagine how such a fishlike animal could have got into our farmyard, especially as we were many miles from the sea.

Some ten years later when I was a student studying geology at the University of London, I discovered Birds Hill stands on a rock called 'Llandeilo Flags' which were laid down in Ordovician times more than 450 million years ago – and that Ordovician rock is one of the oldest rocks in the world. I also learned that the impression of the fishlike animal was a rather special fossil called a *trilobite*.

But, of course, as a small boy I did not realize that the land that was now the farmyard at Birds Hill had long ago been under the sea, and that I had just dug up the fossil of a 450 million-year-old sea creature!

Another item of special interest at Birds Hill was the Roman road which ran along the edge of the farm. It was a road that had been built by the Romans almost 2000 years before and long before the English had colonized England. The road continued as a footpath through the neighbouring estate owned by Lord Dynevor, our local aristocrat, on its way to the local town of Llandeilo. I often walked along this footpath when I was sent on an errand to Llandeilo, and would sometimes stop to look at the cuttings where the road had been originally constructed through high ground. I would wonder what the conditions had been like 2000 years ago, and how the Romans had moved the earth. No doubt the Welsh had been forced to do it, I thought.

Of course, one of the delights of country-life in the old days was to be out in the dark, under the night sky with its sparkling stars and the rising moon above. I well remember one warm summer night lying on my back on the lawn at Birds Hill, studying the stars and looking deep into space and wondering where it all ended.

The moon was of special interest, because on a really clear night, it did not seem to be so far away, for even with the naked eye one could see shaded parts, which I thought might be mountains or forests. Little did I imagine that one day a man would go to the moon, or that I would actually shake hands at the Royal Geographical Society, London, with Neil Armstrong himself, the first man to go to the moon. I asked him if he had been frightened of going to the moon. His answer was that while he had been very confident of reaching the moon, he had not been at all confident that he would ever get off it again!

My early life at Birds Hill (1912–1922) coincided, of course, with the First World War; which raged on the continent of Europe less than 500 kilometres away. I was of course very much aware of the war, for there were German prisoners of war locked up in the mansion at Llangathen, while the sudden confrontation with the German Zeppelin one morning during my cocoa break had given me a bit of a fright.

I was, however, not greatly inconvenienced by the War, although there were certain tasks we boys were called upon to perform to help with the war effort. One task expected of us was to collect the loose wool that sheep had shed in farmers' fields on barbed wire, prickly bushes and so on and to bring it to school. I remember getting a special commendation for a big pile of wool I brought one day. I did not of course tell my teacher that I had got it off a dead sheep!

Although Birds Hill was a very small farm, my Uncle Stephen who 'farmed' it, was required as a war effort, to grow a certain quantity of wheat, even though the soil and especially the climate were not suited to wheat. The Government planted the wheat, but the farmer had to harvest it. I remember how the field of wheat was cut by hand with a special kind of scythe, then stacked in stooks, and finally removed to some place off the farm.

Travelling far from Birds Hill was a rare event, and travelling out of Wales unthinkable. The first long journey I made during the First World War was by train to see my Auntie Jack who was a volunteer nurse in a Swansea hospital, where the patients were nearly all wounded Canadian soldiers.

Then there was a journey I made to Mumbles, a seaside resort near Swansea, where my mother took me to see a certain Dr Knoyle, who had been a friend of my father's in London. We went for a walk along the beach, with his wife and little daughter aged about eight. The daughter and I quarrelled over the possession of a piece of heather and I pushed her into the sea! Not a very noteworthy event you may think, except for the fact that I met this little girl again many years later in London, and eventually married her and never quarrelled again.

But there was one journey I made more frequently, and that was to the upper Cothi valley to see my grandfather and grandmother at Brynteg, in what was then quite a remote and wild Part of Wales. Although, today, the journey takes only about half an hour by car; in 1918 when I was only about six years old, the journey to Brynteg via Llandeilo and Llanwrda seemed to take all day.

There were, of course, almost no cars in Wales in those days, and 'long' journeys were made by pony and trap, or by train, or more likely by both. And so it was, when my mother took me to Brynteg farm.

One day there was great excitement, for news came that my elder brother Tommy had gained admission into a boarding school in England—The Royal Masonic School at Bushey, near London. Then came the sad morning when we all had to get up very early while it was still dark, so that Tommy could be taken in the pony and trap to Llandeilo to catch the train for London.

His coming back from school in England soon became very special occasions. My mother would get very excited, and everything had to be dropped for the reunion with her adorable and innocent Tommy *bach*.

But Tommy *bach* was not as innocent as he looked. To my delight he confided in me that at his school in England, every boy had to join a special class where he learnt some kind of handicraft. He had joined the metalwork class, and had secretly made a key so that he could lock himself in his railway compartment for the long journey back from London to Wales. In this way he was able to have the sole use of his Great Western Railway third class compartment to his own first class self! I began to see the value of English education, at last!

Chapter 2

WE MIGRATE TO ENGLAND

The grass is greener on the other side of the fence.

English proverb.

Soon after my brother Tommy won an exhibition to go to Jesus College Oxford, my mother began talking about how nice it would be if she could go back to London. And especially how nice it would be if we could all go and live in Bedford Park, an attractive area in West London, where each house has its own garden.

I was therefore not surprised when the big decision was made, and my mother and aunt decided (my Uncle Stephen was not consulted very much on such important matters) that they would move to London. The plan was to buy a hotel, that is a respectable hotel where respectable people stayed for a week or so—not an inn or pub where anybody could stay, where alcohol was served and where people got drunk and rowdy!

Much correspondence then ensued with a solicitor my father and mother had known as a friend when they lived in London. His name was Woods and his office was located in Chancery Lane, near the Law Courts, so I thought he must be a very clever lawyer to have his office in such a prestigious locality. In due course a suitable hotel, with the grand name of Hotel London, was found in Lancaster Gate, near Hyde Park—a highly desirable part of London, and where I was told I would be able to ride in the famous 'Rotten Row', a carrot no doubt so that I would readily fall in with their wishes.

And so after much secret to-ing and fro-ing, the great news at last leaked out in Wales that the people at Birds Hill were moving to London. The 'sale' at Birds Hill was a sad landmark in my life, for all that was dear to me was going to be left behind. However, as a special concession my mother said I could take with me, my collection of butterflies, and also 'Jack Sprat' my Welsh terrier, the successor to 'Campbell Bannerman' my old Collie dog, who had recently died of old age.

I remember very little about the train journey to London, but I remember vividly the ticket collector at Carmarthen, where we had to change trains. He was an impressive uniformed gentleman and he not only punched our tickets, but also sold my mother a book he had written about his exciting life as a ticket collector at Carmarthen and of the amusing things that had happened to some of his passengers!

Our first night in London was spent at a hotel near Chancery Lane, and it proved quite exciting, for we arrived in the dark and within an hour Jack Sprat had escaped. My mother promised that next day she would try and find him.

As the wife of a former Detective Inspector at Scotland Yard, my mother was not in the least bit intimidated by police stations, and was off to the nearest one the next morning. To my surprise she was soon back with the news that Jack Sprat had already made history, for according to the police he had been chasing buses along High Holborn throughout the morning, but had escaped capture by the police and evaded death from the traffic. However, after a day-long hue and cry Jack Sprat eventually tired of his new found hobby, and allowed himself to be arrested and tied up in return for some food.

Our arrival at the Hotel London in Lancaster Gate, which my people had bought was, at first, a rather unnerving and intimidating experience for me. But when the porter at the hotel called me 'Sir', and me only a small boy, I felt much better. Nobody had done that to me in Wales, so I began to warm to England.

I also found that living in a hotel owned by one's mother had many advantages. For example, I discovered that if I left my shoes outside my bedroom door at night, they were clean by the morning. And there was no need to make my bed. A young Welsh chambermaid always made it for me, and the daring ones an 'apple pie' bed as well on special occasions!

Of course all the staff at the Hotel London were Welsh, for my mother believed in supporting home industries. In any case, there was much unemployment in South Wales at the time, and so she was able to recruit a loyal hard-working and contented staff without difficulty. Although my mother and aunt treated the staff as if they were part of our family, holidays were strictly limited in those days. Consequently John Jones, our cheerful Welsh porter, was faced with a considerable problem one day when he desperately wanted to return to Wales to see a Wales v England rugby match at Cardiff. So he thought he had solved it when he presented my mother with a telegram he had just received from Wales which read 'To John Jones, Hotel London, Lancaster Street WC2. Return at once father ill. Signed John Jones.' He had absentmindedly signed it himself! My tactful mother ignored this lapse and suggested he should go straight away. And as expected he was back in a couple of days, for he said his father had made an unexpected recovery.

The brochure of the Hotel London was brief and to the point. It described its attractive dining-room, quoted the charges for staying and mentioned some of its virtues, one of which was 'constant hot water'. This latter description was truly prophetic, for although our first few years at the hotel were reasonably profitable, the later years co-incided with the Wall Street Crash of 1929 and the Great Depression of the 1930s which followed it, and was an economic nightmare. Indeed our survival was in the balance for many years and my poor mother was indeed in constant hot water.

As my father had been a Freemason, it was planned that I should go to the Royal Masonic School, Bushey near London. However, I was too young for entry when we arrived in London, so for the time being I was sent to a rather seedy private school at Westbourne Park in London. It was a strange school, for my class teacher administered corporal punishment almost every day with a short stick which he brought down on the offending boy's hand, for the slightest offence. For some reason I was never caned, probably because being a country boy I must have been more amenable to discipline than my classmates, most of whom were rough, tough, cheeky Cockney boys.

In 1925 when I reached the age of 13 years I gained admission, as my brothers had done before me, into the Royal Masonic School, Bushey. This was a school built for the sons of Freemasons whose fathers like mine had died, and which was run on the lines of a public school. I considered myself fortunate to have been accepted, for I had failed at my first attempt at passing the entrance examination. Nevertheless I did not consider myself not good enough, merely that many of the questions in the examination were absurd, such as a detailed knowledge of Roman numerals.

Anyhow here I was preparing for the great step into the unknown, with a long list of requirements such as spare shirts, socks and handkerchiefs, shoes, a tuck box and so on. When I eventually arrived at my first boarding school, I was quite surprised, even pleasantly surprised, for I had never seen a school like it. The school buildings, the school grounds and the school playing fields were most impressive.

The school buildings were arranged in a square around a large grass lawn, across which it was forbidden to walk. At each of the four corners of the square lawn there was a small tower and at the front a large imposing clock tower. Adjoining each small tower there were two houses; consequently there were eight houses in all. Two of the houses were for the junior boys, the remainder were for the senior boys. These houses were known by one of the letters A—H, as well as by names. There were fifty boys in each house, thus making a total of four hundred in all.

I was allocated to the E House, whose housemaster was a Mr Francombe; indeed the house was called Francombe House. But some of the other houses had names of long departed housemasters. My new school was very different from my old school at Westbourne Park. Here there was no time for private shopping or for entertaining one's friends, for everything was done by the clock. We got up at 7.30 a.m., washed in cold water, winter and summer, and then went to the school dining-hall for breakfast at 8.00 a.m. School started at 9 a.m. and the classes lasted three quarters of an hour. When it was time to go to the next class, a bell rang. Every minute of one's life was organized. Leaving the precincts of the school was forbidden, and so we had no time or opportunity for private ventures or thoughts. However, I soon got used to the idea and quite enjoyed it. The idea was of course to keep us so busy that we had no time to get up to mischief. It was, I suppose, a kind of monastery but we were far from being monklike.

My housemaster, Mr Francombe, was strict and on one occasion because we had been rather slow changing into our football shorts and jerseys, punished us by devoting one whole afternoon to practising the art. I suppose we dressed and undressed twenty times that never-to-be-forgotten afternoon, and I remember the air was full of dust by the time the exercise was all over.

But he was also a very kind man, and on Sunday nights he would often read to us weird and exciting ghost stories mainly located in Devon, which I suspect was his birthplace. I was also one of his favourites and he would refer to me as that boy from 'Llan-diddle-diddle-dido' which was his rendering of my home town of Llandeilo in Wales. It was of course not uncommon for the English to regard it odd that the Welsh should have their own language, and joke about it and especially about Welsh place names which they couldn't pronounce. But I decided that it was better to be noticed (for whatever reason) than to be ignored, and did not readily take umbrage when some of the English boys teased me about being Welsh.

After a year in the Junior House I was moved to a Senior House called D or Latham House. The housemaster, a Mr Stephens was a terror! Apart from being very strict, he had an ingenious method of unravelling schoolboy pranks and escapades. His technique was to send for the culprits, call in the first one and place him in a room by himself. Then after the lapse of a few minutes he would call in the second and almost immediately say 'Well, I know all about it, so what have you got to say?' The second culprit would of course be wondering what the first one had said and would talk too much, before being passed in to the isolation room. Then the third culprit would be called in, to be met by the same, 'I know all about it', and he too would proceed to spill the beans. By this devious method, Mr Stephens could unravel the most complicated schoolboy plot! He was much feared.

Fortunately for me, he was mad keen on rugby football. I now showed signs of becoming a good sportsman and soon found myself in the School Rugby XV. I also became a good runner, being the Intermediate Champion and the Victor Ludorum in two successive years, as well as holding the school record for the half-mile for under 14-year-olds at 2 minutes 31½ seconds! In addition my elder brother Tommy, formerly of D House, was also playing rugby for Oxford, so Mr Stephens was well pleased with me and I could do no wrong. Indeed he positively discriminated in favour of those such as I who were in the School Rugby XV. For example, once a week he conducted a Latin test consisting of twenty short questions. For ordinary mortals all questions had to be answered correctly—it was a case of twenty or nothing. But those in the rugby team were allowed two mistakes. So my weekly score was more often than not eighteen or nineteen, when it should have been zero.

Unfortunately I was not so popular with the Headmaster, Mr T. R. N. Crofts. At least I presume so for he denied me a much coveted Honours Cap at rugby (a wonderful looking velvet cap with a gold tassel) because he said I was not in the sixth form, having previously denied me the opportunity to enter it.

I enjoyed my schooldays immensely, but unfortunately my distinctions at school were entirely on the athletic track and the rugby field. For during my last but one year at school the Headmaster got the idea of forming a Commercial class for those he thought could not pass the School Certificate. And that is where I ended up, together with at least another twenty boys who should not have been there.

There was of course a lot to be said for having a commercial class where one could learn useful subjects, such as bookkeeping, shorthand and typing. But the idea that the boys in such a class could not sit for the School Certificate was ill conceived. For by this decision many boys including myself were denied the opportunity of qualifying themselves for entry into a university while at school.

Although my educational achievements at school were disappointing, I nevertheless developed an interest in geography. This was no doubt partly due to my discovery as a small boy of fish fossils on the farm in Wales, but it was mainly due to our excellent teacher of geography. 'Geoger' White as he was known operated from a specially designed geography room, which was full of interesting instruments and exhibits, including a working model of a volcano, which was made to give off smoke when Geoger White was in a good mood! While under him I also gained a little distinction and a modest prize for an essay I wrote on the Tetrahedral Theory for the distribution of the land masses of the world, while I was still just fourteen years of age. In this way I gained his respect and encouragement and a lifetime interest in the subject.

But in 1928 I had to leave school, when I was still only sixteen years of age, slightly demoralized, but determined to make good in the City of London and perhaps like the legendary Dick Whittington, make a fortune. To this end I got a job as a clerk in a Charitable Society, located in the heart of the city, in fact literally next door to the Guildhall. The staff of the society consisted of three persons: the Secretary, the clerk (myself) and of all things a butler. The butler was necessary because it was customary for the Society to meet once a month to deliberate on the affairs of the Society and afterwards to have a sumptuous lunch complete with claret and so on.

The Governors who attended these meetings were, unknown to me, very distinguished people and included Aldermen of the City of London, Baronets, Knights and so on, and it was my humble duty to open the door to them when they attended these monthly meetings. On the first occasion, I opened the door to several, but they walked past me without appearing to notice me. One of them was different; indeed I managed to get into an animated conversation with him, for at least twenty minutes. It might be said I got on with him like a house on fire.

When the meeting and the lunch were over, however, I discovered that the Secretary was furious with me. He reminded me that my job was to answer the telephone and open the door and not to chat up Sir Ernest Wild, the Recorder of London. He fired me on the spot. So within two weeks of getting my first job, I had got the sack!

I was in despair at this sudden turn of events, and considered committing suicide, as I went home on the underground train to Lancaster Gate. But I decided that would upset my mother too much, so gave up the idea. When

I got home and told my mother the terrible news she seemed quite happy, indeed very happy. She then gave me a long lecture saying that I was actually very intelligent, and that all I needed to do was to pass my London Matriculation examination, and then I could go to a university. In fact she went so far as to say that I was more intelligent than my brother Tommy, who was then at Oxford University. Of course I did not believe a word of it, but decided for once to please my mother and do as she suggested.

Although the London Matriculation was considered to be a slightly harder examination to pass than the School Certificate, I decided to study for the former as it qualified one for direct entry into the University of London. However, as I had by now earned my own living for two weeks, I thought it would be infra dig to go back to school even if a school could be found to take me. So I registered with Wolsey Hall Oxford and studied for the London Matriculation through their correspondence course.

I enjoyed the course very much, worked quite hard, took the examination and failed in French! I suppose this was not very surprising considering that I had never spoken to a Frenchman in my life, and that my total acquaintance with the French came out of one book. My mother then decided that I should go to a crammer called The University Tutorial College in London. They were expert at the job of getting students through the Matriculation examination, and I passed after six months.

My period at the University Tutorial College was most entertaining, for there I came across a most unusual bunch of students. They consisted of a mixed bag of both sexes, drop-outs, misfits, late developers, those expelled from school, English, Welsh, Indians and Arabs. In fact one of my best friends was an Arab by the name of Abdullah.

In those days Abdullah cigarettes were very popular in England, and one of their best known advertisements some-times appeared in the non-smoking carriages of the Under-ground and stated 'No smoking—not even Abdullah'. The University Tutorial College was a ramshackle wooden building and very much a fire hazard. So when one day the Principal of the College put a large notice on the College Notice Board stating 'No Smoking' and my friend Abdullah added in his nondescript writing 'Not even Abdullah', he nearly got the sack for his sense of humour.

After matriculating, my first inclination was to take a degree in law, but I soon discovered that a knowledge of Latin (which I had not touched since my schooldays) was necessary for that. I therefore decided to read Economics, for like many young men I had already started to take an interest in politics and economics. At first I was attracted to the Liberals perhaps because Lloyd George was my mother's hero. But I soon switched to the new Empire Free Trade party. Indeed I canvassed successfully on behalf of Vice-Admiral Taylor in the South Paddington constituency by-election in 1937 and he became the one and only Empire Free Trade candidate ever to get into Parliament.

In 1926 my elder brother Tommy had obtained an appointment in the Colonial Service in the Far East, his first appointment being as an education officer at the Anderson School, Ipoh, in the Federated Malay States of Malaya, as it was then called. He wrote enthralling letters about how the native Malays wore sarongs and how they used a special dagger called a *kris* to kill people; about the hard-working Chinese and how they smoked opium which gave them pleasant dreams, and how there were special opium-smoking saloons for this purpose; he also wrote about the mosquitoes and how one had to sleep under a mosquito net at night; and about the heat and the rain.

He also described how a few months after he arrived at Ipoh, it rained for about two months without stop and there was a devastating flood (the famous 1926 flood). He also described how the flood was so bad he could not get to the Anderson School; how the bridge (a pontoon bridge) across the huge Perak river, near Kuala Kangsar had been swept away so that Ipoh was completely cut off from south Malaya; and how a train had been completely submerged by flood water in the Malay State of Pahang.

I soon became obsessed with the Federated Malay States, and started reading any book I could get hold of on this fascinating land, especially those by Hugh Clifford and Frank Swettenham. The postage stamps were also most exciting, and there was one for a district called Sungei Ujong, showing a tiger leaping through long grass which I found particularly dramatic. Even the books, especially if they had spent some years in the tropics, had an erotic smell about them, and some had little holes, pierced right through from front to back by little insects only found in the Malay Peninsula. I found the pull of the Malay Peninsula with its tigers and opium smokers irresistible.

I now made enquiries about how I could get into the Colonial Service like my elder brother Tommy and indeed like my second brother John (for he too went out to the Federated Malay States in 1928 to join the Customs Department) had done. I discovered that it was not going to be at all easy, mainly because of the severe economic depression which hit the world in 1929. Consequently, there were very few vacancies in the Colonial Service and to stand a chance, I would need to have a good honours degree, that is a First Class or an Upper Second Class degree, as well as something to show that I was an above average sportsman—a Cambridge Blue would be perfect, but to be captain of one's college rugby or cricket team might be all right.

I had already decided to take an honours degree in Economics, specializing in Geography, and on the advice of my brother enrolled in 1932 as a full-time student at the London School of Economics. It was good advice, for the LSE as it is generally called is one of the world's leading institutions for the study of economics.

My introduction to the LSE was, however, a traumatic experience—an emotional shock. I had not expected such students. Most of them were rowdy and left wing, a large percentage were Communists, and some were Anarchists. None of them were Empire Free Traders! So I gave up my interest in politics and concentrated on my studies.

Another more serious problem that faced me when I gained admission to the LSE was a financial one. My mother could ill afford to pay the university fees, so I plucked up courage and went to see the Secretary of the Freemasons in Great Queen Street, in London. I told him my story, how I had failed to do well academically at school, but had since matriculated and was now at the University of London. The Secretary whose name was Mallory was a benign and fatherly old gentleman. He beamed approval at what I told him, and without hesitation provided me with more than adequate funds to see me through my university days, enough that is to pay for the university fees, some books and my subscription to Smoky Joe—my night club! 'A friend in need is a friend indeed', and Mallory proved to be a friend indeed. I spent four years at the LSE, the first year was taken up with the Intermediate B.Sc. examination, the other three years preparing for the final Honours B.Sc. (Econ.) degree. In the first year I was introduced to several new subjects such as the British Constitution and Formal Logic. I found them intensely interesting, especially Logic and the intricacies of the syllogism. Indeed Professor Wolf informed me that I had done one of the best papers in the examination, and suggested I should proceed to take an honours degree in Logic and Philosophy.

Although his interest was flattering, I decided to read Economics and Geography—Economics in case I went into business or administration, and Geography in case I became a teacher. I studied methodically and consistently, never cut my lectures, played rugby on Wednesdays and Saturdays, and made merry on Saturday nights, usually until the early hours of the next morning.

Sometimes when I found myself stranded in Piccadilly Circus without any money to get home, or to buy an early morning 'brunch' at a Lyons Corner House, I would call at the Vine Street Police Station where a police friend by the name of Detective Sergeant Fred Jones, would drive me home at His Majesty's expense in a Flying Squad car! Irregular no doubt but a good deed for a deserving case.

As a result of these nocturnal activities I got for myself an undeserved reputation at the LSE for being a devotee of night clubs and the title of NCK (Night Club King). I say undeserved because my 'wild nights' were under control, and restricted to once a week unlike some of my fellow students who did it several times a week. I must also have been a very naive Night Club King, for my favourite night club was 'Smoky Joe' in Gerrard Street, where you could always get a drink any time and was always full of girls. It was many months before I discovered why it was always full of girls— it was a lesbian club!

As Hitler was threatening war in Europe in the mid-1930s I joined the University of London Officers Training Corps, with a view to joining the Royal Artillery in case of war. It so happened that when the final Honours degree results were due to be published in 1936, I was attending an OTC Camp on Salisbury Plain, so I arranged for my close friend Professor Seaborne Davies to send me the results by telegram. In due course the expected telegram arrived, and when I hurriedly opened it, I nearly had a heart attack for it said 'Failed to get your results, as not yet published, Seaborne'. However, a few days later I received another telegram from the roguish Seaborne, 'Got your Upper Second Ged, Well done. Seaborne.'

During the four years I spent at the LSE, my main relaxation in winter was playing rugby for the LSE and occasionally for the University. However, in 1935 I was made Captain of the LSE Rugby XV, and thereafter devoted most of my spare time with the Club, consequently many if not most of my friends were members of the Rugger Club. This was also encouraged by the fact that the Rugger Club had its own table in the Refectory.

One of my best friends was Hugh Wheldon (later Sir Hugh Wheldon), a fellow Welshman, a charming extrovert, who never stopped talking. Hugh was quite a keen rugby player, but he would only play as stand off half, for he said that was the position that best suited his talent and ethnic origins. He of course later distinguished himself as head of BBC Television and as a BBC presenter.

Others of my friends included Peter Ensor, who later joined the Indian Civil Service, Basil O'Brien who made a name in business and especially Philip Adams, who was the Captain of the LSE Soccer XI, and who also joined the Indian Civil Service. He distinguished himself as a District Commissioner with the head-hunting Naga hill tribes in Assam during the Second World War.

Two others of my special friends, with whom I played rugby for the London Welsh were Norman Davies and Vaughan Roberts. Both were outstanding outside halves and both studied law and became solicitors in South Wales. Norman died young, but Vaughan became a colonel in the Welsh Regiment and is still going strong. In fact we have been close friends for over 60 years.

As for girlfriends, like all young men I had a number, and on reflection I must admit they were all extremely nice girls.

The most notable ones were Elizabeth Watkins, whose father Watcyn Thomas was a famous Welsh rugby player; Margaret Carey Evans whose uncle was Lloyd George the former Prime Minister; Sorreno Nicols a daughter of the then Italian Ambassador to the UK and Jacqueline O'Neil Roe whose father was a colonel in the Indian Army.

I also had a close association for a while with a very rich young woman, who insisted that we should patronize at her expense the expensive places she was accustomed to. So for several months I found myself eating out at the Dorchester Hotel, the Cafe Royal, Oddeninos, Simpsons in the Strand and so on.

The Dorchester was the last word in sophistication in the 1930s and my rich girlfriend and I normally frequented a small bar on the first floor where the barman was well known for his exotic cocktails. Little could I have foreseen that one of my former schoolboys, the Sultan of Brunei, would one day buy the whole place! The Cafe Royal was another of our favourite drinking holes and it was also a popular rendezvous for famous musicians and artists. On one occasion we found ourselves sitting at a table next to Charlie Kunz the famous jazz pianist. His girlfriend wore a monocle. But as our equally famous genial Italian waiter 'George' explained, she only wore it for effect, for the monocle had no lens in it!

One of our favourite eating out places was Oddeninos, an expensive restaurant almost next door to the Cafe Royal in Regent Street. Here our special waiter was a Russian emigre called Felix. There after dinner for two, I would be obliged to give him a £5 tip—about £50 in today's money! And so for a while I found out how the rich live.

During my last year at the LSE I made some tentative inquiries about getting a post overseas but not a commercial job, for in those days earning one's living by selling things was considered to be infra dig. Nevertheless I was most surprised when one day I was sent for by the Director of Recruitment at the LSE who asked me how would I like to go to India in the Indian Civil Service. I was most surprised because such plum jobs had in the past been the preserve of graduates from Oxford and Cambridge, and were certainly not offered to students from the notorious LSE. This unexpected honour was probably due to the activities of Professor Harold Laski, who had been campaigning against this discrimination, and I presume I must have been the first surprised beneficiary.

Although loath to turn down such a plum appointment, I decided to keep to my original plan of going to the Federated Malay States. So I applied for the Malayan Civil Service and at my second interview was offered the Nigeria Civil Service, which of course was not what I wanted, for Nigeria was even further away from Malaya than India. I therefore ventured to ask the Colonial Office official who interviewed me whether it would not be possible for me to go to Malaya. His reply was 'We are not in the habit of bargaining' and brought the interview to a close, but then as an afterthought said that if any of those selected for Malaya could not go, I would be offered the post. Malaya, however, was one of the best paid of all the Colonial Administrative posts, and so not surprisingly there were no withdrawals.

So I now found myself in the position of having turned down two good appointments and without anything to show for it. I now decided to try for an educational appointment in Malaya and registered at the Institute of Education, University of London to read for a Diploma in Education in their Colonial Department. To my surprise I found myself studying for the Diploma alongside the three probationers who had just been selected for the Malayan Educational Service: Tony Hill, Bill Jackman and Douglas Muir. I also studied Malay under Sir Richard Winstedt, but of course had to pay my own way.

My decision to study for the tropical Diploma in Education proved to be a fortunate one, for the head of the Colonial Department was a Dr Mumford with whom I got on well. Moreover, when I was placed second in the Diploma examination, he offered me a research scholarship to study the suitability of the existing textbooks in use in the colonies. I also soon found myself as an unofficial assistant author of the *Basic Way to English* although the nominal author was Dr Mumford. This was valuable experience, for it taught me how to write textbooks and that many of the textbooks in use in the British Colonies in the 1930s were obsolete!

While I was doing research, I was treated as a member of the staff and frequently had lunch with three other members of the staff: Dr Mumford, head of the Colonial Department; Professor Laurewys, head of the Science Department; and Mr Lewin, the Librarian and a lawyer by training. Our lunches were always most enjoyable and stimulating, and we would discuss a variety of subjects. The topic I can best remember was when on one occasion we attempted to decide what precisely was meant by being unfaithful to one's wife. I was asked first for my definition and volunteered that being unfaithful meant performing the physical act with a lady other than one's wife. Professor Laurewys who was a Catholic maintained that having the desire was sufficient to be classified as being unfaithful; while Mr Lewin, who later became a Professor of Law said it was just a matter of proving the accusation in a Court of Law. But the maverick Bryant Mumford, however, had an unexpected definition. You were, he said, unfaithful if you were caught.

It was also through Dr Mumford that I met my wife Lyn. One day he invited me to spend the weekend with his family in their lovely country house—Lay House, in Sussex. And there I met a charming dark-haired girl, Eluned Knoyle, who was teaching his children. I fell in love with her; indeed I proposed to her the first time I took her out, but she refused and said I must be drunk. However, she agreed the second time, for on that occasion I made sure that I appeared to be sober! It turned out she was the Welsh girl I had pushed into the sea many years previously when I was a small boy in Wales!

Now that I was engaged to get married, getting a job became more urgent. The next opportunity which presented itself was the post of tutor at Gordon College, Khartoum, for which an honours degree and a Diploma in Education were required. At the interview, the Chairman of the Selection Committee Sir Christopher Cox informed me that there was one appointment and 400 applicants! Spurred by this bit of information I endeavoured to impress the Committee by airing my views on the teaching of English and more especially Basic English. But the result was another failure— I was placed second. Upon hearing of this near miss, my friend Dr Mumford made discreet inquiries as to why I had not been offered the job. Sir Christopher Cox's reply was that they had nearly appointed me, but that the Selection Committee had the problem that they couldn't decide who was interviewing who!

Just as my future was beginning to look black my luck changed. Canon Grace, Principal of Achimota College, Ghana offered me a job on the staff of Achimota College, but I would have to wait a while as the job would not become vacant for six months. I therefore began to prepare myself for Ghana and managed to arrange for Dr Ida Ward, an eminent scholar from the School of Oriental and African Studies to teach me Twi, a language spoken in Ghana. I enjoyed the experience very much, even though Twi turned out to be quite a difficult tonal language to learn, and resigned myself to the fact that I was destined for West Africa.

Fortunately one day Dr. Mumford received an unexpected telephone call from the Colonial Office, with the information that 'If that chap Lewis still wants to go to Malaya, we have a vacancy for him in the Straits Settlements, in the Education Department.' I accepted the offer with the speed of light.

And so by patience and persistence I had at last achieved my ambition of going to Malaya. I realized of course that being a student from the politically notorious LSE was a severe handicap, but had taken the precaution of getting two impeccable referees: my relative Professor Cayo Evans formerly of the Indian Civil Service and Chief Constable Ashley of New Scotland Yard, my late father's best friend.

It took me only a few weeks to get my things together for what was in those days a great adventure, as the only way to get to Penang in 1938 was by ship and a journey lasting a month. There was also no air mail, so letters took a month to reach Penang and replies about two months. My kit included white tropical trousers and shirts, a tin trunk to keep out white ants, and especially a white topee, for there was a firm belief that the failure to wear a topee in the tropics would result in sunstroke and possibly death!

I have already mentioned the Wall Street Crash of 1929. This was the most disastrous stock market crash of recent times, perhaps of all times. Not only did many financiers in

New York commit suicide, but a large number of banks and businesses went bankrupt; indeed things went from bad to worse after the Crash, so that by 1933 there were nearly 13 million people unemployed in the USA, while the proportion was even greater in the United Kingdom. Consequently my mother's sally into business could not have been made at a worse time. Moreover, her particular kind of business—the hotel business—was probably the worst hit by the Great Depression.

I became aware of our financial difficulties in 1930, for as my two brothers were by now far away in Malaya, I was called upon to help and advise my mother how best to weather the storm. The main action we took was to keep our expenses down to a minimum. Thus I prepared the Balance Sheet and Profit and Loss Accounts for the Inland Revenue so as to avoid having to pay accountant's fees. I also became the unpaid resident electrician, plumber, painter and decorator and odd job man at the Hotel London. At the same time my brothers sent drafts of money every month to keep the ship afloat.

But it was a losing battle, for the depression got worse, and as my mother was facing bankruptcy she decided to sell the hotel. She entrusted this to our trusted family solicitor who made a hash of it. Although he was trustworthy, he was also negligent. Having 'sold' the hotel to a 'developer', he advised my mother to close down the hotel and get rid of the guests, which she did. The developer than went back on his word and we made the unpleasant discovery that the contracts had not been exchanged; in other words the sale had not been legally completed.

A few weeks later I read in the *Evening Standard* what must have been the reason for our solicitor's negligence. He had been having an affair with a lady and was being sued in a Court of Law as a co-respondent! The result of course was that my mother lost most of her money, for an empty hotel was almost unsaleable during the Great Depression. But it was eventually sold at a fraction of its real value—to the dishonest developer who had originally negotiated to buy it.

Nevertheless it was fortunate that my mother had been forced to abandon the hotel and move to a flat in Ealing, for within a few months of the commencement of the Second

World War, the Hotel London and Lancaster Street, in which it was located, were completely demolished by two huge land mines dropped by the Germans on one of their earliest air raids on London! The years I had spent growing up in the Hotel London were full of interest. The visitors were many and varied. They included Polish aristocratic refugees, Indian Civil Servants on leave, Welsh teachers on holiday, confidence tricksters, thieves, ballet dancers, actors, actresses, medical and law students and so on.

The unfortunate episode of the dishonest developer who 'bought' my mother's hotel, the crooks and confidence tricksters who never paid their bills taught me some valuable lessons, in particular that it is not advisable to trust people with money, and that you cannot tell a person's character by his appearance!

Chapter 3

PENANG AND SINGAPORE

I wonder what Latitude or Longitude I've got to?

Alice in Alice's Adventures in Wonderland

I set sail from Southampton for the Far East on the P and O *Ranpura* on a sunny day, in early June 1938. The *Ranpura* was a big ship, nearly twice as long as a football pitch, with nearly 600 passengers of whom 300 were travelling first class.

What should have been the happiest day of my life, was in fact a melancholy one, for I was leaving behind not only my mother, but also my fiancée Lyn for what I knew must be many years, as my first leave would not be due for four years. It was a rule that newly appointed officers to the Colonial Service were on probation until they had passed all the necessary examinations, which in my case were two examinations in the Malay language, and it was forbidden for an officer to get married while on probation. So poor Lyn would probably have to wait three or four years before we could get married. Little did I imagine it would in fact be over seven years.

As this was my first voyage on any kind of big ship, it was a novel and exciting experience, and as I was travelling first class, the accommodation and especially the food were excellent. Unfortunately within a day or two we entered the Bay of Biscay, and the ship began to roll and plunge violently in a cork-screw fashion, so that I was seasick and wanted to die. The ship also creaked so much that I feared it was breaking up. But my cabin steward assured me that there was nothing to worry about and that the ship would not sink.

MALAYA: 1938 – 1945

Before the Second World War the Malay Peninsula was divided into the following political divisions:
(a) The Straits Settlements, a British Crown Colony, consisting of Penang, Malacca, and Singapore;
(b) The Federated Malay States consisting of Perak, Selangor, Negri Sembilan and Pahang; and
(c) The Unfederated Malay States consisting of Johore, Kedah, Perlis, Kelantan and Terengganu.

After a few days we reached Gibraltar and I soon recovered from my seasickness and began to take an interest in my fellow passengers. As I was much intoxicated with Lyn, I kept away from the many attractive young women on the ship on their way to India and the Far East, and made friends with two older sophisticated-looking Englishmen. One was a Commander in the Royal Navy, on his way to Hong Kong to supervise the construction of anti-submarine booms to protect the Hong Kong harbours in case of war with Japan, the other was a Major in the Royal Artillery also on his way to Hong Kong.

Gibraltar, of course, was a famous fortress and my two military friends knew it well and showed me over it. I was amazed to discover that this huge rock was riddled with caves, tunnels and passages providing the defenders with excellent protection in case of war. Hitler called it a pirates' lair! It was, of course, one of a series of vital British fortresses guarding the sea route from the Atlantic Ocean via the Suez Canal to the Indian Ocean and the South China Sea.

In 1938 the only way of getting from London to Penang was by sea. There were no passenger-carrying aircraft; there were no air routes between London and Penang. There were just two sea routes: one via the Suez Canal, the other via the Cape of Good Hope, but the Suez route was much shorter and quicker. Britain therefore regarded the Suez route as a vital line of communication between the United Kingdom and its territories in the Far East, and protected it with a series of fortified ports: Gibraltar, Malta, Suez, Port Said, Aden, Colombo, Singapore and Hong Kong.

My military friends told me that Singapore was strongly fortified with many huge 15" guns guarding it from an attack by sea. When I asked them what was to stop an enemy from attacking it from land, they said that the land was covered with thick jungle, which made an attack from the north impracticable. I was not convinced but presumed they knew better than I.

The passengers on the *Ranpura* were almost entirely British. Some were civil servants on their way to the Sudan, Aden, India, Burma, Malaya and Hong Kong; some were British army officers returning to their regiments especially in

India, and many were businessmen on their way to Bombay, Calcutta, Colombo, Singapore and Hong Kong. It was the British Empire at its highwater mark; just before moral scruples, political argument and war persuaded the British government in London to allow everybody to govern themselves.

Fortunately I was in the right job, for the Colonial Office had explained to us that our job was to prepare the people of Malaya for self-government, by which they really meant educate its students so that they would gain entry into universities.

As our ship ploughed its way eastwards, day and night, we called at many ports and I wondered at the diversity of people and places, and the variety of sounds and smells. First, it was Marseilles with its night life, then Malta and its battleships and then Suez. At Suez I went ashore to see the land of the Pharaohs. I met an Egyptian urchin who pleaded, 'Show you a trick, sir. Lend me half-a-crown.' This I did and he ran away with it at the speed of light. Next I went into a shop and bought a small carpet for £30. The salesman described it as 'a genuine handmade Persian carpet'. Later I discovered it had been made on a machine in Belgium, and was worth £3. I soon realized that the morals of Suez were not those of Llandeilo.

The ship continued its journey east and I began to melt in the terrific heat of the Red Sea. Indeed it appeared to me at this point that the further east we went, the drier and hotter it became. Indeed my worst fears were realized when we reached Aden, for I had never been to such a bleak or such a hot oven-like place before. I began to wonder what was awaiting me further east.

Fortunately our arrival at Colombo, with its palm trees and cool sea breeze, was a pleasant surprise. I became confident that perhaps from now on things would get better and so it proved to be. I arrived off Penang Island early in the morning of June 30, 1938. In the distance, I could see a hill covered with tropical rain forest; the air was hot and sticky and I wondered what lay in store for me.

Soon we were alongside Swettenham Pier at Penang to the accompaniment of much shouting and running as the ship was tied to the wharf by huge manila ropes, and a gangway was let down with a crash, while a sea of colourful faces looked up at us, for the crowd that had come to meet the ship consisted of a multitude of races: Indians, Malays, Chinese, Europeans and Eurasians. I soon picked out my brother Tommy in the crowd, dressed in a white suit and wearing the indispensable topee. When I eventually reached him he explained that he had not been able to bring his car on to the wharf, so he had hired a rickshaw.

I had of course seen pictures of rickshaws, and knew they were vehicles pulled by human beings. But I was shocked when I saw our Chinese rickshaw boy, for he was emaciated with sunken cheeks, protruding ribs and a skinny body. My brother explained that this was because he was an opium smoker, and that our rickshaw puller was probably an addict. He also explained that the government was slowly eradicating this practice by supplying opium only to the addicts in special opium-smoking saloons, and that supervising such saloons was part of my brother John's work in the Customs.

After a short ride in the rickshaw, we reached a side-street, where my brother had left his car in charge of his *syce* or driver. I remember the car well—it was a solid tank-like Austin car kept in immaculate condition by the Indian *syce*, whose name was Nair. We reached Tommy's house in a matter of minutes, for he was at that time Headmaster of the Francis Light School, Penang, which was only 3 kilometres from Swettenham Pier. I was enchanted by what I saw: clean and well-maintained roads, beautiful gardens, green and luxuriant vegetation, and white, well-kept houses. Soon after arriving at his house which was built on short pillars so as to keep it cool, my brother's servant produced tea and an evil smelling, prickly looking object called a durian. He explained that the durian was a Malayan fruit, and a local delicacy, and that he always had it for tea! As I did not want to disappoint him, and foolishly believed everything he said, I ate my durian, in spite of its awful smell, and pretended to like it.

Shortly afterwards he switched on the radio (television had not yet reached Malaya) for the six o'clock news. And I was most surprised to hear the announcer say, 'Mr G. E. D. Lewis, brother of Mr T. P. M. Lewis, Headmaster of the Francis Light School arrived in Penang today on the

Ranpura. He is being posted as European assistant master at the Penang Free School.' I discovered that Penang had its own amateur radio station, and that the announcer was the Rev. Colin King, himself a member of the Penang Free School staff.

Of course there were many things that I found very strange, especially the *cicaks*, or small house lizards, that defied gravity and ran about on the ceilings and I was told occasionally fell into one's soup, leaving their tails behind; the ceiling fans which rotated slowly and wearily in the sitting-room stirring up the humid air; the domestic staff which included a Chinese cook, the Indian Nair who acted both as my brother's personal servant (or boy) and his *syce* (or driver), and a Malay *kebun* (or gardener). There was also the mosquito net which completely covered one's bed and protected one at night against mosquitoes, and the 'Dutch Wife' in my bed which I found to be nothing more than a long bolster, which I was told to put between my legs at night so as to keep cool.

I found Penang to be a very hot and sticky place. I also found it difficult to sleep at night not only because of the humid heat but because of the symphony of noise made by the multitude of insects, beetles and birds which live in the jungle. For as soon as it got dark, this jungle orchestra filled the air with the most extraordinary squeaks, shrieks, screeches and squawks. The most annoying noise was made by the nightjar or *tok tok* bird. It *tok tok*'d especially when the moon was up; but its fascination for me was to try and determine how many times it would *tok tok*. Would it *tok tok* once only, or would it *tok tok* a dozen times? I was told that the Chinese placed bets on it.

As my brother was just about to go on six months' leave he took me to the government quarters that had been reserved for me at the Cadets Bungalow. This was a long low bungalow in Macalister Road which was the normal stopping place for bachelor European government officers such as myself on their first arrival in Penang. My accommodation consisted of a bedroom, a bathroom and a portion of the verandah. In addition there was a communal verandah used as a sitting-room, a dining room kept cool by the use of a punkah when someone could be found to operate it, and a long building at the back occupied by our domestic staff. There was one disadvantage of such open living—it was an invitation to thieves. Indeed later on we were paid a visit one dark night by such a person. The thief, a Tamil gentleman, with much foresight, came completely in the nude, so it was difficult to see him in the dark. Moreover, he had also covered himself with coconut oil. Consequently although we thought we had caught him, he was such a slippery customer that we could not hold him and so our fish, or I should say, our oily man got away.

The Cadets Bungalow provided only basic living space for four bachelors, but it had some advantages: the rent charged by the government was modest, and one's companions were normally agreeable.

I soon found out, however, that I was expected to employ an army of personal servants, that is, a 'boy' who cleaned my room and looked after my clothes; a *syce* who cleaned and drove the car when he was allowed to; a *tukang air* who prepared and brought the bath water in a bucket; a *tukang masak* or cook; and a *tukang kebun* or gardener—the latter two being shared by all four members of the Cadets Bungalow. This made five in all; in fact between the four of us we employed fourteen servants. Moreover, one night having a suspicion that there were more than fourteen living at the rear of the bungalow, we carried out a surprise census and found there were over sixty persons! We were informed that they were uncles, aunts, brothers, sisters on a short visit to Penang and that they were just staying for the night! But in fact there were more or less permanent residents living off us.

The salaries paid to our staff were, however, well within our means. My salary was $400 per month, and out of this I paid the following *gaji* or wages to my staff.

Cook (shared)	$30 per month
Boy	$25 per month
Tukang air	$15 per month
Syce	$20 per month
Tukang kebun (shared)	$15 per month

In addition I had to pay about $25 per month rent for my government quarters, while another $30 per month was deducted from my monthly salary to pay off a car loan. The rule was that if a government officer bought a British-made car (and that included one made in the Commonwealth) he could get an interest-free loan from the government to be paid off by monthly deductions from one's monthly salary. So most of us had car loans.

My first car was a British-made Austin saloon, which I bought from the Superintendent of the Trade School, mainly because he had equipped it with a fan. And so I must have been one of the first in Malaya to own an 'air-conditioned' car. My second car was a Canadian-built Chevrolet tourer, which had previously belonged to my colleague Martin Ogle, a car fanatic, so I knew it had been well looked after.

A day or two after my arrival in Penang I proceeded to the Penang Free School to take up my job as an assistant master. I was most impressed with the school buildings and the *padang* or playing field, lined with attractive houses for the senior married staff. I was even more impressed when I saw the school laboratories, which were as good as, if not better than those in many public schools in England.

The Headmaster, Mr Arnold, was kind but slightly eccentric. He was followed by an even greater eccentric by the name of Cobb. The latter distinguished himself one morning during the Cambridge School Certificate Examinations by cycling to the Free School scattering that morning's Cambridge School Certificate Examination papers along Green Lane to the surprise and delight of the schoolboys, because the papers had been insecurely tied on to the back of his bicycle.

The staff was well qualified and dedicated and consisted of five European education officers, who were honours graduates recruited from the United Kingdom and about thirty Asian teachers, nearly all of whom were non-graduates for there was no university in Malaya in 1938.

The European education officers specialized in different subjects and were as follows: the Rev. Colin King (English Literature), J. N. Davies (Mathematics), Patrick Purcell (History), R. W. Bomford and later Ted Barker (Science), Martin Ogle (History) and myself (Geography).

Each of us had our own special interests, and I noticed many of us also had our own peculiar habits. Thus the Rev. Colin King was inclined to preach or lecture us, J. N. Davies to argue, Patrick Purcell to exaggerate, Ted Barker to tease, and

Martin Ogle to write inordinately long letters. But we all got on well together.

Patrick Purcell who had been a close friend of my brother Tommy (better known as TPM or Tiny Lewis in Malaya) decided to take me under his wing and gave me two bits of advice. His first bit of advice was that I should learn Malay as soon as possible—he was a Malay language fanatic; his second bit of advice was that I should get out of Penang and get to know the real Malaya. So within a week or so of arriving in Penang, I found myself on a forced route march with Patrick in Upper Perak, walking from Keroh to Grik. There was no road between these two small settlements in those days, just a footpath winding its way through the jungle and occasionally through kampongs with pretty names like Kampong Lallang. We walked about 40 kilometres in the hot sun, so I was exhausted and footsore by the time we reached Grik. But it was an exhilarating introduction to my new environment, especially as we spoke to many rural Malays on the way, and even saw a tiger—the only wild tiger I ever saw during my twenty-three years in Malaya.

I was charmed by the rural Malays who were polite and smiling, characteristics which make the Malays such likeable people. I was glad I had come to Malaya and not gone somewhere else.

Of the Asian staff at the Penang Free School some notable ones were Ooi Khay Bien, a physics graduate of Hong Kong University and also a stalwart of the school cadet corps; Basha Merican who brought a flock of his children to school every morning in his tiny Austin Seven car, and was much liked by everybody; Captain Mohd. Noor, a religious man and strict with the boys; and Hashim who was the opposite but was nevertheless well liked and popular perhaps because of it. Hashim taught both English and Malay and had an excellent knowledge of both languages. He was therefore a popular *munshi* or language teacher. I had him for a while, and found that he taught best only after he had refreshed himself with a brandy ginger ale.

One of Hashim's jobs was to take the school rugby team on its tours. So I was surprised one day when Arnold the Headmaster asked me to accompany Hashim and the school Rugby XV on its annual tour to Alor Setar, to play against the Sultan Abdul Hamid College. When I asked why, he explained that my job was not to look after the school rugby team but to chaperon Hashim! For apparently on his last excursion to Alor Setar he had indulged himself so much, that he could not be found when the time came to return to Penang, and so the team had to come back without him.

Another Malay teacher was Zainal Abidin. In fact I took over his job as Senior Geography master at the Penang Free School; for he had been promoted to take over from my brother TPM as Headmaster of the Francis Light School. Zainal Abidin was probably the first Malay in Malaya to get a degree in Geography. This he did through a corre-spondence course, probably with Wolsey Hall Oxford—a great achievement. Consequently he was generally referred to as 'Zainal Abidin BA London'.

One of the first jobs I was given by the Department of Education was to write a report on a book he had written in Malay on Physical Geography. To write such a book was no mean task, for there were no Malay words for most geographical terms, and so Zainal Abidin was obliged to invent them. Although he did not write any more geography books, he was a pioneer in the Malay field.

I found the Free School boys a delight. They were almost without exception bright and well turned out, and many were highly intelligent. My job was to teach Geography and English to the best School Certificate classes, which was a pleasure for they were all eager to learn. This was a welcome change from the state of affairs in England, where schoolboys are more inclined to fool about, as indeed I had done during my schooldays.

Although the Chinese, Indian, Malay and Eurasian boys who I was now teaching were industrious, I found that many of them had one failing and that was a tendency to memorize facts without understanding them. This may have been because most Asian children have good memories, but of course relying on a good memory is not a good basis for understanding.

A good example of the danger of such learning off by heart is mentioned by Tan Sri Dr Mohd. Said in his *Memoirs* of his schooldays at the Malay College:

Then there was Abdullah …. he was very studious and it seemed to be his idea that the best way of mastering a subject was to try and learn everything by heart. One day he was asked by the teacher the meaning of the word 'hydrophobia'. Without hesitation he proudly stood up and answered, 'Hydrophobia is a disease bitten by mad dogs'. He was astonished when his answer was greeted by peals of laughter from the rest of the boys.

There were several hundred boys at the Penang Free School, but I only got to know well those I taught in the School Certificate classes and those who played rugby. One class which I can still remember well after fifty years was a School Certificate class to whom I taught English. Some of them, who have since distinguished themselves, were Syed Putra who became the Raja of Perlis and one of the first *Agongs* (or King) of Malaysia. He used to sit at the back of the class perhaps because he was a bit shy. As he was a bit overweight I would occasionally make him run round the *padang*, which he did willingly, for he was a good natured boy. He was also one of the few Malay boys in the class, and as I was learning Malay, I would often try out my Malay on him. He was my unpaid *munshi*!

Another was Eusoffe Abdoolcader. Eusoffe was a keen and diligent student, who always sat in the front, probably the most intelligent boy in the class; he also had a remarkably mature way of looking at things, for such a young boy. I was not surprised when in due course he became a High Court judge.

Then there was Lim Kean Siew, a maverick, who loved an argument, and could be guaranteed to take a contrary view to his teachers. But he was also a very frank and charming boy with a winning smile, and a rare ability to argue his case without causing resentment. In fact he became quite a favourite of mine and eventually a lifelong friend. His chosen profession as a lawyer in Penang, and as a politician were perfect vocations for him.

The Penang Free School also had what must have been the first Sixth Form in Malaya, but it went under another name and was called the Matriculation Class. It was a class for the cream of the school, who were waiting for admission to

Raffles College, Singapore or for something else to turn up. To this class I was allowed by Arnold to teach Logic, which was quite a revolutionary development in those days. One of the boys was Lim Chong Eu who later became Chief Minister of Penang. Like Lim Kean Siew, he was a highly intelligent boy, but unlike Lim Kean Siew he was highly contemplative, that is, he thought carefully before he spoke; indeed one had a feeling that he kept many of his thoughts to himself.

There were of course many other boys such as Gan Kok Liang who was nicknamed the Professor because of his thoughtful and reflective turn of mind; Long Joo who jumped over six feet high on Sports Day, so that the judge, Claude Lyle of the Malayan Civil Service who was about 5 feet 10 inches, had great difficulty in reaching the height; Tan Ah Fee the School Rugby Captain and a good all-rounder and whose brother Tan Ah Tah became a judge; Abdul Latif the school scrum-half who was so exuberant that he tackled with his feet as well as his hands; and last but not least Jagit Singh whose pastime as a schoolboy was to try and trip me up when I tried to teach him the geography of Malaya, after being only one month in the country. Jagit Singh, who when he later became a lawyer was for some reason known as Zig Zag Singh, compelled me to take my study of Malayan geography seriously. So I systematically travelled the length and breadth of the country, from Wang Tangga in Perlis in the north to Kampong Pengerang in Johore in the south, and from Pulau Ketam in Selangor in the west to Pulau Tioman off Pahang in the east, and so ended up knowing it better than even Jagit Singh!

Shortly after arriving in Penang, my brother John who was a Customs' officer in Ipoh, informed me that he would be getting married in Penang and would I be his best man. And so just a few weeks after my arrival I found myself exposed to the high society of Penang, for he married Gwyneth Samuel, whose father was a leading lawyer in Penang. John was in due course married at St. George's Church, Penang, a charming old church built in 1817 with convict labour, while the reception was held at the Judge's House, in Macalister Road. It was all very hot, very civilized and very colonial. However, I was soon reminded that all is not always what it seems, for that evening I attended a smart dance at the lovely and spotless Runnymede Hotel, and as I sat down after dancing with my hostess, observed a rat scurrying across the dance floor.

My brother's wife Gwyneth had interesting ancestry, for Mrs Samuel was a descendant of both Scott and Brown, early plantation owners on Penang Island; in fact the remnants of the Brown estate are still to be seen on the island.

I was at the Cadets Bungalow for about two years and during this period there was much coming and going. Those who lived there during my time and with whom I established friendships included: Claude Lyle, a Chinese Cadet, which meant that he had spent two or three years in Macao, studying Chinese; John Ewart, a New Zealander and a botanist who was in charge of the nearby Waterfall Gardens; Jack Nauen who succeeded him in the same job; Martin Ogle and Ted Barker who, like myself, were both on the Penang Free School staff; and Roger Quixley, an immigration officer.

As most of us had government Malay or law examinations to pass, we had very little spare time. In my case, failure to pass the two examinations in Malay would mean that my appointment in the Colonial Service would be terminated; so passing our Malay examinations was a matter of life and death.

My *munshi* or language teacher was a charming quietly spoken Malay who I think was called Hashim bin Nordin. He was the *Guru Besar* (or Headmaster) of the Malay School, near the Francis Light School and he would come neatly dressed on his bicycle twice a week to the Cadets Bungalow and teach me. As the lessons were usually between 4.30 and 5.30 p.m., it was often still very hot and I would sometimes find it difficult to keep awake.

The first examination I had to pass in Malay (Standard I) was not very difficult, for it was really a matter of building up a vocabulary and learning how to put the words together into a sentence. I found my knowledge of Welsh quite a help when it came to pronouncing Malay words such as *khemah* (tent), *Khamis* (Thursday); *ghaib* (invisible) and so on. I also well remember the first words of Malay I spoke to my 'boy' with the help of a dictionary. I wanted some bath water and so I said '*Sila bawa air panas*' (Please bring me some hot water). He brought me a cup of hot water, and so I learnt my first lesson, for Malays distinguish between hot water (*air panas*) and hot water for bathing (*air mandi*).

The method I found most helpful in building up a Malay vocabulary was to learn together words that were related to each other. For example, I would draw a tree and label all its parts with the correct Malay words, for example: *pokok* or *pohon* (tree), *batang* (stem), *cabang* (fork), *ranting* (twig), *daun* (leaf), *pucuk* (shoot) and *bunga* (flower). I would then stick the labelled drawing of the tree on to my shaving mirror and learn the words every time I shaved. Another method I used was to learn together words that looked alike but had different meanings, for example, *panggang* (roast or toast), *punggung* (buttocks), *pinggang* (waist), *pinggan* (plate) and so on. A knowledge of Malay words was a prominent feature of the Standard I Malay examination, so my *munshi* spent many afternoons testing my vocabulary. One hot afternoon he tested me while I lay on my bed and I am ashamed to say I went to sleep. But my *munshi* was a perfect gentleman and a very understanding *munshi* and continued undismayed to test my vocabulary when I woke up.

The second Malay examination (Standard II) was much more difficult, and included translations into and from Malay, a General Paper on Malay history and customs, *Jawi* (or Arabic script) and an ability to read and write it, letter writing in Malay, Malay proverbs and so on.

Although Arabic script looks difficult, I was surprised to find that it was not so difficult to learn to write it. This is because with our own Roman script there are several ways of writing or printing the same letter, for example, A, a and a; whereas in Arabic script there is only one way of writing each letter; for example, the letter *alif* is always written ا. Of course Arabic letters change a bit when they are joined together, but so do Roman letters.

I fell in love with *Jawi*, partly no doubt because my *munshi* wrote it so beautifully. Nevertheless I was a bit nonplussed when I started to read *Jawi*, which incidentally is written from right to left, and was told that in the sentence: اي بوغ قاسو اين , that اين spelt *ini*, whereas it appeared to me to spell *ain*. Later, however, I was happy to discover that generally speaking *Jawi* is phonetic.

I was also much attracted by Malay proverbs, which show such a deep understanding of human nature in its Malay context. I also went to several Malay weddings, visited padi fields and Malay kampongs and endeavoured to get to know the real Malay. I was puzzled, however, when on one occasion I passed through one Malay kampong, and heard much giggling from some Malay girls, and I heard one shout to another *'Rimau datang'* (Tiger coming)! And so I decided to hire a Malay house in a rural part of Penang where I intended to spend my weekends and so learn the Malay language and idiom at first hand!

Although passing our Malay examinations was a matter of great consequence for our future careers, the supervision of the examinations was traditionally lax. Thus in 1939 when two or three of us took our Standard I Malay examinations in the Education Office in Penang, the presiding examiner, a friendly Welshman by the name of Joseph, announced soon after the examination commenced that he would be out for the next half hour; and by the way the dictionary was on his table! I lacked the courage to take up his kind offer—the thought of an education officer being caught cheating was an inhibition, but some of the others were not so timid.

Dictionaries were often introduced unobtrusively into the examination room. The most ingenious example I came across was when I took my Standard II Malay examination in the Court Room in Singapore. There were about eight of us sitting around a long oval table, with the invigilator sitting at the head of the table. The candidate sitting next to me was a Police Officer. He had placed a large Wilkinson dictionary on the table in front of him, but as he made no attempt to use it, the invigilator seemed content. On the second day of the exam-ination, as he continued not to attempt to use it, I whispered to him, 'What's the use of the dictionary, if you don't use it?'

'Oh,' he said, 'I am not using that one. I've got this one here,' and there on his lap he had another but smaller Malay dictionary. And then gallantly: 'How can I help you?'

Generally speaking European bachelors did not fit in into social life of the European married community in Penang. Consequently most of us were forced to find relaxation play-ing rugby, swimming, joining the Volunteers, visiting cabarets on Saturday nights and so on. The system for making one's presence known so as to stand a chance of being invited to a European couples' home was rather quaint, if not antiquated. One dropped two visiting cards at the house of the married couple who were the object of one's attention and hoped for the best, and if you were lucky, you were invited to dinner. I dropped cards on my immediate superior, the Inspector of Schools, got invited to dinner, and left it at that.

One day, however, I received an unexpected invitation to dinner from the Crown Counsel, Trevor Hughes. He was a bachelor, who lived in great style in a big house in Scotland Road, Penang. He had several Chinese servants who treated him with the pomp and ceremony befitting such a senior legal official. He had invited me, he explained, because I was Welsh, and when the two of us sat down to dinner at the end of a long table, he announced, 'Gerwyn, I suggest we speak only in the vernacular tonight'. The dinner was hysterically funny, because the kind of Welsh we both spoke did not lend itself to pomposity and so I discovered two Trevor Hughes: the pompous and rather distant Trevor Hughes when he spoke English, and the friendly, warm and matey Trevor Hughes when he spoke Welsh.

Rugby was one of my main relaxations, and Penang had quite a good team in those pre-war days. As my brothers, and in particular my eldest brother TPM, had made quite a reputation in Malaya as rugby players, I discovered on my arrival that a lot was expected of me. I started off well by selling a dummy to Johnny Kay, Malaya's deadly fullback, and scoring under his goal posts. But apart from that, I cannot remember doing anything remarkable, though I played for Penang in all the inter-State games during my stay there. Two other members of the Cadets Bungalow who also played for Penang were Claude Lyle (centre three-quarter) and the New Zealander John Ewart (fly-half); between us we often combined to score for Penang.

Others who played for Penang included Ginger Goodrich, Gordon London, Jack Horsburgh—all three of them were killed in the Second World War. Our scrum-half was Keng Chuan. He had learnt his rugby at the Dollar Academy in Scotland; he was also a bit unusual, for he was a Chinese who spoke English with a Scottish accent. He was followed by Pestana, who later became an outstanding player for Penang.

We had several interesting away games. On one such game, when we played Perak on the *padang* at Ipoh, I was much troubled during the game by a Perak player who kept on punching me in the face in the scrums. I eventually managed to get hold of the culprit's hand, and when I followed the arm, was surprised to find a beard at the other end—in fact a Sikh's beard, for the only bearded player in the Perak pack was a Sikh. And so in due course I responded in a suitable manner and left it at that. After the game the Sikh came up to me and apologized, saying 'I am sorry about the fight. I didn't realize you were Mr T. P. M. Lewis' brother.'
'What difference does that make?' I asked.
'Well,' he responded, 'your brother taught me to play rugby.' The Sikh, of course, was Utam Singh, first a schoolboy and later a teacher (and no doubt a rugby teacher) at the King Edward VII School, Taiping—a school well known for its rugby fanatics.

Another occasion I well remember was when we played Selangor on the *padang* at Kuala Lumpur. The wing forwards for Penang were Dr Jerry O'Driscoll and myself, and the main object of our attention was the Selangor scrum-half Frank Smith who, many years later, was British Adviser to Perlis and Terengganu. Half-way through the game there was a violent thunderstorm. There was a flash of lightning, followed by a clap of thunder and the collapse of the scrum. I shouted, 'I've been struck by lightning,' whereupon Jerry O'Driscoll the doctor lifted up my shirt and, with typical Irish wit, said, 'Yes, by God there's a swastika on your back.' Later we discovered that a player playing hockey on the pitch next to us, had indeed been struck by lightning and killed; I suppose I must have felt some of it.

Penang is a paradise for swimming, for the sea water is always warm, and there are many lovely sandy beaches on the north-east coast. So on Sundays I would often go to a beach called the Lone Pine and swim there with some Chinese friends, and less often to the Penang Swimming Club. On one occasion we took Ted Barker, who had recently come from the West Indies to join the Penang Free School staff, with us. As he said he could not swim, we volunteered to teach him, and while two of us held him in the sea, we explained to him how to move his arms. He did precisely as

instructed and swam out to sea out of sight! Couldn't swim—
the liar!

Most able-bodied Europeans joined the Penang Volunteers.
Originally it was not with a view to fighting anybody in
particular, but in 1939 the Japanese invasion of China
obviously posed a threat to Malaya. The Volunteers consisted
of several companies: Europeans, Chinese, Malays and
Eurasians. My company was a machine-gun company and
we would occasionally fire our machine-guns on the rifle
range. There was one special occasion when we manned the
Penang beaches as practice to repel a potential enemy. When
the General from Singapore came to my machine-gun and
asked me to fire our blanks, I threw open the ammunition box
which should have contained a belt of ammunition, but
instead revealed three bottles of Tiger Beer. The General
pretended not to see!

Saturday night was a time for eating and drinking and
sometimes for dancing. For the latter there were dance halls,
generally referred to as cabarets. There were two in Penang:
the Wembley cabaret and the City Lights. The dance girls
sat around the dance floor, and were usually Chinese or
Siamese but occasionally Malay. And in order to dance with
them we had to produce a dance ticket, a book of dance
tickets costing a dollar or so. But dancing in a hot climate
under a few fans was hot work, so many were content to sit,
drink and talk. The habitués of the cabarets were Europeans,
Chinese, Indians, Eurasians and Malays who all got on well
together so that Penang was very much a happy multi-racial
society. The favourite dance tune was without question
Terang Bulan, now the tune of Malaysia's national anthem!

With the surrender of France in June 1940, war with Japan
in the Far East became a distinct possibility. Consequently,
many measures were taken for the defence of Penang, such as
the building of concrete machine-gun posts in the padi fields
around the Bayan Lepas airport, once mistakenly referred to
by some visiting American tourists as 'cute tea-houses', and
the construction of gun emplacements on the north-east coast.

As the building of one of these gun sites involved the
demolition of an unusually tall house on the north-east coast,
the owner invited his friends including myself to a party the
day before it was to be blown up. The party was unusual in

that the guests were invited to do as much damage to the house as they liked. Late that night I came across one of the inebriated guests endeavouring to lift a heavy porcelain pedestal washbasin over the balcony at the top of the house, so that it could fall down the deep well around which the house had been built. He succeeded and I watched with interest as half a ton of porcelain accelerated down the well, before suddenly being riveted with horror as I suddenly saw a guest walk slowly across the bottom of the well completely unaware of the deadly missile that was hurtling down towards him. He escaped death by inches!

The invasion of China by Japan in 1938 also caused much resentment against the Japanese especially from the Chinese community. In fact soon after I arrived, there were anti-Japanese riots in Penang and Japanese goods were burnt in the streets. I took a photograph of one such riot and sent it to the London *Daily Express* by sea mail (there being no air mail) and got paid two guineas for it!

About this time, I decided to take a trip south and visit Malacca and its historic antiquities. I stayed at the Rest House, and one evening was unexpectedly invited to join a stag party on the lawn in front of the Rest House by the Malacca Padre. While we were having dinner I noticed the Chinese Rest House boy come out rather quickly and speak confidentially to the Padre. The Padre came over to me and asked me to accompany him back to the Rest House. He excitedly explained that the Chinese Rest House boy thought there was a German spy in the Rest House and that he was talking in German on the telephone. I approached the telephone room cautiously and there to my surprise was my brother TPM*! The Chinese Rest House boy had been most observant, for my brother is both fair-haired and large and

---

*My brother (TPM) was Headmaster of Clifford School, Kuala Kangsar between 1939–1941. It was a relatively small school, located in the shadow of the famous Malay College, but he was very attached to it and to his students. Indeed he delayed going on leave so that he could teach his School Certificate class up to the commencement of the examination which started on December 1 and so got caught by the Japanese. He took great interest in the welfare of his boys and girls and got great pleasure when they achieved success in life. One of them was a boy called Hamdan, now Tan Sri Datuk Haji Hamdan Tahir, Governor of Penang.

is many people's idea of what a German looks like; moreover he explained that he had been phoning my brother John at Port Dickson and that he had been speaking to him in Welsh!

My friends at Penang consisted of Asians as well as Europeans. But most of them were Chinese, for Penang was essentially a Chinese city. My best friends were probably C. O. Lim and his wife June. 'C. O.' by which abbreviation he was generally known, had studied law at Edinburgh and was a most agreeable companion. He was well read and worldly wise. He was as much interested in the Malay language as he was in things Chinese. I spent much of my time with him and his highly intelligent wife, who was a Raffles graduate.

Another of my special friends was M. Saravanamuttu, the famous Editor of the *Straits Echo*. Sara had a first class brain, and was an engaging personality, and an excellent cricketer. He had few vices except perhaps an overfondness for whisky. In 1917 he gained admission to St. John College, at the University of Oxford, but his trip to England was not without incident. First of all, his ship was sunk in the Mediterranean Sea by a German submarine, on his way to England; then later Sara was sunk for he was sent down from Oxford as a result of some student prank in which he was involved. But I found him a jovial, serious-minded and loyal friend, and I spent many liquid evenings with him. Moreover, when I played rugby for Penang he gave me plenty of the right kind of publicity.

There were also many others, including some delightfully decorative Chinese ladies with whom I occasionally played golf on the Race Course Golf Course.

Golf was a popular game, and I joined the Penang Golf Club at Glugor soon after I arrived. The best game I ever played was the first one, when I got three birdies and an eagle, and my teacher was confident he had discovered a golfing genius. Thus encouraged I started to concentrate on the game but the more I concentrated the worse I got, which is why golf can be such an infuriating game. No wonder Dr Brodie the Penang Medical Officer, and a keen member of the Penang Golf Club once set fire to it. Of course he only set fire to a few square yards to begin with, but unfortunately a sea breeze suddenly blew up, and poor Dr Brodie soon found he had set fire to acres of it! He was fined a few thousand dollars, while the rest of the Club waited for the grass to grow again.

From what I have said so far, I may have given the impression that Penang was a kind of Utopia, and that during the so-called colonial days everybody was happy with the status quo. That of course was not true. Although most Europeans and Asians had friendly personal relationships and mixed freely, for example, they used the same hotels, cinemas and dance halls, the fact that Europeans maintained clubs only for themselves caused some resentment, and of course nobody likes being ruled by another race, no matter how benevolent the administration.

One of the first instances of European-Malay friendships that I came across, was one occasion soon after my arrival when I stayed with a European planter and his wife on their rubber estate near Sungei Patani. The wife mentioned that we would be having curry on Sunday with a Malay who was a close friend. The friend who was an Assistant District Officer, near Sungei Patani, turned out to be a chatty, friendly Malay, who was full of fun and delighted us with innumerable anecdotes about his own eccentric past as well as many jokes at the expense of the British. His name was Tunku Abdul Rahman. It never crossed my mind for a moment that this carefree Malay would one day be Prime Minister of Malaysia.

My transfer to Singapore was unexpected and not exactly welcome. My plans to rent a kampong house near Relau on Penang Island so that I could learn Malay over the weekends in a kampong environment had to be cancelled, and I was soon on my way to Singapore.

No reason was given for my transfer, merely that the 'exigencies of the service' required that I should go to Singapore and that I was to report to the Colonial Secretary. When eventually I met the Colonial Secretary, he told me that the Straits Settlements government was about to introduce a War Tax, or an Income Tax for War Purposes, and that if the law was passed by the Legislative Council, Singapore, I was to become the Public Relations Officer. In the meantime I was to report to Edwin Tongue, Head of the Estate Duty Department, located in the Supreme Court building near by, and await developments.

When I got to the Estate Duty Department I found an embryo War Tax Department staff gathered there, including D. I. Goodwin who had been a student with me at the London School of Economics. The plan now became clearer. The powers that be obviously thought that those of us with degrees in Economics would make good tax gatherers. I spent the next week or so studying the draft War Tax Ordinance, and together with Goodwin prepared leaflets explaining it in simple terms for the use of the general public. It was a novel experience to suddenly find myself an abominated income tax man. Fortunately, the highest rate of tax was only 8 per cent, so although I was shunned by some, I was cultivated by others; very few people objected to it.

When the War Tax Ordinance became law I was the first to take up residence in the Victoria Memorial Hall as the Public Relations Officer, and was photographed by the press as a new celebrity. However, I was soon brought down to earth when a local lawyer phoned me and started talking about his client who was a 'beneficiary in an estate' and so on, in jargon which was Greek to me. So I pretended to be very busy and promised to ring him back. In the meantime I consulted the Collector Dudley Tudor, who was a Chartered Accountant and well versed in such matters. I explained my problem, but assured him if he would give me a book by which I could acquaint myself with the jargon, I could read it up. So I feigned 'flu' for a couple of days and withdrew to my house where I spent 48 hours reading most carefully the book which revealed to me the secrets of estates, trusts and so on.

I returned to my job much enlightened and full of confidence; indeed I soon became an expert on the interpretation of the income tax law. This was mainly because the War Tax Ordinance was designed to be a simple law, but of course such a thing is not possible with income tax, and it soon proved to be most inadequate, so that the War Tax Department was compelled to make a series of rulings. Consequently, the book of rulings soon became thicker than the Ordinance itself, and as I kept the book of rulings, and nobody could be bothered to challenge our rulings, I soon found myself in an unassailable position.

Within a week or so, D. I. Goodwin was sent to Penang to open the War Tax Department there, while I followed to help him recruit the staff. One of those I recruited was Keng Chuan, the Penang scrum-half, for I thought his presence would be good for our image. And so it turned out; for Goodwin put him at the door of the Penang War Tax Department distributing leaflets. This was a clever decision, for as the potentially irate tax payer entered the building, they were soon converted into amenable victims by the garrulous Keng Chuan who knew very little about income tax but a lot about rugby.

There were, however, obvious problems with the existing law, so a War Tax Committee of experts was set up to discuss how best to improve it, and to make recommendations. The Committee included Edwin Tongue (the Collector-General), H. Weisberg (the Financial Secretary) and some local lawyers and businessmen including some really bright sparks such as Datuk Braddell, K. K. O'Connor and Tay Lian Teck, and with myself as a rather inexperienced Secretary.

Of course our deliberations were top secret, for any leakage could result in unscrupulous people benefiting financially. So there was much alarm and despondency when one day the Collector-General informed me that there had been a serious leakage, and asked if I had confided any of our secret deliberations to anybody. I was able to assure him that I had not and that the only person who knew of our deliberations was my confidential secretary who typed the minutes of our meetings.

A few days after this episode, Edwin Tongue asked me to have lunch at the Singapore Cricket Club at his expense, and to report back to him anything of unusual interest. I did as he suggested, and had hardly set foot in the Cricket Club before several members eagerly approached me and invited me to join them for lunch. I soon discovered the reason for my sudden popularity—the Municipal world was agog with excitement, for there was a rumour that we were to prosecute a senior Municipal officer for fiddling his income tax return! Of course I was able to tell them that it was news to me, and they must have been misinformed.

When I returned to the office, I informed Tongue of the rumour and he smiled a well-satisfied smile. He then explained that he had suspected my confidential secretary of the leakage. So he had dictated a letter addressed to the senior Municipal officer, accusing him of fiddling his tax return. My confidential secretary was reminded that the letter was highly confidential, but he had not posted the letter, and had destroyed the carbon copy of it. Consequently the source of the leakage was self-evident, while any suspicion on my reliability was removed. Tongue of course was an outstanding police officer, who had distinguished himself as the Head of the Estate Duty Department before being appointed Collector-General of the War Tax Department. I thoroughly enjoyed working under such an in-corruptible and gifted man. His ship was bombed in the Java Sea after the fall of Singapore, and so Singapore lost a man whom I greatly admired for his integrity and ability.

During my short stay at Singapore I shared accommodation first in Ridley Park with Hugh Turner who was confidential secretary to the Colonial Secretary, a typical Englishman with a dry sense of humour and a very compatible companion; and later with Middleton Smith at 13 Fort Canning Hill, in the slopes of Fort Canning, Singapore, with whom I also got on well.

My colleagues in the business of tax collecting, apart from Edwin Tongue (the Director-General), and Dudley Tudor (the Collector) included Tony Loch and J. G. Rappaport, both of the Malayan Civil Service, of whom the latter was killed in the War, while the former nearly died in the Siam railway; two Chinese Raffles College graduates straight from College, one of whom was Goh Keng Swee who was not particularly good at tax collecting—indeed Tongue proposed to terminate his services, but he was saved from that fate by the Japanese invasion, and later on went to become Singapore's Finance Minister, and a successful administrator; and the friendly Lee Siow Mong. The latter was a highly intelligent young man, one of the few among us who seemed to know what he was about. In fact I much admired Lee Siow Mong for he was a real Chinese, who could speak English, Malay and Chinese fluently and was already an authority on Chinese Art and Ceramics. Indeed on his advice and with his help, I bought some beautiful Chinese porcelain coloured Peking blue. Of course, I lost this treasure with the fall of Singapore; such porcelain is now only found in museums.

As a Public Relations Officer for the War Tax Department, it was intended that I should be the public's friend at court, but of course most tax-payers were suspicious of that concept. Nevertheless, I acquired many new friends especially amongst the wealthy Chinese, whose generous hospitality I accepted, after first getting the permission of my boss Edwin Tongue. To their credit, however, none tried to take advantage of their friendly relationship with me.

Perhaps my best friend in Singapore was Yoxall of the Hong Kong and Shanghai Bank, his wife and their lovely little girl Caroll — to whom I was her Uncle Taffy. She lost her young life getting away from Singapore, after its capture by the Japanese.

Shortly after arriving in Penang in 1938, it became obvious that there was a real possibility of war breaking out in the Far East between Britain and Japan. Japan had already invaded China and was in a very belligerent expansionist mood. An incident which took place while I was in Penang seemed to confirm my worst fears.

What happened was that my botanist friend Jack Nauen caught a python in the Lake Gardens, and wished to have the python's skin preserved. So we took the python to a Japanese taxidermist who had an office and a small shed near Air Itam, Penang. While Nauen was discussing the matter with the Japanese taxidermist, I decided to wait in his office until they had finished. Imagine my astonishment when I discovered that the simple Japanese taxidermist had tucked away in a corner of his office as reading matter, books in English on economics — indeed the very same books I had myself recently studied at the London School of Economic for my honours degree! Clearly this was no genuine taxidermist, but a graduate of a Japanese University! I informed one of my police friends and he replied that they suspected he was a spy, but could do nothing about it as he broke no law!

In fact it later transpired that the Japanese had carefully planned their invasion of Malaya and had set up a network of spies posing as taxidermists, barbers and especially photographers all over the place. In this connection my brother (Tiny) also had an interesting experience.

When he was Headmaster of the Clifford School, Kuala Kangsar in 1940 and 1941, the school photographer was a

Japanese who called himself Robin & Co. However, when the Japanese started to commit atrocities in China in their war against the Chinese, he sacked the Japanese photographer, employed a Chinese one in his place, and explained to the Japanese photographer why. The Japanese photographer was very displeased. He also disappeared in 1941. Later in 1942, after the fall of Singapore when my brother was interred in Changi Jail, he saw his old 'friend' the Japanese photographer again in Singapore, but this time he was in a Japanese officer's uniform—my brother kept well out of his way!

While I was in the War Tax Department there was much military and air force activity in Singapore. But the need for troops and planes for the war already raging in the Middle East severely handicapped the preparations for the defence of Singapore; indeed it later transpired that most of our equipment and planes were obsolete and consisted of what was not good enough for the Middle East.

When the Singapore Volunteers Corps were first called up in November 1941, I was excused on the grounds that my work at the War Tax Department was of national import-ance—obviously one can't do much without money! So when I was called up on my birthday, December 2, 1941, I realized that the political situation must have become very serious indeed. So I rejoined the Machine Company of the Singapore Volunteers Corps on December 2, and within a few days found myself with a few others in a machine-gun pill box on the beach near Kallang Airport. Of course we presumed that this was a temporary alarm only, perhaps a practice, organized by the powers that be. So on the night of December 7, we settled down in a relaxed mood to spend our first night in the concrete pill box and wait. We did not have to wait long, for at about 4 a.m. while some of us were dozing in the moonlight, on top of the pill box, we observed what appeared to be explosions taking place at Singapore. Practice bombing by the Royal Air Force, we thought, and a good thing too. So we dozed off again as the sound of the planes faded away in the distance to the north.

But our conclusions were woefully erroneous, for within a few minutes, the field telephone rang and we re-entered the pill box. An excited voice said 'Singapore has just been bombed by enemy planes. Expect an attack at dawn.' A sudden silence overtook us, as we considered the awful significance of the news. Then one of our team who had apparently been suffering rather badly from constipation during the previous week, asked desperately if we could open the pill box door for him. 'Why?' we asked.

'I want to go to the toilet,' he replied.

Chapter 4

THE FALL OF SINGAPORE

A military operation involves deception.
Even though you are competent, appear to be incompetent.
Though effective, appear to be ineffective.
Attack when they are unprepared.
Make your move when they do not expect it.

Sun Tzu: The Art of War (About 400 BC)

he unexpected bombing of Singapore, and the sudden realization that we were at war, and not playing at war, caught us who were in the pill box a little unprepared, at least unprepared for a Japanese invasion at daybreak. For when we took stock of our position, we found that although we had two Vickers machine-guns and plenty of ammunition, the latter was useless for none of our ammunition had been loaded into their belts.

So there followed a frantic two hours during which we loaded our machine-gun belts with ammunition, and then an apprehensive wait for daybreak. Our instructions were to shoot anything that moved along the barbed wire entanglements along the beach.

Sure enough as daybreak came, the No. 1 on my machine-gun excitedly reported movement and wanted to open fire. I suggested caution, borrowed his binoculars and had a look for myself to see what was happening. And there, as the daylight came, I observed an old Chinese, with the aid of a ladder, climb over the barbed wire entanglements along the sea-shore on to the beach. As he appeared to be emigrating, rather than invading, we decided to hold our fire. We then watched him go down to the sea, have a leisurely bath, and then climb back over the barbed wire the way he had come and disappear, completely unaware that a war had started or how near he had been to his death.

After half an hour or so, as no Japanese invaders appeared, we came out of our concrete machine-gun post and had a look around. We found that our pill box was located at the bottom of a garden belonging to Datuk Braddell, the well-known Singapore lawyer. He was up early and informed us that he had just heard on the radio that the Japanese had not only bombed Singapore, but that they had landed at Kota Bharu in north-east Malaya, and had also bombed Pearl Harbour. The latter bit of news cheered us a bit, for we knew it would mean that we were now no longer alone. We did not know, however, that the Japanese had decimated the American fleet at Pearl Harbour, for their attack had been undeclared and on a Sunday, which though it might have been in accordance with the advice of Sun Tzu was not cricket!

It appeared that a direct attack on the Singapore beaches was now unlikely, so we were given some extra guard duties in the vicinity by Major Swallow. Thus one night I found myself guarding a post office in the Tanjong Katong area. The post office had a hedge around it, and I was instructed to march around it every half hour or so. When it was about 2 a.m., it occurred to me that it was a stupid idea to march as I had been instructed, and reveal myself to any possible attacker, far better crouch amongst the bushes of the hedge, keep quiet and watch. So I did just that, and suddenly woke up to find that according to my watch it was 4 a.m. I had committed the most awful sin: I had fallen asleep while on guard! But nobody seemed to be aware of it, so I decided I had better walk, and resumed my patrol much refreshed after my two hours' sleep!

It was also decided that our pill box needed some local protection, and so we were issued with a number of land mines. These were flat-looking objects that looked a bit like Kelantan Malay spinning tops. We buried them in the ground around our pill box to a depth of about 15 centimetres, covered them with a thin layer of turf, and indicated the danger area by a notice which said 'Keep off the grass'. Later in the war, when we had to leave our sector in a hurry for another sector, and the land mines and the notice were left behind, a lorry with some unlucky Indian soldiers backed on to the grass and were blown up.

The first few weeks of the Japanese attack on Malaya was relatively uneventful, as far as Singapore was concerned. There was the daily high level air raid on Singapore by Japanese aircraft, the roar of our outdated Brewster Buffalo planes as they took off and attempted to intercept the Japanese, and the civilian casualties. I well remember the dismay caused amongst us when one of our Volunteers brought the news of one of the first casualties in the war as witnessed by him. It was that of a pretty young Chinese girl, who had been killed one morning as she went round Newton Circus on a bicycle, on her way to work. It brought home to me that modern war does not discriminate between the young and the old, between soldiers and civilians—it kills anybody who gets in its way.

The next casualty was one of our own Singapore Volunteer Corps. He was woken up from his sleep one night by an air raid, and exploding bombs, when just as he was getting off his bed, a piece of shrapnel whizzed between his legs and removed one of his testicles. After a few days' attention from the doctor, he was none the worse for his experience. I regret to say he got very little sympathy, and a lot of leg pulling about his marital future. But he survived the war, got married and had children!

I had always anticipated that whether I wished it or not, I would in due course get involved in some war, that such an experience was unavoidable, and that the best thing to do in the circumstances was to prepare oneself for it. Consequently, when I was a student at the London School of Economics, I had joined the University of London Officer's Training Corps (OTC) and had I stayed in England, would have been a second lieutenant in the Royal Artillery when the war with Germany broke out.

But things had not worked out as I had expected, for here I was in the Singapore Volunteer Corps, a private soldier. Of course I was in good company, for my fellow privates included directors of leading Singapore companies, lawyers, engineers, professors, university lecturers and so on; but I did not find much consolation in that, now that we were not playing at war, but facing a real war. So when one day I met my old friend Dr Stanley Pavillard, and he asked me if I would care to join his outfit as a corporal, I was interested.

When I was in Penang I had been in the Penang Volunteers, but on becoming seriously ill with diphtheria, had only been allowed to stay in the Volunteers as the doctor's assistant. The Penang Volunteers Medical Officer at that time was Pavillard, and I had worked and got on well with him and knew of his eccentric ways. So it did not take long before we came to an amicable agreement. I told him I would rather be a private in the Machine gunners than a corporal in the medicals, but I would be happy to join him as a Sergeant and so have access to the Sergeant Mess. He agreed.

After some administrative setbacks I became Pavillard's medical Sergeant, and took up residence in the Regimental Aid Post (RAP) in an empty Chinese House in Tanjong Katong Road not far from Kallang Airport. When I first joined we had very little equipment, apart from Pavillard (or 'Pav' as he was known) and an ambulance. However, one day the Colonel phoned to say that twelve stretcher bearers were being sent. These rather surprisingly turned out to be Chinese, most of whom had previously been rickshaw pullers! As they could speak no English and very little Malay, I had to drill them in the most appropriate Malay I could muster for the occasion. They were a motley lot, but we had one thing in common: we were agreed in our opposition to the Japanese invaders. One of them took on the job of driving the ambulance, and another whose name was Gee Bah became my personal assistant. Gee Bah turned out to be an absolute gem, and when things became hectic some weeks later and we were overwhelmed with casualties, he turned out to be a tower of strength, tireless and fearless. This simple rickshaw puller was one of those unsung heroes that come to the surface in war.

After a week or two Pavillard and I decided that we needed more accommodation and noticing that the house next door seemed unattended, I made inquiries and found a Javanese *kebun* in charge. The gardener said that his employer was a Japanese businessman, who had left just before the bombing of Singapore. But he had informed the gardener that he would be back in two months. I laughed at that suggestion, but I was wrong for the Japanese were back in Singapore in two months, and one week. I also searched his house to see if there was anything to explain his real work in

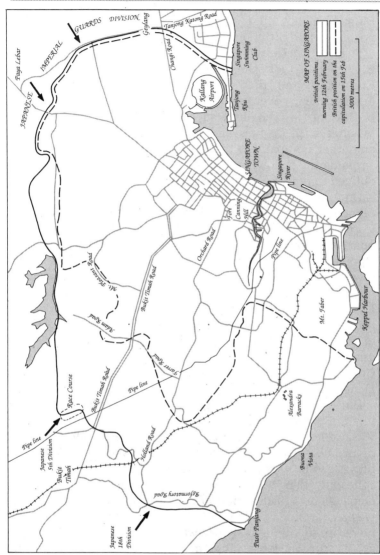

FALL OF
SINGAPORE
FEBRUARY 1942

The map shows the
positions of the
fighting perimeter
around Singapore
on February 12 and
at the capitulation
on February 15.

Singapore, but all I could find was a collection of erotic postcards and filthy pictures.

I have already mentioned that my companions in B. Company of the Singapore Volunteer Corps were Europeans and that many of them were distinguished businessmen, government officers, university lecturers and professors, lawyers and so on. We must have had more privates with degrees and professional qualifications than any other Company in the British or any other Army, which explains the following bizarre court martial in which I was obliged to play my part.

One day the Sergeant Major, a regular soldier from the Manchester Regiment attached to the Singapore Volunteer Corps, informed me that I was to present myself at Headquarters at 2 p.m. to escort a certain Lieutenant-Corporal Oppenheim who had to appear before the Colonel, as he was on a charge for some minor misdemeanour. He also informed me that my other escort was a Corporal Goode. The luckless Lieutenant-Corporal Oppenheim, who was reduced to the ranks, was in fact Professor Oppenheim, later Vice-Chancellor of the University of Malaya, while the Corporal Goode who assisted me in hauling the unfortunate Oppenheim before the Colonel was later to become Sir William Goode, Governor of Hong Kong.

Bottling up such intelligence as privates and corporals in the Singapore Volunteer Corps in the face of a real war was, of course, a criminal waste of talent, but that kind of maladministration frequently happens in war. War also brings with it many sad side effects. One day I met a colleague Glan Williams, who was the Music Master for the Department of Education in the Federated Malay States. He was a charming and highly talented, sensitive musician, with no desire to kill anybody. He was a private, and in rather low spirits, for his job at that moment was to keep the camp drains clean! I did my best to cheer him up, by suggesting that the war would soon be over. In fact he later died working as a prisoner of war for the Japanese on the notorious Burma – Thailand railway.

The Japanese invasion of north Malaya was highly successful from the Japanese point of view. This was mainly because they easily outnumbered us in the air, while their troops were seasoned soldiers having fought for several years in China, and were well supported with tanks. As for our side we had no tanks, and towards the end, very few planes. Moreover, the British, Australian and Indian soldiers involved in the fighting were having their first experience of war.

The most serious setback, however, was the sinking of the battleship *Prince of Wales* and the battle cruiser *Repulse*, two of Britain's largest and most modern warships off Kuantan on December 10, after an attempt to disrupt the Japanese invasion of North Malaya had been called off. When these large ships were originally sent to Singapore, it had been intended that they should have been accompanied by the new aircraft carrier *Indomitable*. But the *Indomitable* ran aground at the entrance to Kingston Harbour, Jamaica, on November 3, and so they were compelled to proceed to Singapore without adequate escort.

Consequently, when these unprotected ships were attacked by over eighty Japanese warplanes off Kuantan on December 10, they were both sunk after putting up a brave fight. The Japanese naval planes dropped a large wreath over the scene the next day! There was no animosity between the British and Japanese navies, for in the First World War the two navies had been allies; indeed previously many Japanese navy men had received their training in Britain! Nevertheless, the sinking of such mighty ships by aircraft marked a turning point in naval warfare. The turn for the Japanese battleships to suffer a similar fate at the hands of American planes came a year or so later.

Soon after the *Prince of Wales* and *Repulse* were attacked, some planes were sent from Singapore to help the doomed ships. One of them was flown by a New Zealand friend of mine, Andy Fleming, but he never came back. I had allowed him to make use of my house at 13 Fort Canning Hill for several months for his weekend leaves, but I never saw him again.

So the progress of the Japanese invasion became ever more serious; some thought inevitable, as they fought their way down the Malay Peninsula slowly but steadily. Thus Penang was evacuated by the military on December 18, 1941, Kuala Lumpur occupied by Japanese troops on January 11, 1942, and Kluang in north Johore reached by Japanese troops on January 24. Personally I never for a moment thought that we would be forced to surrender Singapore. Merely that there would be a hell of a fight, and that in a month or so, reinforcements of planes would come to our rescue. Pavillard on the other hand took a less optimistic view, and as it turned out a more realistic view, and thought that the Japanese would soon capture Singapore. Indeed perhaps because such a possible fate must have worried him deeply, he was soon admitted into hospital with a suspected duodenal ulcer, so I was left to run our Regimental Aid Post as best as I could without a doctor, on my own.

As the Japanese troops got nearer to Singapore so did the intensity of their bombing. Consequently, many of our planes were caught and destroyed on the ground at Kallang airport, while the danger from bombs increased daily. Thus on one occasion while standing chatting to another in a kampong near Kallang Airport, in the rain, I heard an unusual wooshing sound. Thinking that perhaps it was air escaping from a large tyre I thought nothing of it, until I heard somebody shout 'bombs', and literally dived into a nearby slit trench as the bombs exploded all around us, killing many of the kampong people.

One day I decided to return home to see how things were at 13 Fort Canning Hill. On the way I called at Raffles Hotel for a drink. I was surprised to find it crowded; it was business as usual, with a tea dance in operation. The dancing partners were of course mainly in uniform and were presumably on leave or, like myself, on their way somewhere else. I also met a friend, who was a chartered accountant with whom I had dealings while in the Income Tax Department. He was now a Captain in some Intelligence Unit; he mentioned he was looking for somebody who could speak Malay and who knew the country to join his Unit as a second lieutenant. Would I be interested? As it loooked to me that we were in for a long war, I accepted. So he said he would arrange for my promotion, but it would take a couple of weeks to arrange it. But, of course, probably luckily for me, my promotion did not materialize for within about two or three weeks we were both prisoners of war!

I then continued my journey and on reaching 13 Fort Canning Hill, was most surprised to find my house full of strangers. One of them, an attractive European girl, offered me a cup of tea in my own house. I rather enjoyed the ridiculous situation and readily accepted. She turned out to be Katherine Sim, the artist and writer, whose husband was in the Customs Service together with my brother John. Both my brothers were there, as well as some of their friends such as A. H. Gridley (later Lord Gridley) who was also in the Customs.

My brother John had just been evacuated from Penang, and had lost all his possessions, so I gave him my new silk dressing gown as compensation. My brother Tiny had just come back from operations behind the Japanese lines in Perak, and was recovering from Rengas tree poisoning, as a result of cutting his way through the jungle.

When the Japanese reached Perak, he joined an Australian unit called 'Roseforce' as their liaison officer and Malay-speaking guide. It had operated most successfully behind the Japanese lines and had ambushed and killed a senior Japanese officer and his two lorry loads of Japanese soldiers who were escorting him.

Meanwhile the situation appeared to be getting worse. The planes kept coming day by day, usually in the daylight in groups of twenty-seven or fifty-four, but sometimes in groups of eighty-one! The air raids also became more frequent and I found myself having to enter the slit trench at our Regimental Aid Post two or three times a day. While these raids were on, I read Lin Yutang's book *My Country and My People*, which I kept there permanently. British planes were notable for their absence.

February 5 was a particularly bad day, for by now the Japanese had reached the south coast of Johore and were shelling targets on Singapore Island, with their artillery. Moreover, I noticed that one of our large passenger ships was on fire, off the coast of Singapore. It turned out that she was the *Empress of Asia* bringing reinforcements, and carrying some units of the 18th Division. Eventually she had to be abandoned, and all the military equipment on her was lost. But it is an ill wind that blows nobody any good, for one of the units on the *Empress of Asia* was a Field Ambulance. They landed with nothing but their lives.

Fortunately for me, Colonel Newey discovered their plight and knowing that I had no doctor, phoned me up and said,

'Lewis, how would you like a couple of doctors and some RAMC personnel?'

Delighted, sir, I replied and within a few hours I had a Captain Barber and another doctor, several RAMC NCOs who knew their stuff, but who knew not a word of Malay and of course without any kind of medical equipment.

The next morning I had more luck, with another phone call from Colonel Newey. This time, 'Lewis, I believe the RAF have abandoned Kallang Airport, why not go along and see what you can pick up.' So off I went in Pavillard's luxurious Oldsmobile car, with the ambulance and some of Captain Barber's boys. When we got to Kallang Airport, we found the place deserted and in a shambles, with many craters, planes destroyed on the ground, and so on. When we found the Officers' Mess we were even more surprised, for there before us was breakfast laid for a dozen or so people, but completely untouched. The bacon and eggs were cold but not eaten, the coffee was in the cups but not drunk. The RAF lads had obviously left in a hurry. We pressed on and soon found the Medical Centre; in fact we found a superb operating theatre complete with its equipment.

The Field Ambulance boys were overwhelmed with delight and in no time loaded the operating table and its equipment into the ambulance and my car, which we then rapidly transferred to our base in Tanjong Katong Road. Captain Barber was over the moon, and with the aid of his RAMC boys soon set up a going concern. I sat back and organized the general picture, and managed to blend the newly arrived UK residents with the Chinese rickshaw boys and the ever helpful Gee Bah, without any difficulty.

No sooner had we got established, and the news got out that we could cope with casualties, than the wounded started to arrive. To my surprise one of the first was Jack Nauen, my botanist friend from Penang. He had what appeared to be a minor injury—a piece of shrapnel had removed one of his fingers. Apart from that he appeared to be all right, though understandably a bit upset. We gave him our special attention, dressed his hand, put him to bed, while Gee Bah gave him a mug of hot sweet tea. Yet to our astonishment he died that night. I was amazed that such a physically fit and strong person should apparently die so

easily. The doctor suggested it was due to 'shock'.
Another Volunteer who was brought in was Tony Lock, my Income Tax colleague. He had a minor shrapnel wound, but made light of it and lived to fight another day. We were in fact soon overwhelmed with casualties, so much so that by about 2 a.m. Captain Barber fainted from exhaustion at the operating table on to his patient, and so we had to put him to bed, and cease operations for the time being.

Now that the Japanese troops were just across the Causeway, our own artillery started to retaliate and the air was full of the most devastating noise imaginable, especially when the 16" guns that had been brought to Singapore to repel an attack from the sea were turned round and began to shell the Japanese in Johore. Indeed when the shells from these mammoth guns went overhead on their way to Johore, they made a noise like an express train going through a railway station. In addition to all this, the Naval Base was blown up, the dry dock sunk, and the huge stocks of oil and raw rubber set on fire so as to deny them to the Japanese. Consequently, during these last days, the air over Singapore was heavy with black smoke and cloud, which had an ominous and foreboding effect on the whole scene.

A few days after the bombing of the *Empress of Asia*, the Singapore Volunteers manning the machine-gun posts along the south coast near Katong, were moved to face the Japanese who had landed on the west coast of Singapore Island, captured Tengah Airfield, and were moving down along the Bukit Timah Road. The Volunteers were allocated positions somewhere near Farrer Road. Consequently, it was suggested I should set up our Regimental Aid Post in Orchard Road, which I did at the Singapore Cold Storage, where there happened to be a suitably placed air raid shelter, and what was even more important in the circumstances, a plentiful supply of food.

As soon as we took up our new position at the Singapore Cold Storage, I noticed a rather strange phenomenon. Every time a Japanese plane passed low over our position, and we happened to be standing outside our shelter, projectiles of some kind would come whistling and ricocheting off the walls around us. We just could not fathom what they were and presumed the planes were dropping something.

Then one day a wounded Gordon Highlander dropped in for some first aid. Again the plane came over, but this time as soon as our Scotsman heard our mystery pings and ricocheting missiles, he immediately shouted 'snipers' and we dived for shelter. Sure enough after keeping a close look-out, we noticed that when the next plane came over, a shuttered window over a deserted Chinese shop across the road opened, followed by the mystery pings and then shut. We were over the road in no time with whatever weapons we could find, and there on the first floor of the deserted Chinese shop we found the sniper's hideout. He had put a chair on a table in the middle of the room, and presumably with the assistance of an accomplice to open the window when the plane flew overhead, had sniped at us. He had escaped, but the floor was covered with empty cartridges. His idea was brilliant but fortunately for us he could not shoot straight!

One day when the shelling and mortaring had abated a bit I walked down Orchard Road, and entered a large house belonging to one of the Singapore Chinese millionaires, to see how they were surviving or if they needed some help. I was surprised to find it completely deserted—the family had fled. In the hall there was a collection of beautiful jade, which must have been worth a fortune. I wondered how long it would be before it would be looted, and left.

By this time the driver of our ambulance and all the Chinese stretcher bearers had disappeared, 'deserted' would be an unkind word to use in the circumstances, for they were no doubt worried about their families. I therefore advised the now faithful Gee Bah that he too should go home and get rid of his uniform.

In the meantime as we were short of dressings, I decided to go back to the Kallang Airport, for I felt sure the RAF would have left plenty of field dressings behind. So I dashed off in Pavillard's smart car, which I was still safe keeping for his possible return, through Singapore which was under constant shell fire, and along Changi Road.

Just before I reached the junction of Changi Road and Tanjong Katong Road, I noticed some field guns manned by British soldiers in position at a check point on the road. As I drove through without stopping, they waved frantically at me and I waved back. Then to my surprise I thought for a moment they had fired at me, but I put it down to boisterous behaviour. I carried on and then turned south into Tanjong Katong Road and suddenly found myself face to face with an approaching low-flying Japanese plane spraying Tanjong Katong Road with bullets. I speedily got out of the car and squeezed myself into a roadside drain before the plane reached me, and escaped injury. Unfortunately, although the drain was fairly deep it was rather narrow, and although in my desperation to find cover I had successfully squeezed into it, I now found I could not get out of it. I shouted for help and eventually a laughing Chinese came along and pulled me out saying *'Tuan suka longkang'* (Tuan likes the drain). I think he meant I liked the drain for shelter, which of course was very true, for Singapore's deep storm drains made excellent shelters.

I then carried on down Tanjong Katong Road and eventually turned westwards towards Kallang Airport, only to be confronted by some friendly but rather surprised Indian soldiers, who were dug in into some trenches, and who informed me they were waiting a ground attack from the Japanese. I was most surprised for I had no idea that the Japanese had successfully landed on the east coast as well as the west. However, I pressed on, finally reached the RAF Medical Centre and found it very much as I had left it. I made a quick search and noticed a huge crate that looked as if it might contain medical supplies. I opened it and found it full of condoms, thousands of them! I therefore had to make do with some bandages and gauze, and hurried back the way I had come, through the line held by the friendly Indian soldiers whose officer was also most concerned for my safety, and back along Tanjong Katong Road to Changi Road. When I reached the check point held by the British soldiers, I was met by such hoots of laughter, clapping and cheering that it suddenly dawned on me what had happened.

I had without knowing it driven through our lines straight for the Japanese army, then turned south and by so doing travelled parallel to our lines along a strip of 'no man's land' for a mile or so, back through the Indian lines; and then returned by the way I had come. On my first way through, the British soldiers had of course tried to stop me (and were not greeting me), then shot at me thinking I was a fifth columnist, and then almost died of laughter when they saw me return, having realized my error! It was only some time later that I discovered that General Percival had tried to form a perimeter around the town of Singapore on December 12, and that I had charged through it. The Japanese troops that I nearly drove into was a Division of the Japanese Imperial Guards!

After this escape I returned to Orchard Road and decided to visit my house at 13 Fort Canning Hill again to see if my brothers were around.

Japanese shells and mortar bombs were now falling thick and fast while the Japanese had complete air control, so much so that their low-flying pilots were bombing and machine-gunning the streets at will. I therefore decided that going by car in the daylight was too dangerous. So I investigated the drains, and found a lovely, deep, wide, smelly drain that led all the way along Orchard Road to the foot of Fort Canning Hill. I then sprinted the last bit when there were no low-flying planes around, and found both my brothers at home at the back of the house in the kitchen. This, they explained, was the safest place to be, for it was on the leeward side of the house which was under constant shellfire. My house 13 Fort Canning Hill was unfortunately located on the slopes of Fort Canning, the Supreme Headquarters of Malaya Command and a prime target.

I was told that the Chevrolet car I had bought from Ogle had received a direct hit and was finished; John had narrowly escaped being killed by a shell; the house had caught fire but they had managed to put it out, otherwise everything was all right. So I joined them for tea, but when I helped myself to tea from the teapot, I found it contained whisky! This, they explained, was due to the fact that orders had just been issued by General Percival that all liquor must be destroyed, so it was necessary to camouflage it!

My brothers and I, I should add, were in very good spirits! Although all around us seemed to be falling apart, we were after all at war and expected something of this kind; moreover, there was a strong rumour that there were hundreds of American planes on the way—all we had to do was hang on. There certainly was no thought of surrender for we knew that once we had planes, we could more than hold our own. So as soon as it got dark, I made my way back to Orchard Road, convinced that this was the beginning of an historic siege. The next day, February 14, was another hectic day. The sky was covered with great dark clouds from the burning city and the burning oil tanks. The Japanese planes seemed to be able to do what they liked, unmolested. The mortar fire was heavy and persisted all day.

Early that morning while talking to Corporal Baker also of our Regimental Aid Post, we watched two Chinese-looking civilians run across Orchard Road, and suddenly realized that there was something out of character with the clothes they were wearing. They were wearing khaki shorts, but the long type normally worn by Japanese and seldom by Chinese. We ran behind the block and intercepted them. When I said, '*Mana pergi?*' (Where are you going?) there was no reply. And then when I said, '*Apa nama?*' (What's your name?)—again no reply. We knew that even the most Malay language-blind Chinese could answer those questions and arrested them, for they were obviously Japanese. I wondered afterwards, whether they were the two who had been sniping at us! Anyhow they were very fortunate, for they were probably prisoners of war for only a few days.

About midday I received an urgent telephone call from the Australians for help, asking if I could come and pick up two of their 'cobbers' in Holland Road who were seriously wounded. As my ambulance driver had disappeared, I drove it myself along Orchard Road, but had hardly gone 180 metres before I found that the junction of Orchard Road with Scott Road was under heavy mortar fire. To dash through at that moment would have probably meant certain death, so I took cover in a 2-metre deep storm drain which ran alongside Orchard Road. To my surprise I soon found myself joined by George Denaro (Major Denaro of the Malay Regiment) whom I knew well and who was on his way to rejoin his regiment in the Pasir Panjang area. He also had been forced to take cover. While we were chatting, waiting for the shelling and mortaring to stop, I noticed that the frangipani tree that overhung our drain was shedding its leaves like falling snow. So I asked him: 'Why is this tree shedding its leaves, George?' 'Shrapnel,' he answered with a smile, and I kicked myself for being so stupid. I also realized that nobody could live very long above ground, while that shelling and mortaring persisted and kept quiet.

In due course the shelling and mortaring stopped, for the Japanese had obviously found a new target. So I got back into my damaged and slightly bedraggled ambulance and proceeded along Holland Road, where I picked up the two very badly wounded Australian soldiers. I took them to the General Hospital, but when I got there, I found a huge queue of ambulances. I also noticed a huge hole in the ground full of dead bodies, so decided to go elsewhere. Somebody suggested the Victoria Memorial Hall, my former office, and as I knew for sure where it was located, decided to go there.

The drive was hectic for the mortaring and the shelling seemed to be reaching a crescendo, especially at some of the well-known crossroads. But I knew Singapore fairly well and so was able to avoid some of them. Nevertheless when I eventually got to South Bridge Road, it seemed to be a veritable hell for it was full of burning vehicles, fallen telegraph poles, crater holes, and exploding shells; it was receiving the most intensive shelling I had so far experienced. The Japanese would of course have known that this was the heart of Chinatown in Singapore and may well have given it special attention. I had no alternative but to drive through it, and as I did the shells were bursting against the tops of the houses and some of their walls collapsing on to the road, just missing my ambulance by inches. As I drove relentlessly along, I could hear my two patients at the back of the ambulance cursing and blaspheming the Japanese and egging me on with 'Good on yer Sarge,' and so on.

Eventually, I got through to the Victoria Memorial Hall unscathed, but was again met by a queue of ambulances. I was naturally concerned that my two Australians would not survive unless they had medical attention fairly soon. So I left the ambulance in the queue and went inside but could not see a single doctor anywhere—just scores of wounded soldiers. In desperation I shouted, 'Isn't there a bloody doctor here?' and again, 'For God's sake, isn't there a doctor here?'

To my amazement a doctor suddenly appeared. He was Captain Bill Frankland, RAMC whom I had known many years previously when he was a medical student at St. Mary's Hospital, London, and I had been a student at the LSE.

He said, 'I heard your voice and knew it was you.' He came immediately to my rescue and thankfully took in my two Australians. I never knew who they were and I doubt if the poor chaps survived.

On my way back to Orchard Road, I drove past the *padang* and there I saw a beautiful sight—at least a dozen field guns manned by Australians firing non-stop. I stopped and talked to one of them, and asked him what the target was. He just said, 'We are firing off all our ammo,' with no mention of any target. I thought this was a rather ominous sign.

As far as I can remember, February 15 started fairly quietly, with the occasional mortaring and the distant *pom pom* of Japanese field guns. Then about midday I was surprised by a visit from my brother Tiny, who informed me that we had surrendered. I was thunderstruck at this suggestion, and for a moment convinced he had turned traitor, and said 'Tommy, I never thought a brother of mine would be a fifth columnist,' and did not believe a word of it. But he laughed at my response and pleaded with me, saying that he had just been to Fort Canning Hill and had been told the unpalatable truth that we had surrendered. Indeed he elaborated and said that an hour or so previously, together with my other brother John, they had run into an army captain at the foot of Fort Canning Hill who had informed them that we had surrendered. So they had arrested the captain, and frog marched him up the hill to Fort Canning so that he could be locked up as a traitor. However, to their consternation the captain's unwelcome news was confirmed by a Senior Officer of Malaya Command, and so they had to release him!

When I heard this and considered the matter further, and pondered that this day had so far been a rather quiet one, and that after all he was my brother, I accepted that what he was saying must be true. He then told me that he would be joining my brother John, who was still working for the

Government as a Customs Officer and Food Controller. He also said that John had a Customs launch hidden down at the docks, so if I could make my way there before sunset which was of course 6 p.m., we might be able to escape. I therefore returned to 13 Fort Canning Hill and as I approached the house, met a Tamil gentleman carrying on his shoulders one of my large black steel trunks, containing my warm suits, etc. with my name G. E. D. Lewis clearly marked on it in large letters. As he passed me, he politely said, 'Tabek, Tuan,' (Good day, sir.) as if looting was a perfectly normal thing to do. I replied in the same vein and went upstairs, where I found that looters had removed most of my property. There was, however, a loaded rifle on the table and I speculated for a moment that a looter should be shot, but thought better of it and decided that I would rather that the poor Tamil have my property than the Japanese. I then put a few things together in my pack including Lyn's photograph, noticed that the eyes had been removed from a portrait hanging on the wall, went downstairs and sat down on the steps at the front door, and before departing, suddenly uncontrollably had a good cry!

I then made my way down towards the docks, picking my way through abandoned burnt out and wrecked motor vehicles, and on the way, met a young captain of the East Surrey Regiment. As we seemed to like each other's company, we decided to make our escape together. However, when we got to the wharf my brother had mentioned, there was no sign of my brothers or of any boats. In fact there was not a boat of any kind in sight. All the boats had already been taken by the early birds and by deserters earlier on in the week. So the East Surrey captain and I decided that we had better rejoin our units wherever they might be, for nobody could foretell how the victorious Japanese soldiers would behave on the following day, but there might be some safety in numbers.

I eventually arrived exhausted at the Headquarters of the Singapore Volunteers Corps in Beach Street opposite Raffles Hotel late that night to the smell of burning paper. I was told that our senior officers had been burning secret documents, and any papers that might be of use to the Japanese, all that evening. And so with the smell of burning paper in my nostrils, I fell fast asleep.

Chapter 5

PRISONER OF WAR: SINGAPORE

Sarang tebuan jangan dijolok. (Let sleeping dogs lie.)

Malay Proverb

The better part of valour is discretion. (Falstaff)

Shakespeare: Henry IV Part 1

I well remember on the morning of February 16 thinking to myself: I have just lost my house and all my worldly goods. Will I now lose my life? So as soon as we were informed that the Japanese expected us all to be in Changi by 2 p.m., I had a quick breakfast, got into a vehicle and started on my journey. It then occurred to me that I should also take with me what medical equipment I could find, and went back to the Singapore Cold Storage.

Just near the Cold Storage in Orchard Road, I met my first Japanese. He stopped me, seemed to be a senior officer, and spoke to me politely in quite good English. He said, 'Show me Governor's House,' and produced one of our own one-inch maps of Singapore Island which I noticed, to my surprise, had many place names overprinted on it in Japanese characters. I showed him, and he thanked me, and was off in a great hurry.

My first impression of the Japanese takeover was therefore favourable, indeed what I expected, for the Japanese businessmen I had known while I was in the Singapore War Tax Department had always been very polite, with so much bowing and 'excuse me' that I had been bowled over by their apparent courtesy.

I then continued my way along Orchard Road, but in Bras Basah Road, was stopped by a Japanese soldier who rudely shouted '*kurah*' at me, and got into the car. He was a short, aggressive-looking chap, and was wearing strange web-toed rubber boots. Then without wasting any time he pointed at my Omega watch and said, '*clock-o*'. Thinking he wanted to know the time, I tried to oblige but he was not satisfied, and then shouted '*bakayaro*' at me. Of course I thought *bakayaro* which he pronounced *bugero* meant what any English-speaking person would and concluded he was displeased, and when he then withdrew his pistol, decided that he was in fact a highwayman who wanted my watch. So I gave it to him. He then made me drive around a bit, and after a while indicated he wanted to stop, and when he pointed rather coarsely between his legs, I decided he wanted to urinate. I was right, for he wanted it badly and immediately urinated very publicly into the storm drain near by. I had by now decided that I did not care very much for my new friend and thought he would soon want my gold ring as well, so I dashed off towards Changi while he was thus preoccupied, to the accompaniment of more shouts of *kurah*, a word I have never had translated.

Having thus discovered very soon that not all Japanese were gentlemen, I drove straight for Changi, picking up a few wounded British and Australian soldiers on the way. Unfortunately after a few kilometres, we ran into a Japanese checkpoint. They confiscated my vehicle. Moreover, my attempts at retaining the vehicle so that the wounded soldiers would not have to walk were rudely rebuffed and I suffered my first face-slapping for attempting it. Nevertheless we congratulated ourselves that we had not been compelled to walk the whole way to Changi in the hot sun.

When I reached Changi I found that the Malayan Volunteers had been allocated one of the buildings in Kitchener Barracks. We medicals had been allocated the guard room as a medical centre. We started work the next day, with two volunteer doctors, Captain Watson from Telok Anson, and Major Crawford from Johore. We were soon very busy with those war casualties who could still walk. One of them was my old rugby-playing friend Frank Smith (later British Adviser, Perlis and Terengganu). He had received a nasty bullet wound right across his back, just missing his spine, while serving as a second lieutenant with the Malay Regiment. I dressed his wound with 'Eusol' every day for a month before it healed.

Soon after arriving at Kitchener Barracks, I was ap-proached by G. S. Mowatt, previously District Officer, Muar, Johore with a proposal that we should escape. His idea was that as we both spoke Malay, we should be able to make our way up country without much difficulty, and as a medical I could take care of that side of things. I found Mowatt an attractive personality, and was greatly tempted, but thought his plan a bit premature. Far better I suggested to wait until we were perhaps moved up country.

But he was determined to go, so I equipped him as best I could with medical supplies, and he escaped. Unfortunately as I had feared, and discovered many years later, he contracted malaria in Johore, but the kampong Malays, after helping him at first, decided to hand him over to the Japanese, partly through fear of the Japanese and partly so as to collect a reward. When he resisted this idea, he was struck down with a parang, seriously wounded, and eventu-ally ended up in Pudu Jail, Kuala Lumpur.

The first few weeks at Changi were very unpleasant, for there was very little food and there were many times when I was really hungry. There was also very little water, so bathing was only possible when it rained. Consequently, we spent much of our time discussing the war and learning of some of the atrocities that had been committed by our honourable Japanese captors.

I will not describe those incidents of which I have no personal knowledge, but I feel I should record the case of the Chinese who were members of the Singapore Volunteer Corps. Soon after the surrender of Singapore, the Japanese announced that they knew there had been many Chinese in the Singapore Volunteers and that they had not surrendered, but if they did so, they would be treated honourably. Over one hundred surrendered and were immediately tied up to each other, loaded on to lorries, taken out to the Changi beach, forced into the shallow water and machine-gunned, that is, they were murdered: One of them feigned death and when the night came, managed to crawl into our POW camp at Changi. His name was Wong Sin Joon of Whitley Road, Singapore.

Unfortunately, someone must have seen him crawl into our camp because the following day the Japanese came looking for him. I happened to be in the hospital ward where

Wong was being cared for by one of our doctors when a Japanese officer and two soldiers suddenly appeared at the end of the ward. I left immediately, and the English doctor with great presence of mind instructed Wong to play dead and pulled the white cotton sheet over him. When the Japanese came to his bed, the doctor indicated he was *finish-o*, and the Japanese officer passed on without lifting the sheet!

After that escape, there was still the problem of what to do with Wong. The problem was solved when one of our Eurasian Singapore Volunteers called Leonard died of his wounds. The doctor now seized the opportunity and transferred Wong's photograph into Leonard's army pay book. And so the very Chinese-looking Wong Sin Joon became the very Chinese-looking Eurasian 'Leonard'. He got away with it, but the Japanese were always suspicious. On many occasions in later years, Japanese soldiers would poke him in the ribs and say: 'You, China ka?' and Wong (sorry Leonard) would protest 'No, No' and go into a long explanation about his ancestors, saying that unfortunately he just happened to look like a Chinese! I got to know him well and he often helped me with my study of Chinese characters.

The other incident which shocked us took place at the Alexandra Military Hospital when the Japanese troops overran it just before the capitulation. They not only bayonetted the doctors and the patients on their beds, but killed one patient on the operating table. I spoke to one patient; he survived because he managed to hide under his bed. They also murdered several more the following day.

Of course many ugly things happen in the heat of battle, especially when individual soldiers are free to do what they like. But the murder of the Chinese Volunteers disgusted us. For this was a clear case of cold-blooded massacre carried out by the Japanese High Command itself, after a safe conduct of their lives had been promised. It did not take place in the heat of battle; it was cold-blooded murder by the Japanese generals, who prided themselves on Japanese chivalry. What is more, we soon learnt of many more murders, as Chinese and other heads began to appear on poles in Singapore. In fact the Japanese massacred tens of thousands of Chinese after the capitulation.

I must admit I was completely unprepared for this kind of barbarity, from the much-trumpeted land of Japanese chivalry or *bushido*. I thought such barbarous and deceitful behaviour despicable and never trusted them again. And I often wondered what happened to Gee Bah and prayed he had not fallen victim to Japanese duplicity.

In the early days, a favourite pastime of ours at Kitchener Barracks was to estimate how long we would be imprisoned. Some bright spark had drawn a four-year scale on one of the pillars in the barracks, and we were invited to put our names against what we thought was the appropriate time of our imprisonment. Most estimated that we would be prisoners for a year or thereabouts, some two years, a few like myself two-and-a-half years, and one 'mad man' three-and-a-half years. It was the 'mad man' who was proved correct.

After a month or so, conditions improved considerably, mainly as a result of our own efforts. Thus the cooks managed to devise ovens out of Roneo cabinets placed horizontally and longwise over trenches built into the hill slope. I also managed to bring water to the wash basin and lavatory at our Medical Centre. I had noticed that although we had no water in the daytime, there was water available in our tap at night-time, at about 2 a.m. So I scrounged a large tank, put it on top of our guard room and linked the exit from the tank to the in-coming water pipe. During the night as the water pressure rose so the water ran in our tank and when it was full, overflowed thus waking me up. I then turned a stopcock so as to trap the water in the tank and in this way had all modern conveniences during the daytime. When the tank was empty, we repeated the procedure.

The other great improvement was the development of the so-called University of Changi. As we had many of the professors from Raffles College in our camp, we soon had some extremely good lectures going. I attended a short course on Symbolic Logic given by the former editor of the *Statesman of India*, who was well versed in the subject. I then switched to Chinese, my teacher being a Colonel Swanne, who knew some *Kuo-yu*, the other student being a Captain Rawlings who was already fluent in Japanese and whose brother was in the Malayan Civil Service. To assist me in learning Chinese characters, I put a hundred characters or so on to small pieces of white cardboard with the romanized version on the other side.

One day while I was sitting under a tree deeply engrossed learning my Chinese characters, I suddenly discovered I had a Japanese guard at my shoulder. I happened to have the Chinese character *shin* (heart) in front of me, and the guard said, '*Nan-da?*' (What's that?) '*Kokoro,*' I cunningly replied— *kokoro* being the Japanese equivalent of *shin*. '*Yoroshi,*' said the Japanese, well pleased that I was learning *Nippon-Go* (Japanese language).

He then unfortunately picked up my card, turned it over and when he realized I was learning Chinese, blew up with many *bakayaros* and *konoyaros* which, of course, are terms of abuse, with some face-slapping as well in the bargain. So I decided to take up the study of Japanese instead, as it appeared to be the safest language to learn in the circumstances.

One of my companions at Changi was Tom Callam, a former well-known dentist at Singapore, and who was now practising the art as a POW at our Medical Centre. Tom took a different view of the future to most of us; he thought the Russians would rule the roost after the war, and so was assiduously learning Russian. His teacher was a white Russian who had formerly run a band in Singapore.

More important from my point of view, however, at that time when food was short, was the fact that Tom had just started a duck farm and I had somehow acquired two ducks with nowhere to keep them. Tom kindly agreed to add them to his flock on terms to be amicably agreed between us.

I therefore did some research, and found that according to some encylopaedia I had read, a duck should lay 250 eggs per year, so I estimated that two ducks would lay 500 eggs a year. Consequently I argued that as there were 365 days in the year, if he gave me one egg per day, he would make a profit of 135 eggs a year. He agreed. Unfortunately things did not quite work out that way, for his 20 ducks produced only two or three eggs a day, so he asked for a new agreement. I ended up with one egg a week!

After about three months, just as I was settling down to my new environment and beginning to enjoy it, we were told that the Japanese wanted a working party for Singapore.

The party consisted of about 200 POWs drawn from the Singapore, Johore, and FMS Volunteers, while I was part of the medical party. Colonel Newey of the Singapore Volunteers Corps was put in charge of the party; our destination, the Singapore Race Course; and the work, cutting grass for use as fodder for the Japanese horses.

Our Japanese guards occupied the former tea rooms at the Race Course, but we were accommodated in the stand from where we had a good view of the Race Course. I spent about three months at the Race Course camp and accompanied the working parties as a medical orderly and a tea boy. We cut grass all over the place, at the Race Course to begin with, but in the gardens of the more luxurious houses most of the time. This sometimes had very amusing results. Thus one day, one of our party who had previously been Secretary to the Singapore Turf Club found himself cutting the grass in his own garden. The Japanese were delighted and quite sympathetic!

On another occasion we were employed as labourers at a godown in the docks containing medical supplies. I stuffed myself with calcium tablets which I thought would do me good until I was almost sick, and also managed to scrounge (our polite word for stealing) a tin containing about 250 tablets of atebrin, and a Burroughs Welcome wallet of concentrated medicines designed for explorers and travellers in remote areas! The atebrin later proved invaluable, but the Burroughs Welcome wallet was useless without its complementary instruction book or diary. Scrounging (or stealing) was, of course, an honourable profession amongst prisoners of war, for it was regarded as aiding the Allied War effort. Of course, when the war ended the habit took a bit of shaking off, for after three-and-a-half years, we had developed a certain facility at the profession.

The Japanese, who were our guards at the Race Course camp, were on the whole quite reasonable. They had all taken part in the recent fighting, were soldiers of the Japanese Imperial Guard, and were a well-disciplined lot. One day they invited us to a party to celebrate some Japanese festival. Our Colonel was in a quandary, refused to go himself, but sent a small delegation of about ten of us, so as not to cause offence. I was one of those chosen to go.

The party started off quietly with some speeches by the Japanese, and then some rice and saké. After the meal was finished and we thought the party was over, we realized that in fact it had just begun. For we discovered that we were all expected to put on our own individual bit of entertainment for the benefit of the rest. The Japanese soldiers started and sang some excruciating songs, mixed with some play-acting and so on. This went on for some time while we drank more and more saké, which we were not accustomed to, and which made us very drunk. When my turn came to make an exhibition of myself, and having by now lost all my inhibitions and dislike of the Japanese, I showed them a trick I had been taught in Penang. I ate the drinking glass containing my saké! Provided the glass is thin, it is possible to break up a glass with one's teeth and pretend to swallow it by putting the glass under one's tongue. The Japanese were mystified at this performance of mine, and I consequently became a firm favourite of the Japanese Socho (or Sergeant Major), who was a fine-looking soldier called Takei, and whom I must admit I also took a liking to.

The party continued late into the night, with much drinking, shouting and singing. I eventually found my way home, but some were not so fortunate. One of our small POW party, none other than our RQMS, fell over the grave of a Japanese soldier who had been killed in the recent fighting around the Race Course, failed to get up until the morning, and contracted pneumonia! The Colonel was very displeased, the Japanese highly amused, while the RQMS recovered after a week or two in bed.

One of our main preoccupations at the Race Course camp was, of course, the news. And in this respect we were well served by Teddy Yates, who had previously had a radio shop in Singapore, and was now being employed by the Japanese soldiers to keep their radio going so that they could listen in to Tokyo news.

His technique was simple and effective. When the Japanese radio broke down, he would go and repair it at about 9.30 GMT, just before the 10 o'clock BBC news from London. He would pretend that in order to repair the set, it was necessary to wear earphones rather like a doctor wears a stethoscope when attending to his patient, and listen in to the

10 o'clock news. He would then repair the fault, and put some acid on one of the wires so that it would break down again in about a month, and so keep us supplied with news! The trouble with this system was that we were better supplied with news than the Japanese, and it took a great deal of self-control not to contradict them when they gave us their version of the news.

Teddy Yates had the full confidence of our Japanese soldiers, and they even allowed him to have his own little workshop for repairing their wireless set. One evening, however, Teddy Yates and a friend went down to his small workshop under the stairs to listen to the 10 o'clock BBC news. In the middle of this forbidden activity, a Japanese guard suddenly opened the door, which he had forgotten to lock, and asked the friend who was sitting opposite the door, '*Doko Yates-ka*?' (Where is Yates?) The friend indicated vaguely that he was upstairs, and the guard left to find him. But in fact Yates was listening to the BBC news *behind* the door. If he had been caught, he would have been severely punished, and possibly not survived it.

One day in August 1942, I was informed that Colonel Newey wished to see me, and I went along like a schoolboy going to see the Headmaster, wondering what I might have done wrong. When I got to the Colonel's office, he was very affable and asked me to sit down which was unusual. He then informed me that the Japanese wanted a Malay interpreter to work at their Headquarters in the former Outram Road School in Singapore, and that he had selected me for the job because he knew that as an Education Officer, I must have passed the Standard II Malay examination for government officers. Then after some hesitation, he proceeded to say it was a rather a special job, and that as a fellow Welshman, he had selected me for this job because he knew he could trust me and I would not let him down. When I asked him what was special about it he added he wanted me to collect military intelligence. In other words he wanted me to spy. A funny feeling came over me but I tried to keep calm and listened attentively.

He then produced a code which I was to use in sending secret messages to him. It consisted of about six pages of code words with their meanings, and was headed 'Matlockgo'. He explained it would be up to me to find ways of taking it with me into Japanese Headquarters, and suggested I should hide it as soon as I got there. But of course if I was caught, he, the Colonel, would know nothing about it. The military information he wanted in particular was the movement of warships in Singapore Harbour.

At first I was elated that I should have been picked for the job, then a bit scared when I pondered what would happen to me if I was caught. It never occurred to me to refuse to do it, or to suggest that perhaps somebody else would be more suitable. I suppose it was a case of orders are orders.

As I had to report for duty the next day, I had very little time to decide how to take the code with me. I finally decided to fold it neatly and put it into the breast pocket of my shirt. Only a fool would report at Japanese Headquarters with a secret service code in his breast pocket. So I did just that. When I finally got to the Outram Road Headquarters, I was met by a friendly and polite Japanese interpreter, who took me to his boss the Japanese officer who did not look so friendly, and then to my quarters with some two hundred Australian RAASC prisoners of war who were employed driving vehicles for the Japanese. I found I was sharing a small room, or lean to, with the senior Australian sergeant Jack Lee from Toowoomba, Queensland. And so I had succeeded in getting my 'hot potato' to its destination without being detected.

But I now had to let my Australian companion into the secret. He took the news that he was harbouring a spy with a certain amount of calm amusement. I had, of course, to let him know where I had hidden the code, so that he could keep well away from it, and promise not to involve him in the affair. But he proved an excellent companion and conspirator, as were all the other Australians.

It was a novel experience living with 'fair dinkum' Aussies, and I enjoyed their company immensely. They were a fine group of men, not disciplined in the way British troops are, but disciplined nevertheless by their own code of ethics. They didn't suffer fools gladly, but if you could fool the Japanese, you were accepted enthusiastically.

And so it happened to me, for on the first day when the Aussies were chased out early in the morning by the Japanese for *tenko* (roll call) and they tried to get me out as well, I responded by saying 'English soldier no *tenko*'. I had observed that the Japanese were often susceptible to suggestion. So on this occasion, the Japanese took me at my word, and left me alone to stay in bed. The Aussies thought such bluff was the sign of a superior brain, and nicknamed me the 'Count', from then on.

My official work at the Japanese Headquarters in Outram Road was that of Malay interpreter working with the Japanese interpreter, who was a decent Japanese called Uchida Masahiro who could speak English but knew no Malay. The Senior Japanese Officer, always referred to me as 'O-San' which I gathered was not offensive, and treated me rather like a pet dog. The Headquarters administered all the POWs in Singapore, while Uchida and I were required to prepare all the paysheets for the POWs (Officers thirty cents, other ranks ten cents per day), as well as assist as interpreters with any problems of discipline that might arise, of which there were many.

As far as I can now remember, there were two main POW camps in the urban area of Singapore; one at the Great World, a former entertainment park and the other off the River Valley Road. The first was a most extraordinary camp, with mainly Australian prisoners of war living in buildings that had previously housed a variety of entertainment booths with their garish signs still up. The River Valley Road camp was located in a swampy frog infested area, and consisted of rows of rickety huts made out of bamboo and covered with attap, with a muddy passageway in between, and which had originally been built in a hurry to accommodate up-country refugees, during the recent war. Here the prisoners were both British and Australian, and the conditions awful.

The POWs housed in these two camps, worked in various places but especially in the docks and in the godowns (or warehouses) where they sometimes had a field day, furthering the Allied cause by pilfering and stealing anything that came their way. One such POW who worked at these docks was the Australian Russell Braddon, the author of *The Naked Island*, whose book gives an excellent account of the Japanese invasion of Malaya, from a young Australian soldier's point of view. His description of a day working in a godown is also worth quoting:

> For eight riotous hours, as we worked under the justifiable suspicious eyes of our guards, we ate chocolates and cough cubes, drank bay rum, cough mixture, cod liver oil and the essence of vanilla—in equal and indiscriminate quantities; applied hair tonic to the hair, face cream to the face, and iodex to almost anything; mixed handfuls of sugar with handfuls of herrings in tomato sauce and devoured the resulting mess; and sold lipsticks by the dozen to the Chinese outside the back door.

Of course many POWs were caught. When the thief was caught by a Sikh guard or the crime was considered serious, the culprits were brought to our Headquarters where Uchida and I were called upon to interpret between both side in front of the Japanese officer. Of course I did my best to help the POW culprits by misinterpreting the evidence, for as I have already said we regarded stealing from the Japanese as aiding the Allied cause.

There on one occasion an Australian 'thief' was brought before the Japanese officer at our Headquarters by a Sikh guard, with Uchida and me in attendance as interpreters. When the Sikh guard found that he had to give his evidence in Malay before a Malay-speaking white soldier, who was obviously a former Malayan resident, he was very embarrassed. As I cross-examined him, I was able to make him contradict himself quite easily as his Malay was rather limited. Moreover, when I discovered that he had formerly been a policeman in Singapore, I enjoyed his discomfort. The Japanese I discovered had no more respect for the Sikh turncoats then we did, and just made use of them. I therefore had no difficulty in persuading Uchida that the Sikh guard was lying, and the Aussie soldier got off, much to his surprise.

Although I now found myself in the role of a spy, I was in fact a rather reluctant spy, not so much because I was not prepared to do what somebody had to do, but because I had had no training in the business. I therefore embarked on a Teach Yourself course. The Outram Road POW camp had a small library with several books on spying in the First

World War, so I read them all, and found one book written by a German master spy quite instructive. He maintained that the best code was the code that one designed for oneself. I therefore spent some time wondering how the code I now possessed could be converted into a form that I had myself designed, so that nobody else could recognize it as a code. After much thought I finally worked out what I considered to be a brilliant solution, but to carry it out I would first need a Japanese dictionary. I spoke to Jack Lee, my Australian companion from Toowoomba, and he made it known to his Australian truck drivers that the Pommie 'Count' needed a Japanese pocket dictionary. Within a week or so they had stolen or 'scrounged' about ten dictionaries! One of them was ideal for my purpose. It was an English–Japanese dictionary, consisting of one thousand pages of words but as it was printed on India paper, it weighed very little.

The new version of the code that I now devised consisted of numbers as follows. Let us assume the code word for *aircraft carrier* was the word *good*. Then the code number for the word *aircraft carrier* would be $26.10 where 26 was the page upon which the word *aircraft carrier* appeared in my Japanese dictionary, 10 the number of lines down the page upon which it appeared, and the dollar sign $ a bit of camouflage! Similarly the code number for the code word *good* might be $200.12 indicating that the code word *good* was on page 200, the 12th line down.

I then transposed the whole of my code into numbers, camouflaged as dollars and cents, but in reality referring to locations in my English–Japanese dictionary. But there still remained the problem of how I could justify carrying such a list of numbers around with me, for it was too long to represent a shopping list! I solved that problem too by getting into a friendly argument with Uchida.

I worked every day in the Japanese Headquarters in Outram Road with Uchida, helping him prepare the pay-sheets for the POWs. He used an abacus, and I used an adding machine. One day I teased him about using such an out-of-date device, and he replied that he could add up quicker on his abacus than I could on my adding machine. So I challenged him to a friendly contest, and volunteered to produce some numbers for us to add up. Of course I produced my code numbers! I added them up on my adding machine, with the numbers conveniently recorded on a long slip of paper; Uchida added them up on his abacus. Uchida won and I lost, but we were both happy, for different reasons!

Indeed I was very happy for I was now in the matchless position that I could explain to any inquisitive Japanese not only why I possessed the English-Japanese dictionary, (for was I not an enthusiastic student of *Nippon-Go*?), but also the list of numbers, for they were the result of a friendly competition I had with the Japanese interpreter, by the name Uchida Masahiro, in Singapore. It was with great relief that I destroyed the potentially lethal code as delivered to me by my Commanding Officer Colonel Newey. But I was sorry about my treatment of the kind Uchida. He had been very good to me and I regarded him as a friend, and this was no way to treat a friend, even though it was but a minor dirty trick.

Apart from that bit of unavoidable deception, my relations with Uchida were excellent. I would often spend an evening with him and teach him Malay, while he would respond by teaching me *Nippon-Go* (Japanese). He also introduced me to some interesting books on Japan such as *Things Japanese* by Chamberlain, and the famous Japanese author Koizumi Yakumbo, who was in fact an American by the name of Lafcadio Hearn.

Although Uchida was nominally a samurai, and always carried a sword, he was in fact a cultured and unaggressive person. He was the only Japanese with whom I ever had a close personal relationship as a prisoner of war and I have always treasured his memory.

As for gathering military information, the Colonel was quite right in thinking that I would be in an excellent position to acquire it. For the Australian truck drivers, with whom I was closely billeted, travelled all over the island and especially the docks, and came home every evening with information about what was going on and how many ships there were in the harbour. Indeed they came home one evening with an extraordinary story of how they had spoken to some German sailors, off a German submarine, who gave them cigarettes. They wanted to know why the Australian prisoners allowed themselves to be pushed around so much by the Japanese. Generally speaking, there was no difficulty in passing information on to the Colonel at the Race Course camp, for one of our drivers visited the camp almost every day delivering rations and so on. During the whole five months that I was at the Outram Road Headquarters, I cannot remember sending more than a few messages in code.

The underground activities in Singapore during those days of Japanese occupation were legion; the blackmarket was in full swing, stealing and much worse were commonplace. I can now remember only a few such activities. One was the Australian truck driver who stole a tin of M & B 693 while at a godown. He then carefully disguised it as rubbish by wrapping some old paper round it, and deposited it in the Outram Road POW camp refuse bin, which was taken away by the Chinese swill collector the following morning. The Chinese swill collector then sold the tin of M & B 693, kept his commission and returned the money due to the driver at the bottom of the swill bin.

Australian and British working parties, especially those working in the godowns became expert thieves or scroungers, as they preferred to be called. Favourite hiding places were water bottles, and in the case of the Australians, under the rather large Australian hat on top of one's head. One amusing incident I witnessed was when a thirsty Japanese guard attempted to drink out of a POW's water bottle, found it rattled, and poured out a bicycle chain!

Another ingenious deception came to light when some British POWs took over some road work and a steamroller from an Australian unit. On the first day, the British soldier who had been given the job of driving the steamroller was asked by the Japanese soldier in charge how much petrol he required for the steamroller for the next week's work. He was informed that the Australian driver of the steamroller managed on two gallons of petrol a day!

Our Outram Road POW camp was plagued with bed bugs, which were impossible to eradicate, under the conditions that we were living. So occasionally there would be a big clean-up, or perhaps I should say a big pick-up of bed bugs. Thousands of bed bugs would be collected by the Australians, put into match boxes, and then deposited surreptitiously in the Japanese sleeping quarters. There was some satisfaction to be gained from sharing the discomfort.

After spending about four months at the Japanese Head-quarters in Outram Road, there was a sudden big move, brought about we suspected by the onward advance of the Japanese Imperial Guards towards Australia. I returned to the Race Course camp in January 1943 only to find that Colonel Newey and the Volunteers had returned to Changi. In their place, there was a small party of Pathan POWs who had bravely refused to join the Indian National Army, in spite of short rations and threats to their lives. We became bosom pals in distress! I was left with about ten Australian drivers and reverted to being a medical sergeant again. I had very little to do, as my patients were well able to look after them-selves, and spent most of our time playing chess. Then suddenly and with little warning, we were informed that we would all return to Changi in a few days.

Before returning to Changi, however, our small group of British and Australian POWs received a most unexpected invitation. We received an invitation from the Pathan POWs to afternoon tea! The Japanese, of course, would have suffered apoplexy if they had got wind of it, so we wondered how our Pathan friends were going to manage it.

We had tea that evening in the part of the Race Course grandstand furthest away from the tea room where the Japanese guards were housed. We had tea and cakes. The table was covered with a white table-cloth, which looked as if it had been made out of a Japanese tent, which it undoubtedly was. The table was also decorated with flowers. There were some quietly spoken speeches of loyalty from the Pathans, and then as if to tempt fate, a comic sketch of Japanese soldiers on parade, with a Pathan mimicking a tiny Japanese officer with a very long wooden sword. It was a hilarious spectacle, and a fantastic farewell for us, but very rash. Nevertheless, our Pathans assured us that there was nothing to worry about, that they had sentries posted, and that if any Japanese were seen coming in our direction, the tables would have been cleared and all the cakes and flowers removed out of sight. I must say I was greatly relieved when the tea party was over, for these loyal soldiers would have suffered greatly if they had been caught entertaining us to tea, especially on table-cloths made out of Japanese tents.

We started our journey by going to the River Valley camp which was occupied by Indian POWs, most of whom were supposed to have joined the INA, and some, for example, the Gurkhas who most definitely had not. We were lodged for the night in the bamboo and attap camp chapel, so as to be isolated from the Indians. But after dark, we received a clandestine visit from one of their senior officers, carrying a copy of the INA newspaper. We discovered that carrying the INA newspaper was a bluff, and that he had come to explain that the Indian soldiers had been forced into joining the INA and that the Japanese had threatened to shoot them if they didn't join. He wished us to deliver a message to his old commanding officer, who was an Englishman in the Changi POW camp.

Then later in the middle of the night, I was woken by the sound of marching feet just outside our small chapel. I got up and looked out, and there about 6 metres away, I watched in amazement a small group of Gurkha soldiers march past in the moonlight, while the Japanese were asleep. They were fully dressed, no words were spoken, but as they passed us, they gave an 'eyes left' and disappeared. Tears came to my eyes at this extraordinary gesture of loyalty and solidarity.

The next day, on March 1, 1943, we returned to the Changi POW camp. Our truck was loaded high with rice bags and our *barang* (luggage), and I sat on top of it all so as to get a good view. We passed several civilian working parties, but I did not see any of my brothers, but my brother Tiny apparently saw me, for in his secret diary* he made the following entry:

March 1. All Welshmen in the camp had a meeting on St. David's Day. On the outside wood fatigue, I saw my brother Gerwyn on a lorry which passed us on the Tampenes Road and he appeared to be well. I am not sure whether he saw me. Hopes of repatriation have been raised again....

---

*T. M. P. Lewis: *Changi: The Lost Years. A Malayan Diary 1941–45* (Malayan Historical Society, Kuala Lumpur 1954)

Soon after arriving at Changi, I received the welcome news that I was in any case going to be allowed to see my brothers in Changi Jail. And so on March 13, 1943, I and some others were marched out to Changi Jail, where I found my brothers Tiny and John sitting rather quaintly on tiny homemade folding stools, looking very small and timid at the foot of the giant Changi Jail walls. I said, 'Dr Livingstone I presume,' not knowing what to say on such a grotesque occasion, and quickly brought ourselves up-to-date with our own personal news, I gathered that my brother Tiny had sent me several packets of vitamins, and even produced more. But I asked him not to worry about me as I had a better opportunity for scrounging such items than he. And so after a brief half hour, our meeting was brought to a sudden end by the Japanese guards, and I returned to the Changi POW camp. The next time we met was two-and-a-half years and many Japanese *bintoks* (face-slaps) later!

I now found that the Changi POW camp was a much better place to live in. This was because many thousands of POWs had left for Japan and upcountry and so there was no overcrowding. There were also many lectures and concerts to go to, as well as leisure and news. In the circumstances it was positively the best place to be. As there was not much medical work for me to do, I managed to persuade the Medical Specialist at the POW Hospital to allow me to do some psychological research on some of his patients. I acquired a copy of *Ravens: Progressive Matrices* which is an Intelligence Test, and tested about one hundred POWs suffering from malnutrition such as beri-beri, stomatitis, angular stomatitis, pellagra, etc. The result was negative; in other words it would appear that the intelligence of our POWs had not suffered as a result of their relatively short term (about one year) exposure to malnutrition.

My most interesting occupation, however, was as the official News Representative for the building in which I was living. Every evening, provided there was no emergency, I reported to the top floor of a building which had previously been a married officer's private accommodation, to hear the BBC news. As the possession of a radio and listening in to a radio was punishable with death, the building had sentries posted around it, the sentries being prisoners pretending to be gardening, sweeping leaves, playing chess and so on. They were posted in depth and as soon as a Japanese appeared within 270 metres or so of our news building, an alarm was given; then if he got closer, the news committee would disperse.

The news was half-an-hour old and was given verbally by the person who had actually listened to it. The briefing was often illustrated by maps which were hung up on the wall. I well remember that the news I was responsible for distributing, for it was concerning the defeat of the redoubtable Rommel at Tunis in North Africa.

Unfortunately just as I was beginning to enjoy life at Changi, the Japanese decided to send another party of five thousand prisoners up country. They said that this party (called F Force) was going to Thailand where there was plenty of food, and that the camp would be located in pleasant hilly country. They also said it would be OK for the slightly sick men to go, for they would have an opportunity to convalesce. They recommended prisoners to take their musical instruments with them, and even suggested taking a piano would be a good idea. It sounded most attractive, but I did not volunteer and I was not sent. I was quite happy where I was.

However, about one month or so later after the departure of F Force, there was talk of more parties going up country. Soon the Japanese called for more men, but this time it was to be an entirely medical party (K Force). One of the doctors on this party was a Captain Wallace of the Indian Medical Service whom I had got to know through Clancy of the Methodist Mission of Malaya. He asked me if I would go with him and three Anglo-Indian boys as his medical sergeant, so I agreed especially as we were going to the same delightful place in the hills as the F Force.

And so we left Changi on June 25, 1943. We were a party of thirty doctors and two hundred men, some of them Australians, with Major Crawford of the Johore Volunteer Engineers in charge. We drove past Changi Jail early in the morning just at daybreak, and I wondered how my brothers were getting on in jail, and whether I would ever see them again.

When we reached the Singapore railway station and were lined up on the platform, I suddenly found myself face to face with the Indian station master. We recognized each other, for he was the same station master with whom a year and a half previously, I had arranged for the all-important War Tax Committee of which I was the Secretary to travel to Kuala Lumpur. On that occasion we travelled first class in a special coach; on this occasion he had made arrangements for us prisoners to travel in metal cattle trucks. He looked distressed. I was sorry to cause him embarrassment, for I had by now acclimatized myself to my new circumstances and was looking forward to the trip to our promised Utopia in Thailand.

A. SOME OF MY FAMILY, BRYNTEG FARM, PUMPSAINT, WALES 1911

The picture shows my father (centre back) and some of his brothers and sisters; also my grandfather and my grandmother (centre front).

B. THE WEDDING DAY, BIRDS HILL, WALES.

My father and mother were married in 1903.

C. FAMILY GROUP, WALES 1914

My mother and us three brothers Tommy, John and Gerwyn.

A. LONDON SCHOOL OF ECONOMICS (UNIVERSITY OF LONDON) RUGBY XV 1936–7

The photo includes Sir William Beveridge, Director of the L.S.E. and the father of the British Welfare State (Centre); Professor Seaborne Davies, President of the L.S.E. Rugby Club (to the left) and myself, Captain (to the right).

B. JOHN'S WEDDING, PENANG 1938

The photo taken at the Judge's House, Macalister Road, Penang shows (left to right) Judge Howes, Mrs Samuel, Myself (bestman), Myfanwy Samuel (bridesmaid), John (bridegroom) Gwyneth Samuel (bride), Mr Samuel, Mrs Howes and the Padre.

A. ANTI-JAPANESE RIOTS, 1939

Photo taken by myself of rioters burning Japanese goods, Beach Street, Penang.

B. MY BROTHER TOMMY (TINY) 1939

As a member of the F.M.S. Volunteers, he spent some weeks behind the Japanese lines with the Australian "Roseforce" and survived.

C. JAPANESE TROOPS ENTERING KUALA LUMPUR, JANUARY 1942.

Kuala Lumpur was occupied by the Japanese unopposed. Photo: Imperial War Museum, London

A. OUR WEDDING DAY 1945

Lyn and I got married in May 1945 after a record wait of seven years!

B. TUANKU MUHAMMAD SCHOOL K. PILAH STAFF 1948

Sitting (L to R): S. Ponniah, Tengku Syed Jong, V.M. Francis, Ng Yoke Ying, Myself, Lyn, H.R.H. Stafford, Lim Joo Hock, P. Gunaratnam, S.P.S. Kannu, V. Murugasu, Paul Asivaratnam.

A. INTELLIGENCE TESTING K. PILAH

Some of the thousands of Chinese pupils whose intelligence I tested.

B. TUANKU MUHAMMAD SCHOOL, KUALA PILAH, NEGRI
SEMBILAN 1947

The second post war School Certificate Class. It shows a teacher,
myself, and some of the successful pupils, such as Tengku Zainab
(to my right), Noordin b. Keling (to my left) and Yunus Maris
(extreme right).

C. THE AGONG'S 64th
BIRTHDAY

In August 1959 the Agong invited a few of his old K. Pilah
friends including Lyn and
myself to his birthday party.
Lyn and Katherine Sim in left
foreground.

A. TASEK BERA, PAHANG

Starting our adventure down Tasek Bera. Lyn, and Adang the Semelai guide, in the foreground.

B. TRAS VILLAGE, 1952

Tras was a hornets' nest of Communist supporters, so all the people were removed in 1952.

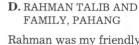

C. SENIOR INSPECTOR OF SCHOOLS 1950

Myself and some Inspectors and Headmasters at Pekan. Photo taken by Rahman Talib.

D. RAHMAN TALIB AND FAMILY, PAHANG

Rahman was my friendly Mal assistant when I was Inspect of Schools; later he became t Minister of Education in 196

A. CLIFFORD SCHOOL, KUALA LIPIS, PAHANG UNDER WATER

During the 1926 flood, the school hostel was half submerged in the flood, while Osman Ngah, the school clerk's house almost completely submerged!

B. DATO ABU SAMAH AND MYSELF

We spent a lot of time gossiping about country life.

C. MY BROTHER JOHN

Taken on his unexpected visit to Kuala Lipis at the height of the Communist troubles.

A. ANDERSON SCHOOL, IPOH, RUGBY XV 1954

One of the best rugby teams the school had for many years. It beat all rivals except King Edward VII School Taiping. Captain:Lai Wah Seng.

B. NG SIEW KEE, SCHOOL CAPTAIN

Now a distinguished Old Boy, a Ph. D. and a world authority on tropical agriculture.

C. ANDERSON SCHOOL PERFECTS 1953

The school captain to my left is V. Sivalogantham.

A. CLUB 21 VICTORIA INSTITUTION, KUALA LUMPUR 1959

These were the star performers at the VI in 1959.
Standing (L to R): Chew Meng Ian, Thavaneswaran, Gan Kong Eng, Lim Chooi Tee, Sha Kam Choy, Cheong Yeng Young, Thiruchandran, Raja Ismail, Ho Wing.
Sitting (L to R): Leong Min Tuck, Billy Tan, Cheong Yong Kuay, myself, Kok Lit Yoong, Bobby Lee, Thiruchelvam.

B. MUSTAFA ALI, SCHOOL CAPTAIN 1958

Now a Director of Malaysia's largest multinational company.

C. CADET CORPS, VICTORIA INSTITUTION

Inspection of the Cadets by the Sultan of Selangor, April, 1957.

A. VICTORIA INSTITUTION, KUALA LUMPUR PREFECT'S BOARD 1961

To be a prefect at the V.I. was the next best thing to Paradise. School Captain: Chung Cheong Hoy.

B. SWIMMING TEAM, VICTORIA INSTITUTION, KUALA LUMPUR 1961

As the V.I. had its own swimming pool, it excelled at swimming. Captain: Lam Ah Lek.

C. V.I.CADET CORPS 1961

The Commanding Officer of the 5th Malay Regiment replies after I present him with a gift as a token of our thanks for training our cadets, at a passing out parade. On my left Hasanuddin Aziz,our efficient OC., V.I. Cadet Corps and rugby master.

A. LOYAL RETAINERS

Timah and Awang, together with Megan (our daughter) and "Poppy". Awang was my fearless bodyguard in Pahang, and together with Timah, our loyal retainers for 12 years.

C. MY DAUGHTERS MEGAN AND RHIANNON

In the garden in K. Lumpur, where they entertained many imaginary guests to tea in their miniature Malay house.

B. HEADMASTER (MYSELF) AND TWO DISTINGUISHED OLD BOYS

Tan Sri Yaacob b. Abdul Latiff (left) and M.F.G. Leembruggen (right), both Malaysian Ambassadors.

A. THE RAJA OF PERLIS, MYSELF AND TUNKU HALIM

Former schoolboys: The Raja of Perlis to whom I taught English at the Penang Free School in 1938 and Tunku Halim, one of my former V.I. schoolboys in 1961.

B. THE GOVERNOR OF PENANG AND HIS WIFE

Tun Haji Hamdan, my brother's former schoolboy at Clifford School, Kuala Kangsar in pre-war days and now a friend to both of us.

C. THE SULTAN OF BRUNEI AND I

My former schoolboy at the Victoria Institution 1960–2. Then a shy, thoughtful and likeable schoolboy; now the wealthiest man in the world.

Chapter 6

THE RAILWAY OF DEATH:
THAILAND AND BURMA

Ten wa mizukara tasukuru mono o tasuku.
(Heaven helps those who help themselves.)

Japanese proverb.

The train journey from Singapore to Bampong in Thailand took exactly one week. It was a very unpleasant experience. This was because about twenty-eight to thirty of us prisoners were crammed into each truck, so that there was no room to lie down. For one week we were compelled to sit on our army packs, and sleep as well as we could sitting up.

Even more unpleasant was the shortage of drinking water and a complete lack of toilet facilities. Consequently, whenever the train stopped we were forced to squat along the track wherever it might be, and in full view of whoever there might be. The Japanese soldiers were amused at our predicament, and *benjo* (WC) became an addition to our Japanese vocabulary. Those who developed dysentery or diarrhoea endeavoured to *benjo* while the train was moving. It was a taste of things to come and of their complete indifference to the embarrassment and discomfort of our situation.

The train was delayed for two days at Ipoh. There were rumours that Chinese guerrillas had blown up a bridge further north and that it would take some time to repair it. The delay was welcome for the Japanese very 'generously' allowed us to have a bath. The bath consisted of standing underneath the hydrant that supplied the railway engine with water. About ten to twenty were made to stand under it, the Japanese guard pulled a lever and a ton of water fell on us. It was like a terrific cloud burst and it was all over in thirty seconds, but it was better than nothing. Crowds of locals gathered at Ipoh station to witness the performance.

In due course we arrived at Bampong, a small railway station on the Singapore–Bangkok line and about seventy kilometres to the west of Bangkok. We also now discovered that it was the starting point for a new railway to Burma that the Japanese had started building, and it dawned upon us why we had come to Thailand. We had come not to have a good time in the green hills of Thailand, but to work on this railway. As soon as we realized that this was our destination trading started at the Bampong railway station between the POWs and the Thais. I sold a motor car inner tube which I had acquired in Singapore, and which I had intended using as a lifebelt in case I was torpedoed on the way to Japan. I sold it for quite a large sum of money, which proved invaluable later on.

We also discovered what our work was to be in Thailand. We were to provide medical care for the thousands of Tamils and other conscripted labourers who were working on the railway. Of course we had no idea what the conditions were like, but the rumours flying around were rather discouraging.

When the Japanese first invaded Burma, they had complete command of the sea and air, and supplied their troops in Burma by sea via Rangoon. Then when the sea route became dangerous, they decided to build the railway line linking Bampong in Thailand to Thanbyuzayat, near Moulmein in Burma. The distance was 415 kilometres and the topography, rugged limestone country covered with tropical rain forest.

They commenced work on the railway in June 1942. First of all, thousands of prisoners of war were sent, then thousands of Tamil, Burmese, Chinese, Malay and other Asian labourers. Altogether, over 51,000 British, Dutch and American prisoners, 9,500 Australian prisoners and over 250,000 conscripted Asian labourers were sent to work on the railway. Of these, 13,000 prisoners of war and an estimated 70,000 Asian labourers died. That is, 83,000 people died in about two years working on the railway, which is why this notorious railway has been called the Railway of Death.

Of course, when I arrived at Bampong I was not aware of all this. I had no idea I was about to enter this valley of death. The Japanese now informed us that our K Force of thirty doctors and two hundred medical orderlies were going to be split up and to my delight, I discovered that our team of five, headed by my friend Captain Wallace was being posted to a POW camp at Nikki, near the Burma frontier. So was an Australian team headed by Captain Jock Frew (later Sir John Frew) who came from Melbourne, Australia. Nikki was one of the furthest camps up the railway, and I suppose being young and foolish, it sounded like an exciting adventure.

We started on our journey on July 2, 1943. The first 125 kilometres was not unduly arduous for we went on a train piled high with rails; then at a river jungle camp called Wan Yi, we transferred on to large river barges towed by motor-boats we called *pom poms*. The barges were heavily loaded with railway sleepers and railway lines which we noted were marked FMS Railways. As the South-West Monsoon was now at its height, and it was raining cats and dogs, we were happy to be travelling by boat, even though the barges seemed to be overloaded and often swayed alarmingly when our barges met a strong river current. Nevertheless, the journey was full of interest for the Menam Kwai Noi was in full flood, the surrounding vegetation thick tropical rain forest, while the jungle reverberated from the cries of the *wah wah*s or long tailed monkeys, and the toucans which flew overhead in formations like flying fortresses.

We passed many riverside POW camps, some of them perched on high river banks, all of them made of bamboo and attap, and most of them looking dilapidated. Occasionally we would get feeble waves from the POW occupants, and sometimes dire warnings of what lay ahead.

On July 20, we arrived at the POW. riverside camp of Kinsayok where we disembarked in a downpour of monsoon rain, and suddenly came face to face with the full brutality and the unbelievable barbaric conditions under which the POWs were being forced to live and work. Owing to the continual downpour of the monsoon rain, the camp was a quagmire, the huts leaking, while the toilets consisted of nothing more than long trenches covered with rickety bamboo, most of them open to the sky, the rain and the flies.

The prisoners' work lasted all day, seven days a week and was extremely heavy. For most of them, it consisted of clearing the jungle, hauling huge jungle logs by hand, building bridges and roads, digging cuttings and building embankments with the most primitive of tools, that is, *cangkuls* (hoes) and baskets only.

Under such brutal conditions the prisoners, who were normally fit and strong young men, soon succumbed to overwork and diseases such as malaria, dysentery and diarrhoea as well as tropical ulcers on their legs and feet. But the sadistic Japanese engineers in charge of the construction work were completely without sympathy, for their orders were to construct the railway whatever the cost and 'speedo' was their clarion call. Even the sick were forced to work and consequently they too died like flies. The daily British bugle call of 'Last Post' was the only indication we had that some poor devil had just been tipped into a grave in the nearby jungle.

I spent a very uncomfortable night, not only from the appalling wet conditions, but at the thought of the alarming prospect in front of me. My apprehension was well founded, for the next morning I witnessed with my own eyes three sick prisoners being carried out by their mates on stretchers to work on the railway, for the Japanese guards said if they were fit enough to sit up on their stretchers, they could break stones for ballast on the railway. When I witnessed this brutality, I was overcome with hatred of the Japanese.

We were also informed that we would be leaving for Nikki immediately, that it was a long way, and that we would be marching. And so early in the morning, after a most meagre of rice meals we started off in single file in the pouring rain for Nikki—over one hundred kilometres away. I counted myself fortunate that I was not a slave labourer under the jurisdiction of the Japanese engineers and was much relieved to get away.

As many thousands of prisoners and especially labourers from Malaya had already marched along the route we now followed, the track which passed through virgin jungle was by now well worn, muddy and sometimes so wet as to be almost impassable. The Japanese engineers had established a series of staging camps, at intervals of approximately

THE THAI–BURMA RAILWAY OF DEATH

Built in 1942–43 by 51,000 prisoners of war and over 250,000 Asian labourers. Estimated number of deaths: 13,000 prisoners of war, 70,000 Asian labourers, a total of 83,000.

twenty kilometres, along the track, where a rice meal was available. So if you wished to live, you had to reach these camps. If you did not and fell by the wayside, then you just lay down in the jungle and died from starvation. Many thousands of Malayan labourers did just that, and in some cases it was no doubt a happy release. I saw many such bodies, but I caught the odour of hundreds more lying dead in the jungle.

The march to Nikki in the heavy rain and along the muddy track was a nightmare, and I was thankful that at that stage I was able to withstand the strain, for I had only recently given up playing rugby and so I suppose I must have been reasonably fit and well.

One of the unexpected hazards of the march were Thai *dacoits* (or robbers). They would attack any POW or Asian labourer who lagged behind because of sickness or exhaustion and rob him of his money and his worldly goods. One day as we were laboriously making our way through the jungle, I was surprised to come across a Thai sitting cross-legged on a bamboo platform under an attap shelter and in a praying position. I thought it odd that he should be alone in such an isolated and deserted location, and then as we got closer, noticed a knife stuck in his back but we kept going with hardly a comment. He was no doubt a *dacoit* who had quarrelled with his friends over the spoils.

I cannot remember all the horrible details of that march, for I have until now endeavoured to put it all out of my mind, but I remember two fairly large POW camps* on the way named Tha Khanun (215 km) and Konkuita (260 km), and some of the incidents that took place on the way.

Thus soon after leaving the ghastly camp at Kinsayok, we had to climb a steep hill which was hard going even for the fittest. So we had to help each other and fortunately nobody from our party dropped out. It had not been so with the poor Malayan labourers, however; for their goods and chattels were strewn all along the hilly track, as they had given up the ghost, entered the jungle for a rest, and died from starvation. Many of them appealed pathetically to us for

---

*For a description of some of these camps see Robert Hardie: *The Burma–Siam Railway* (Imperial War Museum, London, 1983).

THAKHANUN CAMP, AS DRAWN BY DR ROBERT HARDIE

This is the camp where I first experienced the dreaded cholera, on the march up the railway track to Burma. The railway line was, of course, not built when I reached this camp.

help in Malay (*Tolong Tuan*) but we were all in the same boat, and struggling for survival.

Later at one of our overnight stops, and just as we were about to move off, I was told that there was an FMS Volunteer in a hut who was desperately in need of medical help, and his camp had no doctor. So I saw him and found he had a huge tropical ulcer on his leg, which, without treatment, would undoubtedly eventually cause his death. I had a small quantity of iodoform with me, which was a secret supply, I had kept for my own use in case of an emergency. These yellow crystals were like gold dust on the Death Railway, for it was the only known available cure for tropical ulcers. I sprinkled half my supply on his wound, marched on, and never saw him again. Well not until I was stationed in Pahang many years later. Then I met a chemist called Allen at a curry lunch on the Selbourne Guttapercha Estate, near Kuala Lipis. When I was introduced to him by the manager of the Selbourne Estate, he welcomed me warmly and said, 'You saved my life.' He was the anonymous FMS Volunteer I had doctored with my iodoform on the railway!

A few days later we arrived one evening at ThaKhanun. This was a small camp on the banks of the Menam Kwai Noi, consisting of a POW camp and a Japanese camp. Dr Robert Hardie, formerly a well-known private practitioner in Kuala Lumpur and a Medical Officer for the FMS Volunteers made an excellent drawing of it, which appears in the secret diary he kept on the Death Railway. When we arrived I was pleasantly surprised to discover that the British adjutant of Tha Khanun POW camp was an old friend, Captain Close, with whom I had played rugby for Penang in 1938-9. He gave me the frightening news that they had just suffered from a severe outbreak of cholera, that ten POWs had died the first day, and that as there were only three hundred of them in the camp altogether, they (now we) should all be dead in a month! He also informed me that he was lousy, and showed me for the first time what lice looked like, and explained that they were impossible to get rid of under our living conditions!

My friend Captain 'Wally' Wallace also gave me some instant advice on how to avoid contracting cholera—drink only boiled water. Later that evening, feeling thirsty, and warned off water, I went to the cookhouse where two POWs (an Australian and a Briton) were permitted by the Japanese to sell hot sweet 'coffee' (made from burnt rice) at ten cents per mug. I bought a mug full of artificial coffee from the Australian, but as he had no change for my Thai currency, he suggested I pay him the following morning before I moved off, when he would have change. So the next morning about 7 a.m., I called to see him to settle my small debt, only to be told by his partner, 'Sorry, mate, Blue died last night of cholera.' The Australian had contracted and died of cholera in the space of less than nine hours!

We were glad to leave Tha Khanun, in spite of the monsoon downpour which continued unabated for one whole week. But our main preoccupation was with any signs of the dreaded cholera. I was delighted, however, for my problem was with the opposite condition. I had not been to the toilet for days! The Australian Jock Frew (Captain Frew, later Sir John Frew) and I competed for the honour of leading our dwindling medical party, for by now most of the K Force had taken up their duties at the various Tamil camps on the way.

As we crawled along in single file, in the heavy rain, with myself in the lead, I suddenly found myself face to face with the framework of a large wooden bridge which was under construction. It was half completed, with only the long beams, made out of tree trunks, and upon which the railway would rest, in position. Down far below was a large menacing-looking swiftly flowing river in full flood. I looked around, could see no other way, and presumed that crossing by the unfinished bridge was the only way. So balancing myself carefully I walked along one of the lines of tree trunks as far as the middle of the river, where the flattened top surface became narrow and then non-existent. So with a thumping heart, I just managed to cross over to the other line of tree trunks which looked less dangerous, and finally made it to the other side of the river amid cheers and clapping from both the Japanese engineers and the British and Australian prisoners of war. Then when I looked behind me for the rest of the party, I realized why I had received such a welcome—there was nobody there! The correct route was a hundred yards upstream, where there was a low level bridge; but it was not visible because it was under a few centimetres of flood water. I had performed a hair-raising trapeze act without knowing it. If I had slipped on the wet wooden framework of the bridge, I would surely not have survived the swirling flood water below, loaded as I was with my pack on my back. So my cat burglar training as a small boy had come in handy after all!

Another two days' march brought us to Konkuita on August 11, 1943. It was one of the worst camps I had so far experienced. It was occupied by some of the F Force who had left Singapore a few months ahead of us. They were suffering terribly from Japanese maltreatment and disease. To make matters worse, it was pouring with rain; the whole camp was water-logged while the air was overcast with mist and smoke. The smoke came from two funeral piles of burning wood and human bodies, for cholera was taking a heavy toll not only of the POWs but of the Malayan and especially the Tamil labourers in Konkuita.

The Japanese were terrified of cholera, and those thought to have cholera were taken to primitive shelters in the jungle to die, unless they had friends still alive to look after them. The helpless labourers from Malaya were treated even worse than the British and Australian prisoners of war, in spite of the much vaunted Japanese claim that their invasion of Malaya was to create a New Order and to liberate the people of Malaya from British rule.

In case anybody should think that I have exaggerated the sufferings of the F Force, the facts are these. The F Force consisted of 3600 Australians and 3400 British prisoners of war. They arrived in Thailand towards the end of April 1943, and were forced to march over three hundred kilometres to Nikki near the Thai–Burma frontier, in two weeks. They suffered from very brutal and inhuman treatment at the hands of the Japanese and had a horrific death rate, for in the space of one year out of the 7000 prisoners in F Force, the number that died was 3000, yes 3000!

The death rate amongst the Tamil and other Malayan labourers was even greater, but nobody knows for certain how many labourers from Malaya died. But from conversations I had with some of the survivors later on, I estimate that the death rate amongst the labourers who left or were conscripted by the Japanese from Malaya to work in the 'pleasant hills of Thailand' was over 70 per cent. I met many who said they had left Malaya in parties of two hundred but now there were only thirty or forty left. Many of them also told me how they had gone to free Japanese cinema shows in Malaya and were conscripted as they came out of the cinema – *tangkap* (caught) was the word they used. They were then sent to work on the railway, without being able to inform their families and treated more or less as slaves.

My friend Wally was by now finding the march very exhausting. This was partly because we carried all our worldly wealth on our backs, and were loath to part with any of our treasures. We therefore both decided to start lightening our loads. Wally had a copy of Manson Bahr's enormous book on tropical medicine. So he broke it in half, kept the first half which included *cholera*, and gave the other half which included malaria to another doctor in our party called Dickie Dawson who had volunteered to carry it. I got rid of a copy of Gide: *Political Economy*, and felt much better.

The last lap to Nikki was about twenty-five kilometres, but the track we followed was very muddy and we made very slow progress partly because the heavy monsoon rain continued to fall unremittingly and partly because we were exhausted. I well remember one stretch that was so muddy, that we were up to our knees in mud and so it took us over half an hour to struggle a distance of only about 200 kilometres! As a result we failed to reach our staging post that night, and had to sleep in the jungle on the wet ground, soaked to the skin. Moreover, none of us slept a wink, for during the night we were attacked by a plague of sandflies, which made our life a misery. I expected to get pneumonia, but apart from being stiff and wet, was none the worse for the experience and when the morning came, continued our march while our wet clothes dried on our back!

When we finally got to Nikki, we found it was a large dilapidated camp on a piece of flat land near a river, which was probably a tributary of the Menam Kwai Noi. Nikki was the headquarters of F Force and there were many British and Australian prisoners there, as well as Malayan Tamil labourers living under the most awful conditions. We were given two leaky tents, and our medical team under Captain Wallace shared one of them with the Australian team under

Captain Jock Frew. The camp was the usual quagmire while the monsoon downpour continued for another month.

One of the first jobs I had was to look after a hut full of Tamil labourers dying of cholera, with one of the Australians Wally Handley, who had a nice sense of humour which enabled us to tackle our ghastly job with equanimity. Taking the matter too seriously certainly would not have helped, for there was nothing we could give our poor Tamils except sympathy and a few jokes. The Japanese treatment for cholera, dysentery and diarrhoea was all the same—creosote tablets. These may have been a help with the latter, but they were useless for the treatment of cholera, so all our cholera patients died. We also protected ourselves from cholera by taking off all our clothes and spraying each other with carbolic acid which, I gathered later, should have caused us to die of carbolic acid poisoning.

Soon after I arrived at Nikki, as I was on my way down to the river to have a wash, I passed two prisoners followed by a Japanese guard. I discovered they were two escaped POWs, who had been recaptured. As I passed them, one of them suddenly said to me, 'Hello, Lewis.' His skin was quite dark and he looked very ill, but I had no idea who he was. He had just had a bath and was kept overnight in a filthy bamboo cage not fit for a dog and given the minimum of food. Later I discovered he was Lieutenant Machado of the FMS Volunteers and formerly of the Malayan Education Service.

He had escaped from the dreadful camp at Sonkurai. The escape party consisted of about ten POWs, mainly officers, including Machado. They had noticed that the town of Ye on the Indian Ocean, was only about 65 kilometres from Sonkurai according to the map, and so they had thought they could reach it quite easily. Unfortunately most of the intervening ground was rough hilly limestone country, and so the apparently short journey proved a nightmare of vertical limestone cliffs and gorges. They were soon in serious trouble and recaptured. By good fortune the two survivors which included Machado were not executed. Machado later became Headmaster of the Government English School, Tapah.

On another occasion we made a day-long visit to an isolated party of Australians from Sonkurai who were cutting down the virgin jungle near the Burma frontier and who were under suspicion of having cholera which, of course, terrified the Japanese. We walked several kilometres along the railway track to reach them and then carried out the Japanese test for intestinal disease, which was the rather embarrassing procedure of pushing a glass rod up the backside of the patient. Just after I had done that to one of the Australians, the Australian officer said to me with a smile, 'I think you ought to know you have just buggered one of Australia's famous Test wicketkeepers,' and so I had so to speak, for I believe he was none other then Ben Barnett, the famous Australian wicketkeeper.

The informative Australian officer also told me that the previous day, when one of his working party had tried to saw a log lying on the jungle floor, the log suddenly moved and turned out to be a huge python! They had trouble in killing it, and eventually had it for lunch, which is probably true, for I ate several small snakes myself while I was in Burma.

Soon after I arrived at Nikki, I went down with malaria for the first time in my life, the first of many attacks of malaria I suffered while I was a POW. Then as if that was not enough, I also got dysentery. The two together made me very ill and very weak, so weak that I could only walk a few yards. Jock Frew, however, thought of a good idea; he dug a small slit trench a few yards from the tent which served as an air-conditioned lavatory for my personal use. I was resigned to the fact that I was going to die in this remote jungle camp, but consoled myself that the nearby bit of flat land near the river would make a nice site for my grave. But I had overlooked the fact that I had two doctors looking after me—Wally Wallace, the malaria expert and Jock Frew the Australian former Superintendent of the Royal Melbourne Hospital. Between them, and some emetine that Wally had secreted for his own use in case of an emergency, I pulled through.

I did not get dysentery again, but my attacks of malaria recurred twenty-five times before the war ended. I also developed beri-beri on several occasions, and picked up hookworm, but of course I managed to avoid cholera, otherwise I would not be alive writing this. But my tribulations were minor as compared to those who had to work on the railway as labourers in the F Force.

One of our most common tasks was to carry forty-five gallon oil drums across a portage, which passed through the nearby but remote Thai village of Wang Ka. The drums of oil were very heavy, and two of us would have to carry them slung from a long bamboo, for a distance of about two kilometres. The only consolation on this job was that our Japanese guards usually overlooked any shopping we made as we staggered our way through the village carrying the oil drums. The choice of goods that we could purchase was very limited and, was mainly restricted to a kind of tobacco we called Sikh's beard, a kind of sugar similar to *gula melaka*, Thai cigarettes and so on.

One day while I was doing some illicit shopping, I noticed a Sikh having a cup of coffee at a small table in the corner of the shop. Thinking that perhaps he was a Sikh from Malaya, I said, 'Do you speak English?' He answered quietly, 'A little.' So I asked him where he came from and he said, 'Kuala Lumpur.' I then went on in Malay and said, '*Mana pergi?*' (Where are you going?) but got no answer. So I said, 'Why can't you speak Malay?' He surprisingly answered me in good English and said, 'Actually I am in the East Surreys.' He was a British soldier from the East Surrey Regiment camouflaged as a Sikh, complete with a long beard and a turban. He informed me that he hoped to get to India soon, and had so far walked and hitch-hiked all the way from Singapore!

The carrying of the oil drums along the portage was back-breaking work, especially as the track was very muddy. So when one day my Australian friend Wally Handley and I in a state of extreme exhaustion were beaten with a bamboo by a small Japanese bully, Wally's patience burst, and he said to me in a subdued but angry voice, 'Let's do the little bastard in.' This we could have done quite easily for we were passing through some thick jungle undergrowth, but while I was considering the 'proposal', the Japanese left us in a hurry without more ado. However, an hour or so later, as we were crossing a flooded river in a small boat perched like birds on its side, our little Japanese came unexpectedly from behind Wally Handley, and pushed him into the river. We managed to pull him out only with some difficulty, for the flooded river was flowing fast. We decided our little Japanese could speak English and had tried to drown Wally.

Our experiences at Wang Ka village were always interest-ing. Thus one day a small Japanese platoon of Mountain artillery came through, manhandling their mobile artillery with some difficulty along the portage. Their young officer spoke to me and after a short chat, we discovered that we had both studied Economics at University. He confided that he thought the war a crazy idea, and was looking forward to the day when it was over.

One morning in October 1942 we woke up to the whistle of a railway engine, and we realized that the railway line had been completed and a train had actually reached Nikki. This surprised us greatly in view of the shoddy work the POWs had put into the construction of the railway, and the match boxes of white ants that had been installed at the base of nearly all the bridges.

Nikki now became the 'Wild West' camp of the Death Railway, where illicit trading, illicit stealing, bribery and corruption were the order of the day. One special reason for this was the existence of the remote Thai village of Wang Ka, that I have already mentioned and was not far from our POW camp. The object of our activities was of course survival; it was a case of the survival of the fittest and heaven helps those who help themselves!

The Tamil labour force was paid one dollar a day, the prisoners ten cents per day, so there was an inducement to supply the Tamils with the consumer goods they demanded, as they were the only people with any money. The chief consumer goods the Tamils wanted were *cappatis*. So a complicated *cappati*-making industry was set up by the POWs to alleviate the Tamils of their shortage of *cappatis* and relieve them of their money. The Dutch prisoners took a leading part in this industry. Several Heath Robinson machines were devised to grind stolen padi into rice flour, while others supplied other ingredients. My team fitted into the scheme quite nicely for we were able to supply the new industry with Thai *gula melaka*, which we were able to buy on our visits to Wang Ka. Nikki became a thriving capitalist society.

Another illegal activity was the night-time poaching of Thai bullocks. This was the special preserve of the Australians, for many of them were cattle ranchers back home, and so they were well trained for the job. Their procedure was to spread rumours that tigers had been seen at sunset near the camp. This ensured that the Japanese guards neglected their duties after dark, thus making it easy for the Australians to go out at night, kill a Thai bullock, skin it and cut it up into manageable pieces, bury the bones and offal in the jungle, and return to the camp with their swag before daybreak. Some of the guards at Nikki were Koreans, and they were also easily bribed to co-operate in return for a share of the loot.

The POW cookhouse at Nikki was run by some Dutch POWs. Most of them had formerly been rubber planters in northern Sumatra. They were a friendly crowd and all spoke Malay, so I was a welcome visitor. They were entrusted with the job of cooking the stolen bullock meat, and the Australians for its distribution. I was once a beneficiary. I was woken up in the middle of the night. An Australian voice in the dark said, 'Give me your hand, Serg.' And upon so doing, I found I had a large piece of hot steak in my hand. I never discovered the identity of my benefactor—I presumed he was a grateful patient!

But the most successful plundering at Nikki was our weekly train robbery. Once a week a train called at Nikki at night time in case of an attack from Allied planes, which delivered the weekly supplies of food for the Japanese troops. The Japanese would always call for forty men from our camp to unload the train, but we always sent forty-one men—the extra man being carefully selected and given the title of Ali Baba for that evening's operation. It was Ali Baba's commission to select something edible as he helped unload the train, such as a case of tinned food, or better still a case of condensed milk. Then instead of carrying it to the Japanese godown, he would in the dark make his way to the Dutch cookhouse in our camp, where a small team would be waiting discreetly. When the stolen case arrived, it would be opened immediately and the box burnt. Then the tins would be opened, the contents emptied into a bucket and taken for distribution among the patients in our POW hospital. In the meantime, the empty tins would be flattened, put into a sack and taken into the jungle where they were buried. The whole operation would take about fifteen minutes. After some weeks the Japanese realized that somebody was stealing, and so they counted our party very carefully before we left, but of course always found forty men and nobody missing!

Soon after the railway was completed on October 16, 1943, the F Force left Nikki and were sent down the railway back to Thailand to lick their wounds. But some were too sick to leave and remained at Nikki. These included eight Australians who had suffered severely from dysentery and were near skeletons. I decided to try and keep their spirits up by supplying them with Burma cheroots which I was able to buy at the Thai village of Wang Ka. Everybody expected them to die, but to our surprise they slowly recovered and eventually followed the rest of F Force down the railway back into Thailand. They used to tell me that they waited all day expectantly for me to return from the Thai village with their supply of Burma cheroots, which goes to show smoking is not always bad for you.

In November there was a most surprising development. The two medical teams headed by Captain Wallace, with myself and the three Anglo-Indians, and by Captain Jock Frew and his four Australians were transferred to the adjacent Japanese camp to carry out anti-malaria work. We were informed that from now on we were in the Imperial Japanese Army and were given Japanese names! When we reached the camp we paraded before the Japanese officer who was a doctor, and lined up as follows: Captain Frew, Captain Wallace, Sergeant Lewis, etc., and numbered *ichi, ni, san*, etc. Consequently the names we were given were as follows: Captain Frew *Ichiro*, Captain Wallace *Niro* and myself *Sabro* and so on.

The move was a change very much for the better, for we now found ourselves on Japanese rations, while the Japanese officer in charge treated us very well. Unfortunately it looked as if he meant it when he claimed that we were now in the Japanese Army and tried to get us to swear allegiance to *Tenno Heika*, that is, the Emperor of Japan. Jock Frew handled the situation very well for he was a very charming person with a disarming personality. He managed to avoid upsetting the Japanese officer, by getting him to agree that while we could not swear allegiance to *Tenno Heika*, we would willingly thank the Japanese Emperor for sparing our lives.

This we did every morning on parade and honour was satisfied. Our unexpected posting to the Imperial Japanese Army was a most interesting experience for me, and I have yet to meet any other Briton who has served in the IJA. The routine was rigorous. *Sho* (getting up) was at 6 a.m., followed immediately by *tenko* (roll call) and physical exercises for about five minutes, followed by washing and shaving at the river and then *meshi* (rice) or breakfast at 6.30 a.m. Hardly any time was allowed for dressing in the morning, so most of us went to bed partly dressed. Our POW section was under the charge of a Japanese NCO, and we were regarded as being one of the smartest and quickest off the mark. The last on parade in the morning was always the same little Japanese, who consequently suffered a lot of bullying from the others because he was such a slow moving little chap.

Although we were at first a little dubious about our new role, we felt that as we were mainly engaged in anti-malarial work, and this benefited the POW camp as well as the IJA camp we could not be accused of collaborating. In any case as every POW knew we had very little choice on the railway, we did what we were told if we wished to survive.

Nevertheless we were obliged to wear our Japanese names on our breasts for all to see. One day I met a grinning and exceptionally short Japanese soldier and the following conversation ensued:-

Japanese	:	*Anata Sabro-ka?* (You, Sabro?)
Me	:	*Hai.* (Yes.)
Japanese	:	*Watashi Sabro.* (I am Sabro.)
Me	:	*So desu-ka.* (Is that so?)
Japanese	:	*Anata big Sabro,*
		Watashi small Sabro. (You are big Sabro, I am small Sabro.)
Me	:	*Hai.* (Yes.)

And so I made a new friend, which was welcome, for they were very scarce on the ground. This of course was because he was only a one-star private, the lowest of the low in the Japanese Army, and so he was happy to make friends with a POW.

As was to be expected, we were given the least attractive jobs. Thus one day I was taken to a small compound in the jungle where one of the officers had his attap 'house' hidden under some large jungle trees and told to sweep the compound clean of leaves. The slightly unpleasant Japanese NCO told me that I could finish as soon as the compound was clean of leaves. But of course this proved to be an impossible task, for by the time I had swept it clean, more leaves would have fallen in the parts I had cleared. So I was there for an eternity.

Then a most unexpected occurrence took place. A young Japanese girl appeared from nowhere and with a friendly smile gave me a bunch of bananas and disappeared almost as quickly into the Japanese officer's attap house. I was overcome with her friendly gesture and had no idea there was such a female of the species within a hundred kilometres. So I have naturally a special affection for Japanese ladies, and have always excluded them from any unkind things I may have said about the Japanese.

When Christmas and especially the New Year arrived, there were modest celebrations and our gentleman Japanese officer whose name I have now unfortunately forgotten treated us like his own men, for as he had explained to us several times we were now in the Japanese Army. The New Year in particular was an occasion for celebrations and *yasumi* or rest. We also had a party on New Year's Eve, with the Japanese officer seated at the head of the bamboo table, then the Japanese soldiers and ourselves. We had rice and saké and in no time were well on our way to getting drunk, a condition we had not experienced since fraternizing with the Japanese Imperial Guard at the Race Course camp in Singapore in 1943. And of course we were all expected to provide some entertainment for the benefit of the others. I sang some Welsh songs, and Wally my doctor friend recited a long-winded poem which nobody could understand. I didn't eat glass this time probably because we only had mugs, and in any case it was not that kind of party! When the party came to an end, we were most surprised to discover that the Japanese always celebrate New Year by singing a song, to the tune of Auld Lang Syne. When we did that, I almost forgot for a moment that I was a prisoner of war in the jungle on the Burma–Thailand frontier.

The civilized Japanese officer under whose protection we now sheltered, had a junior officer under him called *Sato*

Mina Reiskang, the latter words indicating his rank. We
called him 'Sato, the Twirp' probably because he was a
rather quiet chap. One day he informed me that he wished
me to help him with some research work. I reported as
instructed and discovered that the work he was doing was
post-mortem examination of the bodies of some of the
Tamils, with a view to finding out the cause of their death. It
was rather gruesome work, but he was delighted when he
was able to show me what he was looking for, perforations
in some intestines caused by dysentery.

As was always the case with the Japanese, when we made a
move, it was always sudden, unexpected and not in the
direction expected. And so towards the middle of January
1944, we were suddenly informed that we were moving, and
that we were not going down the railway line to Thailand,
but to Burma. We would be returning to our former Japanese
guards and would be taking charge of coolie camps in
Burma. Moreover, as there were not enough doctors to go
round, all *Gunsos* (Sergeants) would be doctors and would
be in charge of their own camps.

So on January 19, 1944 we left for Burma on the newly
built railway line. While waiting at Nikki for our train to come
and take us to Burma, another train suddenly arrived from
Burma, crammed with Japanese soldiers. I was astonished to
see their condition, for most of them were emaciated, sick
and wounded. I was standing within a few metres of them and
could see their terrible condition, when one of them pathetically begged me for *mizu* (water). As I always carried a
water bottle with me when on the move, I naturally moved
towards him and gave him my water bottle. Within seconds
of this, a Japanese guard with a fixed bayonet, rushed at me
and chased me away. '*Mizu nei*' (No water), he said. '*Orl
men*, bad men.' I was astonished at his inhumanity to his own
Japanese wounded, and decided I would never understand
the mentality of the Japanese. The explanation was that all
Japanese soldiers were expected to die and not to get ill or
wounded. This attitude of course went a long way to explain
why the POWs were so often treated with barbarity, and also
why the sick were never paid.

The train journey to Burma was most interesting, but I
was disappointed to find that the three pagodas at the Three

Pagoda Pass were only about six to nine metres high. The weather was by now delightful, for the monsoon rain had stopped and we were entering Burma in the dry season. The vegetation included many large trees, some of them teak trees with large leaves as well as a lot of bamboo. I noticed some beautiful wild fowl amongst the clumps of bamboo. Burma looked a promising land.

I was posted to a camp called Mezale, and my assistant was Jack Ambrose, one of the Anglo-Indian boys in our team. Jack was a quiet, solid companion and in civil life had worked on the Indian railways as an engine driver. Our new camp was a large one with over a thousand Burmese labourers, but they were in a bad way and were dying like flies at the rate of about ten to fifteen per day.

I immediately set to work to find out the cause for such a high death rate and came to the conclusion that they were dying from malaria and dysentery. I asked the Japanese for some quinine tablets, was given a bottle of 250 tablets, used it up two days, then asked for more and got beaten up by the Japanese soldier in charge for using up two months' supply in two days! As for dysentery, I was given a bottle of their more or less useless creosote tablets. It was clear that I was not going to be given adequate medication to care for the sick and dying Burmese labourers, so I decided some other course was called for. It then occurred to me that both malaria and dysentery are preventable diseases and so embarked on a policy of 'prevention is better than cure'.

I persuaded the Burmese in charge of the camp, who could speak a little English and had once been a teacher in Burma, to clean up the camp so that the mosquitoes could not breed. We even checked all bamboos that had been cut down, and made sure that there were no little cups left where water could collect and the mosquitoes could breed. This action was highly successful and within a fortnight or so, the incidence of new malaria cases declined dramatically. My attack on dysentery required more drastic action. All Burmese labourers were informed that in future anyone wanting drinking water had to collect it from the Burmese cookhouse (where they were given boiled water) and that anyone found drinking any other water would be flogged by the Japanese. This action also produced excellent results. Consequently, within a fortnight or so the number of deaths, from malaria and dysentery declined dramatically, to just one or two a day, and the 'English douctor's' reputation went up by leaps and bounds.

There were of course no medical records, so I gave each Burmese a numbered bamboo tag, and kept a record of any malaria they suffered by entering on to a sheet of paper their temperatures on a three point scale as follows: Slight temperature = +; High temperature = ++; and Raging temperature = +++. I had no thermometer, so I assessed their abnormal temperatures by putting my hand on their foreheads. It was a useful guide, but the Burmese labourers were a devious lot and traded their disc numbers when it suited them.

They were also inclined to be indifferent to the suffering of each other. Thus on one occasion I was called to the assistance of a Burmese whose friends obviously thought he had 'died' for they had stolen all his clothes. When I examined the 'dead' patient I found his pulse still beating, so gave him an injection of camphor, whereupon he recovered and his friends were obliged to return to him all his clothes and belongings!

The Burmese were well pleased with their 'douctor' as I was called, and were convinced that I could create miracles, so when they heard that I only received ten cents a day, immediately increased my salary to ten rupees a day which was considerably more, but on one condition, and that was that I should join them every night on a nearby hill where they gambled. I could hardly refuse such generosity and for a while joined them every night on the hill, where they solemnly handed over the ten rupees to me, and I then proceeded to lose it all in the space of about ten minutes gambling. The only person who always made money was the Burmese who owned the pack of cards. He hired it out every night at one hundred rupees a time! The whole business came to a sudden end, however, when the Japanese got wind of it, carried out a raid one night, and scattered all the gamblers, leaving me to pretend I was attending to a patient. To my surprise I was not touched by the Japanese soldiers. Perhaps they were impressed by the silk shirt and stethoscope I now displayed for their benefit.

I got on very well with the Burmese. One day they informed me very proudly that the British now had a very clever Burmese general fighting for them against the Japanese. When I asked them his name, they said Maung Ba Thin. I did not of course disillusion them that he was actually an Englishman by the name of Mountbatten. As there was only one Burmese in the camp who could speak English, I made every effort to learn Burmese. I found plenty of volunteers ready to teach me; unfortunately the words they taught me were, generally speaking, most inappropriate. Thus for a while I was going around the camp thinking I was saying 'Good morning' in Burmese, but in fact saying 'Balls to you'. However, I eventually persuaded them to take my attempts at learning Burmese seriously and soon became fairly fluent, with phrases such as *Be-u belaule* (How much are these duck eggs?) and *Kinbyar sa-thi athe* (You must eat liver) for my patients suffering from beri-beri and so on.

The Burmese, however, often ill treated any of the hill tribes that might come their way. I met a Karen in our camp, who begged me not to mention it to the others that he was a Karen. On another occasion I came unexpectedly upon a group of Burmese who were whipping another but pale-skinned Burmese tied to a tree. Thinking that the victim was a thief, I asked them what he had done wrong. 'Nothing,' they said. 'So why are you whipping him?' I asked. 'He is a Talaing,' they replied. When I remonstrated that they shouldn't beat an innocent man, they reluctantly released him, and would undoubtedly have killed him if I had not intervened.

The Burmese themselves were also badly treated by the Japanese, and any Burmese who tried to leave the camp was flogged. I had to dress the wounds of one such Burmese who had tried to escape so as to rejoin his family near Rangoon, but in spite of my best efforts, he died.

A most extraordinary happening took place one day, while I was dressing the wounds of the flogged Burmese. I noticed that the Burmese who slept alongside him on the bamboo bed appeared to be trying to read a little green book. One day I casually had a look at this book and to my utter astonishment found it was the Burroughs Welcome diary that complimented the Welcome wallet of medicines I possessed. The Burmese could not read, neither did he want to give it to me. After much bargaining I finally managed to buy it for thirty rupees. It was certainly the most extraordinary coincidence to find this book in the jungle! It was a heaven sent gift for me, for from now on I was able to make intelligent use of my Welcome medical wallet.

The hut where my companion Jack Ambrose and I lived in was quite near to the small attap quarters of the Japanese guards responsible for the camp. So one day, when their field telephone rang and nobody answered it, I went over and boldly picked up the phone. The following conversation then took place:

Me   :   *Moshi, moshi.* (Words I had heard the Japanese use many times on the phone, meaning 'hello'.)

Voice :   Japanese words I did not understand.

Me   :   *Anone.* (More words I had often heard the Japanese use on the phone, but did not understand.)

Voice :   More Japanese words I did not understand.

Me   :   *Sore-kare-ne.* (Another phrase I had often heard the Japanese use on the phone.)

Voice :   Angry voice shouting down the phone.

Me   :   I put the phone down and retired.

The next day I heard a terrible rumpus coming from the Japanese quarters, and could see a very irate *shoko* or Japanese officer shouting at and slapping some of the Japanese soldiers. After twenty minutes or so the noise died down, and one of the Japanese two-star private friends came across in a state of excitement. So I asked him what the trouble was. 'Oh,' he said, 'Japanese soldier speak bad words to Japanese *shoko* on the telephone.' I looked surprised, and thanked my lucky stars that although my Japanese vocabulary was limited, my pronunciation must have been good!

About this time Jack Ambrose and I seriously considered escaping; indeed one afternoon we followed the river which flowed past our camp deep into the jungle. As it was the dry season, we were able to walk along the river-bed. The river was very low, with occasional deep pools, which we swam across. Our idea was to follow the river-bed and set up a small camp in the deep jungle before the monsoon arrived, for I had a supply of atebrin sufficient to last a year or so, and to wait for our forces to overrun our location. We also planned to steal enough rice to last us a year. Unfortunately after about three months at Mezali, and before we had got very far with our plans, we were on the move again; this time to another Burmese camp called Ronshi several kilometres along the railway line towards Moulmein.

So in early April 1944 I moved to our new camp at Ronshi. Like our old camp, it had a large number of Burmese slave labourers doing maintenance work on the railway, and suffering especially from malaria and dysentery. I followed my previous practice of 'prevention is better than cure', cleaned up the camp and introduced the regime of boiled water only for drinking purposes. In this camp, however, the Japanese in charge had introduced the compulsory use of chopsticks. He proudly claimed that now there was no danger of the Burmese getting diarrhoea or dysentery from eating rice with dirty hands. The idea was sound, but its implementation was impossible, for they only used their chopsticks when a Japanese appeared. Indeed I always knew that when I found them using their chopsticks, there must be a Japanese on the horizon!

I quite enjoyed my stay at Ronshi; the weather was fine for the first month or so and the sickness not so bad as at Mezali or 'Misery' as we called it. Moreover, the Japanese left me alone to get on with my job.

At the end of the month they informed me that if I wanted to collect my monthly salary of three rupees (30 days × 10 cents), I would have to go and collect it at Anan Kwin about twenty kilometres along the railway. So one day, after I had seen to my patients, I set off for Anan Kwin along a rough dusty road running parallel to the railway and got there rather tired just before dark. I then collected my pay from a rather unpleasant Japanese, and then in my best and most humble *Nippon-Go*, asked him where I could sleep for the night. He exploded at the suggestion, and with many *bakayaro*s (damn fool) and *konoyaro* (also damn fool) chased me away. I was of course now faced with another twenty kilometres' walk back in the dark, but decided I would be better off in the jungle than with my *Nippon* paymaster.

So I set off along the road, but soon found I could not see in the dark and so walked along the railway line, where the white limestone ballast between the railway sleepers showed the way. I walked like this for over an hour or so, stepping from wooden sleeper to wooden sleeper in the pitch dark, but guided by the white limestone ballast. I then suddenly noticed that the ballast had changed colour, the rocks seemed to be black; so thinking that perhaps it was some kind of black lava rock I bent down to pick it up. To my horror I discovered there was no rock; there was nothing between the sleepers. I was in fact walking across a railway viaduct, that the Japanese were so fond of building. Moreover, as I could now just see the tops of the trees far below, I knew I was high up, so that I faced an uncertain future if I slipped and fell in such a godforsaken place.

Having realized my predicament, I concentrated on not missing my footing and within ten minutes or so got myself on to *tierra firma* again. But it was not too soon, for just as I was congratulating myself on my escape, I heard the whistle of the night mail of our Burma–Thailand railway in the distance.

Of course I got off the track as the night mail rattled by, and now actually began to enjoy my walk, as the moon began to rise and I felt free of any Japanese tormentors. As I walked along in the moonlight I began to hear various noises in the jungle, and in particular a screechy-squealing noise in the far distance, which I had never heard before. Moreover, after an hour or so, and as I got nearer to my camp at Ronshi, I realized that the animal making the screechy-squealing noise was getting nearer and nearer and was indeed now quite close behind me. When I finally reached the Burmese camp, I found them in a great state of excitement. So I asked them what all the fuss was about and they said, 'Leopard, leopard, can't you hear it?' I then realized that I had been stalked by a leopard, and that I had narrowly escaped ending up as his midnight meal!

Although Ronshi was not such a medical black spot as Mezali, malaria was a serious problem while scabies was also a minor irritant. For malaria I managed to invent my own effective treatment. One day when I was given a bottle of quinine by the Japanese, I noticed it said on the outside of the bottle 'Quinine de-hydrochloride. Soluble.' So I decided it meant what it said, took the sugar coating off the tablets, dissolved them in sterile (i.e. boiled) water, and injected the solution intravenously into one or two of my important patients, that is, headmen. As the treatment seemed to be highly effective, I decided that perhaps a small charge of ten rupees per injection would not be unreasonable in view of the inequality of incomes as between myself and the Burmese, and started a small private practice. My new treatment proved to be most acceptable, and my reputation as the 'English douctor setore' (English injection doctor) spread like wildfire, so much so that I started getting patients from camps as far as ten kilometres away along the railway. When this happened, I became most apprehensive that the Japanese would get to hear of it, and reluctantly decided to close down a promising private practice.

As for scabies, the treatment was simple. All I had to do was to swallow my pride. Every evening the Japanese bathed in a 45-gallon drum of warm bath water, the water being warmed by the simple expedient of lighting a fire under it. The bath water contained sulphur, which prevented the development of scabies. The officer bathed first, then the NCOs, then the privates in order of seniority and then me. I never inquired very much whether the Japanese peed in their bath water and I never got scabies.

My first few weeks at Ronshi were notable for their moonlit night, the kind of romantic nights one would normally take one's girlfriend out. I had by now been a prisoner of war for several years and felt very much isolated from all those I loved. I had not, for example, received a single letter or postcard from England or from Lyn since the fall of Singapore two-and-a-half years previously. I occasionally heard heavy bombers flying overhead at night, but of course had no way of knowing whether they belonged to friend or foe.

One sunny day, however, while I was walking across an open space in the middle of our camp, I heard a most unusual noise coming along the railway line. It sounded like a train coming at high speed or perhaps a runaway railway engine. I had no idea what it was, but I did not have to wait long for an answer, for suddenly three very fast low-flying planes, without propellors, flashed past and opened fire on the railway trucks parked at our modest railway halt. I nearly had a heart attack, for the markings were British and I jumped and waved at them like a lunatic. I then ran down to the railway line and sheltered behind a huge teak tree, and noticed huge holes in the railway trucks. A few minutes later the planes came back again and machine-gunned the Burmese camp—no doubt thinking it housed Japanese troops, but the firing seemed strange to me. Some of the bursts of fire were like machine-guns, but some had a much deeper tone. Finally, after another sweep over our railway halt they flew off at great speed, leaving me gasping but exhilarated, for they were the first British planes I had seen for many years.

I now sat down and wondered what I should do. I presumed that many of the Burmese in the camp would have been killed or wounded, that the Japanese would blame me for it and perhaps execute me as revenge. But I decided there was no way out but to go back to the camp and deal with the wounded. So I hurried back full of apprehension; but when I got back I found the camp completely deserted, there was not a soul in sight. The Burmese had all sprinted into the jungle at the first attack and not one person had been hit or wounded in any way. When they came back they thought it a huge joke, especially when they saw the Japanese railway wagons with enormous holes in them. The Japanese soldiers did not say a word and made no mention of it. I decided it was diplomatic to do the same.

I stayed at Ronshi until July, by which time the wet monsoon was in full swing again and conditions muddy, wet and miserable. Fortunately, my duties were not very arduous by POW standards. But both Jack Ambrose and I got beaten up one day for no apparent reason, but probably because this was the month when the Japanese suffered their first big defeat in Burma at the hands of the British and Indian troops at Kohima.

Anyhow I well remember the occasion. That night Jack and I felt miserable after our maltreatment as we prepared to go to sleep in our attap hut, while the monsoon rain poured outside and leaked inside. Suddenly we heard a noise outside, and then two tiny soaked brown-skinned Chins appeared out of the darkness. They both bowed and then one of them held my hand and said, 'England, America, Chin *adudube*' (England, America and Chin are altogether) and disappeared into the night. I was overcome with delight to discover that I was after all not alone, and had such loyal allies close at hand, even though they were so small. I slept like a top.

When I was at Nikki I had become friendly with a Japanese *Gunso* of the same rank as myself, who I used to call 'Joe'. When I moved to Burma, I met Joe again several times for he seemed to have a roving commission and we became quite pally. Then one day I met Joe and he gave me a cigarette and he confided, '*Astar orl men kaeru*,' (Tomorrow all men return). And so it turned out for on August 1,1944 we were put on the train and started for 'home' which was, of course, Thailand.

Unfortunately a bridge must have collapsed, or perhaps had been bombed by our planes; consequently our trip was interrupted, so we ended up with about twenty other members of our medical K Force in a tent in the wet jungle. To my surprise I discovered that most of the others were quite ill with malaria, for I had overlooked the fact that my intake of atebrin had saved me from malaria. Consequently, the rest were too weak to keep a fire going for boiling water, etc. So the job of keeping the rest of the party warm and supplied with boiling water devolved on myself and another. Fortunately, I remembered something from my Boy Scout days. Together the two of us found long logs in the jungle, which we carried with difficulty to our tent, and then placed them end to end along the length of the tent. We then lit a fire where the two logs met, and by moving them as their ends burnt away kept a fire going for a whole week without much exertion.

On August 7, the monsoon downpour eased off a bit, and once more we embarked on a train. This time there was no interruption, and we made our slow but rickety way along the railway line, picking up odd numbers of our K Force as we went along. Although the journey was quite enjoyable, we were of course a bit apprehensive about the reliability of some of the large creaking bridges and viaducts, and wondered how the white ants the POWs had installed the previous year at the base of all the bridges were getting on! We saw one or two railway engines upside down in defiles where bridges had collapsed, and where the white ants had no doubt done their work. We were greatly relieved when we finally reached Kanburi and found ourselves once more with the Tamils or rather in a Tamil hospital camp.

Kanburi is an old walled city, with a pleasant location, on the banks of the Menam Kwai Noi, and here the reassembled K Force rested for the next six months, together with another similar medical party called L Force. I now found myself part of Wally's team again, and we spent much time talking about our trials and tribulations in Burma. We had of course had considerable freedom in Burma, and now began to look upon our Burma experience with nostalgia.

Kanburi was a completely different environment to Burma. In the first place it was in the egg belt, where fruit of all descriptions was also available if you had the money to buy it. It also had excellent bathing facilities. We were marched down to the river every evening for a swim, and on the way sang various songs uncomplimentary to the Japanese, which fortunately they did not understand.

The work was mainly for our own benefit, and was not particularly arduous, such as digging latrines, building attap covered huts, cutting down bamboo and so on. I was in charge of a lavatory-building party, much favoured by the Japanese because we had the reputation of being good workers, and so we were employed at this work for several months. Our technique I regret to admit was deception, which was, of course, acceptable behaviour for POWs. The lavatories were in fact long deep trenches, covered with attap roofs. So our procedure was first of all to put up the attap roof, so as to provide shade from the hot sun, dig down as quickly as possible, and then as soon as all the diggers were out of sight, stop work!

As the *honcho* or person in charge of the working party, I would sit at the top of the trench, keep a look-out for the Japanese in charge, and conduct various discussions or seminars amongst those down below out of sight. We were the most respected working party in the camp and also the one that did least work. The secret was always to be seen to be working when visible, and idle when invisible. The object of course was to conserve our energy and survive.

One of the best jobs I was employed on was floating bamboo down the Menam Kwai Noi. We were taken upstream for several kilometres by truck, where a pile of bamboo had been stacked by another POW party. Our job was to build a raft in the water one day, and then float it down to Kanburi the following day. Then another party of POWs would dismantle the raft, carry it to a nearby site and build a hut. Of course while floating the bamboo raft downstream, we could bathe and swim in the river as much as we liked. The only hazard was a large fish which frequented the river, and was inclined to nibble those parts on one's anatomy that one treasures most, for we swam with nothing on.

One of the members of our bamboo party was the Chinese survivor of the Japanese massacre of the Chinese Singapore Volunteers, and who was still giving me the occasional Chinese lesson. As we sat on the bank one day, a large Thai boat loaded with rice went by, and on it were three large Chinese characters. Wong (alias Leonard) immediately asked if I could read that. So I slowly read it out to him, 'Wo Ai Ni' and laughed because that had been one of my first lessons, for as every student of Chinese knows Wo Ai Ni means I love you.

It was while I was on the bamboo raft floating job that I had a most interesting experience. One day while resting on the riverside I got to know a young Thai schoolboy who could speak Malay. He asked me a lot about myself and was most interested when he heard that I knew the railway well, had been to Burma, and knew where the Japanese hid their railway engines in the day time, and how they did it by sheltering them under trees adjacent to the line.

Nevertheless I was most surprised when one day he said he had a brother in the Thai army who wanted to speak to me urgently. After some hesitation I agreed, and one day during my *yasumi* (rest) period, I sneaked off into some nearby jungle with my young Thai friend where I was confronted by a Thai in a resplendent uniform, waiting for me in a hut. He told me that the Thai army were against the Japanese, but could do nothing at the moment.

He requested me to come the following day and bring with me in my pack my bare necessities, and then said, 'I will take you to your friends.' I was nonplussed at this unbelievable development. Was the Thai soldier a Japanese agent sent to trap me, or did he belong to some underground anti-Japanese organization? I found it difficult to sleep that night as I considered the suggestions. I was inclined to believe that his was a genuine proposal, as I had become very much aware of the fact that all ordinary Thais seemed to dislike the Japanese as much as we did.

I did not of course know that there was a *Seri Thai* (Free Thai) underground movement in existence and that the Thai chief of police was already fully on the side of the Allies and was actively plotting the overthrow of the Japanese.

I also reflected that if I escaped, my companions who were left behind would suffer, and no doubt some would be tortured by the Japanese in the mistaken belief that they were a party to it. So I decided not to accept the kind offer of the Thai soldier, and my Thai schoolboy friend seemed very disappointed and disappeared.

In the meantime my camp at Kanburi was fast becoming a capitalist bedlam. Although it was an unwritten law that no POW exploited another, stealing and cheating the Japanese of their property was an honourable thing to do, with the Thais as the unlimited receivers of all stolen property. Of course not all the Thais were what they appeared to be, for some of them were Chinese with Thai names, and with no love for the Japanese who had invaded their homeland. But it mattered very little whether they were Thai Thais or Chinese Thais—they were all eager buyers of stolen Japanese property. So there was a brisk trade, the biggest haul being a Japanese truck loaded with medical supplies which a POW drove away, while the Japanese driver was having his *meshi* (lunch). The truck was discovered a few days later several kilometres away in some dense scrub, completely denuded of its contents.

The widespread stealing and pilfering soon proved catching, for one evening my quiet law abiding teammate Jack Ambrose suddenly announced that he intended to steal a duck from the Japanese duck farm. I tried to dissuade him from such a reckless venture, but he was determined to go, for he said he would go at night and strip so that nobody could see him. I begged him to go during a rainstorm, but that was easier said than done for we were now well into the dry season.

One night, however, there was a heavy thunderstorm and Jack took off all his clothes. As he was an Anglo-Indian he was ready-made for thieving in the dark, for he had a very dark skin; in fact so dark that at night he was completely invisible in the nude even at a distance of three metres, provided he did not show his white teeth. So reminding him on no account to smile, I saw him off late that night in the heavy downpour. Listening to his progress was nerve wrecking. First, we heard the Japanese guard at the entrance to the camp challenge a noise he had heard go by in the thunderstorm, no doubt thinking it was a dog, then some restlessness from the ducks at the duck farm, so we knew he had reached his objective. There was then a long wait, no more disturbances in the night except for the distant rumble of the receeding thunderstorm, and then the sudden return of the rain-drenched Jack with his duck. I was now really alarmed, but Jack reassured me that he had made arrangements for the surreptitious cleaning and cooking of the duck. He was as good as his word, for the following day we had roast duck with our rice for lunch, for the first time in three years!

Of course, the object of most of the pilfering was for food, or to get money so that we could buy some of the consumer goods available in Kanburi. I was reluctant to steal and restricted my income producing activities more in keeping with my qualifications as a graduate in economics by gambling on the exchange rate. When I sold my rubber tyre on my first arrival in Bampong for about a hundred baht, it was possible to buy Burmese rupees at ten to one, so I invested thirty baht in Burmese rupees. Then when I was providentially sent to Burma, I found that in Burma, Thai baht, Malayan dollars and Indo-China currency were all available at huge discounts, so I acquired Thai, Malayan and Indo-China currencies. In this way I was able to acquire, in a more or less legal way, pocket money for the purchase of eggs and fruits.

Our Japanese guards were of course well aware that we were stealing things on a massive scale, and became infuriated when one day a tin full of M & B 693 much treasured by the Japanese for treating venereal disease, disappeared from their office. They carried out a massive and most thorough search lasting several hours but found nothing. When the search was over and much to everybody's surprise, the missing tin reappeared in the hands of one of our Cockney pilfering experts called 'Busty'. When he was asked where he had hidden it, he answered, 'Oh, just under the Colonel's bed,' —the only place the Japanese had not searched.

Our K Force and L Force officers were in fact nearly all doctors and they were a considerate lot. They also voluntarily subscribed part of their meagre pay into a fund for the benefit of those on lower pay and those, for example, the sick, who got no pay at all. The British Colonel who endeavoured to keep this gang of rustlers and kleptomaniacs under control was a Colonel Benson, a good natured pre-war vintage Colonel Blimp type of officer, who was well liked even by the Australians who normally did not venerate their officers very much.

One of the most popular officers was a Captain McGarrity, a spitting image of Groucho Marx, whose character he had successfully portrayed on the stage in the halcyon days of Changi in 1943. He was also a favourite of the Japanese, who liked his moustache and his loud words of command at the troops. Fortunately they did not realize that it was all play-acting on his part and at their expense.

Another who I particularly admired for his good nature and skill as a surgeon was Captain Tim Hogg, an Australian from Launceston, Tasmania. He once removed a corn from my foot after much play-acting and fooling around. He also bullied me into assisting him with an operation while I lay ill in bed with one of my many attacks of malaria. He brought the patient along, and laid him alongside me on my bamboo bed, and then proceeded to take his appendix out with some kind of local anaesthetic. He informed me that the patient's life lay in my hands. I had to keep the flies off. One fly settling on the wound, he warned, would probably result in the death of his patient. I am glad to say I successfully kept all the flies at bay and the patient lived; maybe he is still alive! And of course there was my own friend Wally (Captain Wallace IMS) who was a pessimist and a worrier but a very good friend through very difficult days. I kept his spirits up with a constant supply of Burma cheroots; and it was he who saved my life at Nikki. He later joined the Colonial Medical Service and served as an eye specialist in Sarawak and Sabah after the war.

In February and March 1945 our Japanese hosts became very touchy. I suffered a beating when in a misguided act of generosity I took the blame for some misdemeanours committed by another working party, and ended up with a busted ear-drum and a deaf ear for the rest of my life! But our worst clash with the Japanese took place in mid-March 1945. One night having already been prisoners of war for over three years, and in need of a little relaxation, we decided to have a party. So we drank a lot of Thai liquor, got very merry and sang a variety of songs late into the night. One of the songs we sang was the 'Road to Mandalay', the first five lines of which go as follows:

By the old Moulmein Pagoda looking eastward to the sea,
There's a Burma girl a-settin and I know she thinks o'me,
For the wind is in the palm trees and the temple bells they say:
Come you back, you British soldier; come you back to Mandalay
Come you back to Mandalay.

This particular song apparently infuriated the Japanese and the following morning we were all lined up and beaten violently across our backs with pick-axe handles. Pick-axe handles are extremely hard, and when I received my beating, I was hit with such force that I fell to the ground, and for a moment thought I wouldn't be able to get up. Fortunately, I suffered no serious damage, apart from the loss of the use of one of my kidneys, and have managed quite well with the use of only one kidney!

I often wondered why they took such umbrage at our innocent drinking party in 1945. I discovered the reason forty-four years later when by accident I found myself a guest at the 19th Indian (Dagger) Division Officers Reunion Dinner at the Oriental Club in London. I discovered that this 19th Indian Division commanded, I am pleased to say, by a singing Welshman by the name of Major-General Peter Rees captured Mandalay Hill on March 11, 1945. Our drinking party and our Mandalay singsong unfortunately took place a few days after the capture of Mandalay by the 19th Indian Division. It was a case of *post hoc ergo propter hoc* or as the Malays would say *Enggang lalu ranting patah* (The hornbill flies past, the branch falls off), that is, it was a most unfortunate coincidence.

Shortly after the unpleasantness over the Mandalay song,

we were moved to a proper POW camp at Tamuan near Kanburi. This was a high security camp, for it had an enormous deep ditch all the way around it, as well as guards. The British camp commander was surprised when we arrived to find that we were not three hundred *orang hutan*, for the Japanese had informed him to expect three hundred wild men from Borneo, although I suspect he must have actually said three hundred wild men from Burma. We were, however, well received by the others in spite of our bad reputation as a gang of thieves. I was made a camp policeman on the basis, so I was told, of 'set a thief to catch a thief'. I was happy in my work, but not flattered by the criterion, especially as there were many better qualified than I.

I got my first mail at this camp, that is, I got my first mail from home for over three years. It consisted of a letter and a postcard from Lyn, telling me that she still loved me and was waiting for me. She also said she had written every week, so I often wondered what the Japanese did with those 150 letters. The postcard was especially touching. Many years ago, in England, we had gone for a walk together, and while walking across a field in a friend's farm in Sussex called Layhouse Farm, Lyn tripped and fell and asked me to pull her up. For some perverse reason I refused the offer, suggested she could get up quite easily, and walked on. When I got back to my host's house, he asked me where Lyn was and I said she was following. After half an hour as she had not put in an appearance, I retraced my steps, peeped through the hedge and found her still sitting in the field! So I had no alternative but to go and pick her up and so she had won. Her postcard said:

Went to Layhouse for the weekend and revived old memories. Walked across the field I sat. All my love.

The huge ditch around the camp was an object of some suspicion. The Japanese said it was to keep us in the camp, but we believed that in an emergency it might be our grave. I was therefore quite happy when on June 12, 1945, we were on the move again, this time to a camp to the north-east of Bangkok. We travelled by a slow train, and on the way had to over come an obstacle—a railway bridge which had been bombed by Allied planes. This called for some very hard work, first unloading the train of hundreds of very heavy rice bags, carrying them across a ravine and then loading them on to another train about a hundred metres away. We also spent an uncomfortable night in the godowns at Bangkok, not only because we had to sleep on rice bags with rats running over us at night, but because we knew it was a favourite target for our Allied planes.

After a few days we arrived at our new camp called Pratchai, which was near Saraburi about 120 kilometres to the north-east of Bangkok. We arrived late one afternoon, and when we were shown the site for our new camp, we found it hard to believe that our Japanese guards were serious and really meant it. It was a large flat padi field under 15 centimetres of water. In spite of our protestations we were forced to spend the night in tents in 15 centimetres of water. So we placed our packs round the tent pole, and tried to sleep sitting upright on our packs, with our feet in the water, while it poured with rain all night outside.

The following day, we were paraded in the watery padi field and during *tenko* (roll call) while we were numbering in Japanese I heard one POW say *ni-ju ouch* (twenty ouch). The explanation was that as one of the barefooted POWs numbered 20, he was bitten on his toe by a padi crab, much to the amusement of all concerned. We were then informed by the Japanese in charge that we had two days to get the camp organized, that is to build a cookhouse, lavatories, etc. but they had no ideas of how to get rid of the water.

Fortunately, we had Gunner Charlie Webb, formerly Professor of Physics at Raffles College, Singapore in our midst, and the British camp commander called him in for advice. He quickly devised an ingenious level made out of a long piece of bamboo, carried out a rapid survey, and discovered that the padi field had a gentle slope in a certain direction. All the fit men in the camp then set to and dug an enormous drain in the direction of the slope, and, hey presto, within one day all the water had run off into the drain, while during the next day the hot sun dried out the padi field into a bone dry camp site. The Japanese were flabbergasted! I must admit I was also amazed at the transformation of the padi field into such a beautiful dry camp site within a couple of days.

As soon as the camp site was ready, most of the POWs were put to work digging tunnels into the adjacent mountain range. There was much speculation as to the purpose of these tunnels. The most popular theory was that we were building a line of defence for the Japanese army, and that the tunnels would house Japanese field guns which would fire from the mouth of the tunnel and then withdraw into the tunnel for shelter.

I never found out, for one day in mid-August 1946 as I was chatting to a friend while sitting in a shallow drain in our camp, I noticed unusual goings on in the Japanese soldiers' camp which had recently been established next door. They were busily burning their papers and things. I watched with increasing interest and said to my friend, 'Can you remember when we last burnt our papers and things?' But we dared not jump to conclusions. Then a wave of excitement swept the camp when our ration team of POWs came back from Saraburi with the news that the Chinese Thais had put up Chinese flags, and were saying that the war was over, and that a big bomb had been dropped on Japan. But we were apprehensive and carried on as before; even though the Japanese had informed our camp commander that there would be no more work that week—all men *yasumi* (rest). Then we noticed that the Japanese guards were no longer guarding our camp, and wondered what was up.

Finally, on August 16, 1945, there suddenly rang out a bugle call, not a Japanese bugle call but the British bugle call, 'Come to the cookhouse door, boys, come to the cookhouse door.' At the sound of this call we all ran out tremendously excited on to the parade ground where our British camp commander was waiting for us. Then during a deathly silence when you could have heard a pin drop, he announced to a thunderclap of cheers that Captain Suzuki the Japanese Commander had just informed him that the war was at an end. He also begged us to stay in the camp, do nothing rash, and keep well away from the Japanese soldiers whose future actions were unpredictable. Having heard so much from the Japanese soldiers that they never surrendered, and fearful that if they decided to commit hara kiri, they would first kill us, we were only too ready to keep well away from them.

I immediately rushed for my pack, for at the bottom of my pack I had a surprise for everybody. I had a small Union Jack secreted there. I had carried it with me for three-and-a-half years, through thick and thin, for such a day. When I produced it, there were no lack of volunteers to climb on to the top of our attap hut to fly it from there. The Dutch also produced a flag, but to my dismay it was ten times bigger than mine! However, this was no time for envy, but I have often wondered how the Dutch had secreted such an enormous flag.

We slowly adjusted our behaviour to the now delicate situation, 'discretion' became the order of the day, while we tried to pretend that nothing much had happened. Then one day one of the notorious Korean guard bullies, by the nickname of 'Silver Bullet' came into our camp and tried to fraternize. We felt like murdering him, for he had made our life a misery at Pratchai, but everybody showed wonderful self-control and completely ignored him so he slunk away.

Then after ten days, which seemed ten years, a solitary British plane flew over our camp and dropped some food and a bundle of papers. I was called to the camp commander's office and asked to unpack the bundle of papers. I did so speedily and expectantly, eager to read what the papers at home had to say about us heroes in Thailand. I went through the *Sunday Express* carefully, page by page, but could find nothing about the War in the Far East. Indeed I could find absolutely nothing about any prisoners of war in Thailand, or about any prisoners of war anywhere. The paper was all about the people of England enjoying themselves on an August Bank Holiday. The camp commander and I looked at the other papers, with the same result. It looked as if we had been forgotten. To say that we were most disappointed is an understatement. We were devastated. My camp commander gave instructions that all the papers should be destroyed as soon as possible, and any knowledge of their existence suppressed.

The following day, an officer of one of the Guards Regiments together with a wireless operator complete with his transmitter landed by parachute into the middle of our camp. He sat on a truck and we gathered around him, treating him as if he was a God from heaven. We watched his every movement, especially when he withdrew a cigarette from his cigarette case and nonchalantly lit it with a cigarette lighter, which drew a loud laugh. Our POW smokers had for many years rolled their own home-made cigarettes made of any old leaf, and spent much time looking for a light.

A day or so later we had another surprise; we had an unexpected visitor. Lady Louis Mountbatten herself came to our camp, bravely escorted by just two Gurkha soldiers. We lined up still wearing the minimum of the clothes that we still had left to wear and cheered her. As she walked past me, she suddenly stopped as if to speak to me. But, alas, it was my good-looking friend of the Armoured Cars, standing next to me and still wearing his beret and looking a dashing young prisoner, that she had spotted and spoke to. Although mortified, I took some consolation from the fact that it was a near miss.

After what seemed an interminable delay, we were taken in trucks to Bangkok Airport for transit to Rangoon by an organization called RAPWI (Repatriation of Allied Prisoners of War and Internees) but which we designated as Retain Allied Prisoners of War Indefinitely. Unfortunately, when we reached the airport, we were subjected to a medical inspection before flying which I failed because of my ear-drum which had been broken by a Japanese a few months previously and was still giving off pus. The doctor said it was too dangerous for me to fly with such an ear condition, and as I was the only one left behind, took me into Bangkok for a drink. He took me to the smartest hotel in Bangkok and asked me what I would like to drink. I said boldly a Tuborg beer, and to my amazement, the bar boy produced it. He explained that he had hidden this particular beer from the Japanese for over three years.

After more delay, I decided to doctor my ear myself so that it looked as if it had healed, passed the medical inspection and was flown to Rangoon. When I arrived I felt most uncomfortable getting into a proper bed between clean white sheets after so many years, and having a meal without being able to sterilize my dixie. In fact some POWs refused to eat their meals until boiling water was provided so that they could sterilize their eating utensils. As one of them said to me, 'I am not going to get cholera now after all we've been through.' Our British army hosts thought we were mentally deranged and met our every word with sympathy.

At long last, the time came when we had to wish goodbye

to many of our Aussie friends and we embarked on an old P and O passenger ship at Rangoon bound for home. At Colombo we were met by a bevy of beautiful 'Wrens' and given some money for shopping. The young lady allotted to me took me into town and I suggested we visit Colombo's best shoe shop, so that I could buy some shoes in place of my home-made sandals made from an old rubber tyre. As I self consciously put my bare feet on to the stool to be fitted, a British army officer happened to come and sit along side me. When he saw my bare feet with no socks on, for my socks had worn out a year previously, he made some most uncomplimentary remarks about me. My 'Wren' was furious, told him I was a recently rescued prisoner of war from Burma, and he, of course, was then most distressed, poor chap.

The voyage home was a most wonderful experience, with plenty of food and no work. Even the most haggard skeleton like POWs started to look good, as they began to put on weight on what amounted to be a holiday cruise. Moreover, when we got to Suez we were issued with cold weather uniforms and so began to look like soldiers again. I must have looked very odd, for my jacket and trousers were British army issue, but my cap was American!

We also got our first proper mail for years at Suez. I got a letter from Lyn saying she was very excited at my home coming, but many of the others were not so lucky. Many husbands got letters from their wives to say that they had remarried, many unmarrieds that their girlfriends were now married with two children, and some husbands that their wives had unexpected additions to their family. It was ecstasy for some and tragedy for others. For me it was the former, for when I disembarked at Southampton and finally reached Victoria Station, there on the platform to meet me was my lovely looking Lyn, looking as sparkling as ever. She had waited over seven years for me! Also at Victoria Station was my eldest brother Tiny, still wearing his home-made sandals made out of an old rubber tyre, and my poor mother and her sister who had spent so many years wondering whether we were dead or alive.

Lyn and I got married* after a short period of getting to know each other again. Then one day I felt cold and knew I was going to have another attack of malaria. I called a doctor but he refused to believe I had malaria, so I took a sample of my blood, put it between two glass microscope slides, and posted them to Professor Manson-Bahr, the distinguished expert in tropical medicine. He phoned Lyn and said I was the first patient ever to send his own blood slide, confirmed I had malaria, and added I also had something else, hookworm or elephantiasis he cheerfully suggested. So I was admitted to his hospital for tropical diseases and was treated for malaria by the great man himself, as well as for the other complaint which turned out to be hookworm. I recovered and was never again troubled by either.

I now decided that my rusty brain needed exercise, registered for a Ph.D., and started on a course of lectures in educational psychology at the University of London. One day when visiting the refectory with Lyn, I was suddenly startled to find myself sitting down to lunch opposite three Japanese in uniform. When I first saw them I bristled as a cat does when it sees three unexpected dogs, and then upon looking at them more closely found they were Japanese in British army uniforms. They were Canadian Japanese! I had been prepared for anything on returning home from the Burma–Thailand Death Railway, but I was completely unprepared for Japanese in British uniforms!

Of course, I did not at that time know that over 20,000 American Japanese (*Nisei*) had fought so bravely on the Allied side during the Second World War that their 422 Regiment was the most decorated unit in the American Army!*

---

*My brother Tommy followed my example soon after and also got married. He married Pat, a daughter of the popular Director of Education Hong Kong, Tom Rowell. They had two sons David and Roger. David my godson later distinguished himself as a leading corporate lawyer in the City of London.

*Masayo Umezawa Duus: *Unlucky Liberators* (University of Hawaii Press, 1987).

Chapter 7

RURAL PARADISE:
KUALA PILAH

Seperti tikus jatuh ke beras.
(Like a mouse fallen into a rice bin, or in Clover)

Malay Proverb

After enjoying several months of idyllic leave with Lyn and on full pay, the Colonial Office made suggestions that officers might perhaps like to consider returning to Malaya before their leave had expired, in view of the difficult conditions still prevailing in the country. So some time before my leave was up, I found myself on a P and O ship on the way back to Malaya, sharing a cabin with three other similarly altruistically minded government officers, and living under rather spartan conditions.

After a voyage lasting about three weeks, and under rather cramped conditions, we finally arrived in Singapore in July 1946 to find the place under British Military Administration; with Japanese prisoners of war much in evidence, scurrying about doing as they were told in an exemplary manner.

I was met by a young self-important Major in uniform who informed me that he represented the Director of Education in Kuala Lumpur, and that I was posted to Kuala Pilah in Negri Sembilan as Principal of the Tuanku Muhammad School. I was, of course, delighted at this news, for I had heard of Kuala Pilah and that it was considered to be one of the most attractive rural spots in Malaya. I put this good fortune down to Mr H. R. Cheeseman, the Director of Education, and who I had reason to believe had me down on his list of favoured education officers. Those not on the approved list were traditionally sent to Kuala Lipis, Pahang.

I travelled to Seremban by train, where I was met by a Malay *syce* from the Education Department with a car, for transporting me to Kuala Pilah. Some Japanese prisoners of war had, however, the misfortune to be at the Seremban station when I arrived, so I instructed them curtly in Japanese to carry my luggage to the car. But I did not say much more in spite of my past intentions of getting my revenge on them. I find I can't harbour a grudge for very long!

Kuala Pilah turned out to be what I had been led to expect, a mainly Chinese small town set in a beautiful district of padi fields, coconut trees, Malay kampongs and smiling Malays, crowned so to speak with a royal *istana* (or palace) at the secluded Sri Menanti and an equally charming royal family. To me, it was a rural paradise and a welcome change from the Burma–Thailand railway.

The Tuanku Muhammad School was named after the father of the Sultan, Tuanku Abdul Rahman, also known officially as the *Yang di-Pertuan Besar* or *Yam Tuan* in Negri Sembilan. The medium of instruction was English and the pupils, Malays, Chinese and Indians of both sexes. Most of them came to school by bicycle, but some came to school in special school buses run by the local bus company, although the Sri Menanti children had their own bus.

On arrival I reported to the District Officer, who was a British Military Administration appointee, and so he spoke no Malay and knew very little about the job. He informed me that as I was the first civilian to return to Kuala Pilah I could take up residence in whichever house I liked, so I picked the best, then found that it had been the Headmaster's house before the war, and so took possession of it. I was soon joined by several other European government officers. They included Stewart Angus the District Officer, Martin Read the Medical Officer, his wife Alison the Lady Medical Officer, and Leon Comber the OCPD.

Stewart Angus, Martin Read and myself had all been prisoners of war of the Japanese, while Leon Comber had seen service as a Major in Burma fighting the Japanese. So we had a lot in common and appreciated the tremendous welcome that we received at the hands of the people of Kuala Pilah, especially the Chinese community who had suffered most under the Japanese occupation. For a month or so we were wined and dined at innumerable Chinese dinners, some out in the open along Main Street, some in Chinese restaurants, and some in one of the many clubs so popular in Kuala Pilah. At these dinners we learnt of the terrible sufferings of the people of Kuala Pilah during the Japanese occupation, how the Tuanku Muhammad School had been used as the headquarters of the Japanese *Kempetai* (or secret police), how hundreds of people had been tortured at the school, and how over three hundred mainly Chinese victims lay buried in the small rubber plantation at the back of the school.

When I arrived at the school I found it in a lovely location, overlooking a well kept *padang* and surrounded by shade trees. One of its former teachers (Mr Francis) had success-fully re-opened it, but it was operating under many difficulties, especially the lack of books. So my earliest efforts were directed at acquiring textbooks and building up a school library.

One day when I took one of the senior classes, I recognized one of the Malay mature students. He had worked like myself on the Burma–Thailand railway as a medical dresser. His name was Mohd. Sharif bin Ishak. He wrote an article in the first issue of the school magazine about it, and described his experiences as a dresser in one of the Japanese jungle 'hospitals' as follows: 'I have never seen such suffering of human life as I did in that hospital which could be called a living hell.' But we never discussed our mutual experiences, for we both wished to forget that nightmare.

There was keen interest in education, especially from the kampong Malays, which was a welcome development. In fact they were so enthusiastic that many were forging the dates of birth on the birth certificates of their children so as to qualify for entry into the Tuanku Muhammad School. One parent even offered me an envelope which, when I opened it, contained a bundle of ten-dollar bills, perhaps one hundred dollars in all—a lot of money in the 1940s. So I gave them all a lecture on the evils of forgery and bribery and told them not to do it again! Some were a bit ashamed of themselves, but all were puzzled how I knew they had tampered with their birth certificates, as the forgeries, had been beautifully executed. They had overlooked the fact that the serial number at the top of the birth certificate, also included the year of issue as a part of it!

As many of the pupils were still suffering from several years of malnutrition, free Klim milk was issued to all pupils every day. I found a cheap source of Klim milk for my own use in the town at a shop run by a shopkeeper with whom I was on friendly terms. I thought I was getting my milk cheap because of our friendship, until Stewart Angus the District Officer told me one day that someone had stolen a lot of his Klim milk that he had stored in a building in his garden!

There was also a great shortage of all kinds of consumer goods, and in an attempt to alleviate this shortage fairly, I was supplied with bales of cloth for distribution amongst the pupils. As for myself I had no car, for none were available, and often walked to school or cadged a lift from Martin Read who was allowed a car because he was the Medical Officer, or Miss Bunty Coupland, my so-called 'European Mistress' who also had a car for some of her special duties.

We were, of course, short of many other things, especially cutlery for special occasions. Consequently our Malay servants frequently borrowed each other's employers' cutlery. Thus one evening at a formal dinner party at the doctor's house, I unthinkingly admired his cutlery and remarked that we had a somewhat similar set. It was only later I discovered that it was in fact our cutlery, and that Puteh our Malay servant had lent it to the doctor's house. *Pinjam sahaja* (borrowed only) explained Puteh in her loud infectious laugh!

Almost a year after my arrival at Kuala Pilah, Lyn who had so patiently waited for me for such a long time during the war, was allowed to come out and join me. I went to meet her at Singapore in March 1947 and we travelled from Singapore to Seremban by train. When we had gone about half way, Lyn asked me why our Tamil Station Master travelled with us on the train. I explained that the Tamil Station Masters she had seen at our various halts were not the same one, but different ones who looked the same because they all came from Ceylon!

We arrived at Kuala Pilah in a thunderstorm. She described it in her diary after her arrival at Kuala Pilah as follows:

We eventually set out on the 25 mile drive to Kuala Pilah and home. There is a range of hills between us and Seremban and we had to cross them. The road wound between jungle covered hills, the sun was setting and the view was wonderful. It got dark before we arrived and the rain poured down in sheets and there was tremendous thunder and lightning to herald my arrival. I can't remember much about the journey, I was too excited.

At the door was Puteh—she is now an old friend though our conversation is extremely limited, and the old gardener and his wife. Puteh gave me a beautiful bunch of flowers, white wax-like flowers, the petals white at the edges but yellow at the centre and giving out an exquisite perfume. They grow on a tree in the garden and I can't remember the name. Puteh is charming and has a lovely sense of humour and a very infectious laugh.

Lyn loved Kuala Pilah and was fascinated by her new environment, by the friendly people and the variety of customs. She also made friends very easily, including one of the royal family at Sri Menanti. She was also asked by the District Officer if she would like to help, on a voluntary basis, with the social welfare of the kampong Malays and readily agreed. In this connection she visited many kampongs, some of them very much off the beaten track. One of these, not far from Kuala Pilah had suffered a traumatic experience. Apparently when the Japanese were defeated and the Chinese Communists came out of the jungle, there was trouble between the Malays and the Communists at this kampong, as a result of which some of the Malays took the law into their own hands and killed several of the Communists. British justice being what it is, with its insistence on the rule of law, the Malays involved were had up for murder and sent to jail at Kuala Lumpur. Unfortunately the poor wives of these kampong Malays had no idea how long their husbands had been sentenced to jail and were in a great state of economic distress. Lyn and the Welfare Nurse eventually sorted things out for them, found out how long their husbands would be in jail, and arranged for them to get some economic assistance from the Social Welfare Department.

Our house was located on the side of the hill at Kuala Pilah and overlooked a Malay kampong. Consequently the kampong noises and the sounds of popular Malay songs such as the delightful one called *Rasa Sayang*, would often drift up towards us providing a romantic background to our home. We were also located a few metres from the jungle and on moonlit nights wild pigs would often come and feed off the nuts which fell off a nearby palm tree in the garden. Puteh was full of superstitious beliefs and folklore. One moonlit night she came hurrying upstairs where Lyn and I were having a drink with Stewart Angus, the District Officer, and announced that she had just seen a tiger. So I rushed to an upstairs window with a strong torch, and there below me walking along the road leading away from the house I saw not a tiger but a large dog. When I informed Puteh of this fact, she became even more distressed, and said it confirmed her fear. The tiger she informed me was *Datuk Gaung*; who when necessary could change himself into a dog!

In May 1947, soon after Lyn arrived at Kuala Pilah, we were invited by the Sultan, Tuanku Abdul Rahman together with some others, to dinner at the *Istana* (or Palace) at Sri Menanti.

Although Lyn had learnt some Malay in London before she came out, under the guidance of none other than the famous Sir Richard Winstedt himself, I felt it would perhaps be advisable for Lyn to have some more tuition in Malay and engaged first of all one of the Malay boys at the school, and then one of my Malay teachers. The Malay schoolboy was Mohd. Noordin bin Keling (now a Datuk), who later became the Director-General of the Veterinary Service; the Malay teacher was Che Mansor bin Othman (also now a Datuk) who later first became *Mentri Besar*, Negri Sembilan and then Deputy Speaker of the House of Representatives. Of the two, I think Noordin bin Keling must have been the best value, for the idealistic Mansor was overcome with the problems of the world, and spent a lot of time with Lyn, building castles in the air instead of teaching her Malay.

As there was only one Teacher Training College in Malaya in 1947—the Sultan Idris Training College at Tanjong Malim for Malay school teachers, education officers such as myself were expected to train the teachers in the so-called 'English schools' ourselves, whether we were qualified to do so or not. I volunteered to teach Educational Psychology as it was my special interest at that time, as well as 'English as a Foreign Language' of which I had some knowledge by virtue of the fact that I had many years previously been a part author of the *Basic Way to English*.

I therefore travelled forty kilometres to Seremban every Saturday morning, where special teacher training classes called 'Normal Classes' were held at the King George V School. Among the instructors were E. M. F. Payne (later Dr Payne), Headmaster of the KGV School whose special interest was science and mathematics as well as Malay and linguistics, and L. I. Lewis (a namesake of mine but no relation), the Senior Inspector of Schools but in fact the Chief Education Officer for Negri Sembilan. L. I. had a lively and entertaining personality with the gift of the gab and could talk convincingly on any subject.

We normally foregathered together for lunch after the classes were over, and discussed the educational problems Malaya *ad infinitum*. We came to the conclusion that the existing Malayan educational system was archaic, needed restructuring, but as there were no signs of this being done from above, decided to send up our ideas on the subject to headquarters at Kuala Lumpur. We proposed that the existing eleven-year course finishing with pupils taking the Cambridge School Certificate should be split into two stages: (i) a Senior course consisting of five years study and (ii) a Junior course consisting of six years. I followed it up by drafting a suggested Geography Syllabus for English schools on these lines, which was circulated and slightly amended, and then finally published by the Government Printer in August 1950. Our suggestions for restructuring the education system were adopted and soon all schools in Malaya were split into Primary (six years) and Secondary (five years). Moreover in due course syllabuses were drafted for all subjects within these parameters and so we were well pleased with our efforts.

The three of us remained friends all our lives and eventually ended up in Kuala Lumpur. Payne became Director of Education, L. I. became Chief Inspector of Schools and I became Headmaster of the Victoria Institution, after successfully refusing the job of Deputy Director on several occasions.

One unexpected result of the Japanese occupation of Malaya was the flourishing of the wildlife in the jungle, because of the Japanese prohibition of the possession of firearms by private individuals. Consequently soon after my arrival at Kuala Pilah, I found there was an abundance of wild pig, mousedeer, wild duck and wild fowl in the jungle, with even tigers and elephants much in evidence. So I went on several shooting trips, the most successful was one when all my companions missed a flock of wild ducks as they flew overhead and then invited me to shoot at a solitary wild duck, which I did with success, much to the approval of the local kampong Malays; the least successful was when I had hurriedly to seek the safety of a tree after a close shave from a nasty looking wild boar!

My life at Kuala Pilah was extremely busy, indeed I don't think I have ever been so busy in my life. At long last I had the opportunity to do the things I had wanted to do for so many years. Apart from running the school, training teachers on Saturday mornings, playing rugby with the boys and our local Kuala Pilah XV consisting of some local planters, the Medical Officer Dr Martin Read, and his assistant Dr Abdullah, the OCPD W. Strathairn, and some of my schoolboys on Saturday evenings, I was also involved in various projects such as educational research, textbook writing, and the study of Chinese. Of these activities the former, that is, educational research, took pride of place while I was at Kuala Pilah.

Since my first arrival in Malaya in 1938, I had become concerned with the position of the Malays in Malaya, for they seemed to be second class citizens in their own country. Although some government positions were reserved for Malays, in general there was no discrimination in favour of the Malays, and the best jobs went to those with the best qualifications. When I asked why the Malays did not seem to be able to hold their own in open competition, I was told that the Malays lacked the intelligence of the other races. I was not, however, thoroughly convinced of this, for these observations were based on opinions and not scientific evidence.

I therefore decided to carry out a comparative survey of the intelligence of Malays and Chinese in the Kuala Pilah district by means of intelligence tests. I used two tests (i) a non-verbal test which I had myself designed (Lewis: *Non-Verbal Test of Mental Ability*) and (ii) a well-known Army test (*Ravens Progressive Matrices*, published by H. K. Lewis). I used non-verbal tests because a knowledge of language did not therefore form part of the test, while they could be administered in any language. In this way, I was able to test the intelligence of Malays in Malay schools; Chinese in Chinese schools; and Malay, Chinese and Indians in English schools and compare the results.

I tested over 4500 boys and girls of school age: 3000 Malays in Malay and English schools; 1500 Chinese in Chinese and English schools. Tengku Syed Jong the teacher of Malay at the Tuanku Muhammad School administered the test in English and Malay, and Lee Chong Goh a teacher at the local Chung Hwa (Chinese) school administered the test in Chinese (*Kuo-yu*). It was a mammoth task especially for Tengku Syed Jong who visited about twenty Malay schools in the Kuala Pilah district, some of them quite remote and accessible only on foot. I accompanied Tengku Syed Jong on all his trips, and took great care to ensure that the dates of birth of those tested were supported by valid birth certificates. The scores were then entered on to cards by Lyn and filed in a cabinet.

The survey proceeded smoothly, until just before it was completed, when the OCPD arrested my Chinese assistant as being a suspected Communist. This, of course, spelt disaster for my research work. So I visited the OCPD who was W. Strathairn and fortunately a good friend of mine, explained the position, and obtained the release of my unfortunate Chinese assistant.

When the survey was finished, a group of about twenty Tuanku Muhammad School pupils were marshalled under the supervision of Mr Selvaratnam the Senior Mathematics master, and the mean scores and standard deviations calculated for both Malay pupils and Chinese pupils, by age groups.

The results proved most interesting. They showed that although Chinese pupils were age for age undoubtedly superior to Malay pupils in the early stages, this superiority decreased with age so that there was no significant difference at 16 years, that is, it could be said that Chinese pupils appeared to be precocious rather than superior in mental ability as compared with Malays. This, however, did not end the story. I now endeavoured to look for factors that might account for these differences. I was not entirely successful in that, but my research revealed one important factor—rural pupils were at a serious disadvantage when seeking secondary and consequently higher education as compared with urban pupils. Moreover, as most of the Malay pupils lived in the rural areas, and all the secondary schools were in the towns, it was clear that they were handicapped. This was something which might account for the difference in achievement as between Malays and Chinese, and I suggested that it was something the Department of Education could put right. Although it was obvious what action was called for, I did not make any concrete suggestions for fear of offending the Director of Education. Some years later, however, while I was an Assistant Director of Education in Kuala Lumpur, I felt free to elaborate and suggested in a short memorandum that the way forward in this respect was to build bigger and better hostels at the large secondary English schools for the rural Malays. Unfortunately the Communist insurrection which overwhelmed Malaya in 1948 no doubt delayed any serious attempt at solving the problem.*

I, of course, recorded the mental ability of all the pupils at the Tuanku Muhammad School and soon found that some of the best Malay pupils were highly intelligent. Thus there was one family of Malay girls who excelled in this respect. They were Tengku Zainab, the Headgirl who had charm as well as intelligence, and her sisters Tengku Zoe, Tengku Zailah and Tengku Zailan. The latter got a very high rating in intelligence, and distinguished herself academically in later years, obtaining many degrees!

Some village schools also seemed to harbour pockets of high intelligence; for example, Gunong Pasir, for some reason produced some quite remarkably intelligent children. I also,

---

*For an interesting discussion on the problems facing the Malays 25 years later, and especially the Malay dilemma, that is, the relative poor economic performance of the Malays as compared to the Chinese, see *Mahathir Mohamad: The Malay Dilemma* (Asia Pacific Press, 1970).

unknown to the authorities, took intelligence scores into account when selecting rural Malays for entry into the Tuanku Muhammad School, which is perhaps why the Tuanku Muhammad School produced a record 14 candidates with Grade I School Certificates in 1953! But such a policy sometimes created problems. I remember one small Malay boy came top in the intelligence test and near the bottom in the written exam. I made inquiries and discovered that my problem boy habitually played truant at his Malay school, so I admitted him, knowing that I would ensure that he would have to change his ways when he came to the TMS! It's a pity I can't remember his name.

Many highly successful Malays came from Kuala Pilah, such as Tunku Shamsul Bahrin, Professor of Geography at the University of Malaya—(perhaps he was the boy who played truant at his Malay school); Noordin bin Keling who became Director-General of the Veterinary Services, Yunus Maris who became a Senior Lecturer in the Malay Department at the University, Raja Alias (now Tan Sri) who became Director-General of the Federal Land Development Authority, Zainal bin Deli (now a Datuk) who became Senior Assistant Commissioner of Police, Asidin bin Ali who became a Lieutenant-Colonel in the Malay Regiment and so on. Some of my Malay teachers also shone. Thus Mansor bin Othman became *Mentri Besar* of Negri Sembilan. But I often wondered what happened to a small boy called Mohd. Nor bin Kadir. I have lost track of him. He scored very high marks in the intelligence test and should have become a minister.*

One day the Director of Education, Mr H. R. Cheeseman, paid a visit to the school. Although he had no degree, he was a highly respected senior officer, a scholar and a born teacher. He was also a pioneer writer of textbooks for the Malayan scene. I suppose he came to see how good or bad I was at running a school. I had been warned that he was a very perceptive person, and had a habit of leaving something behind when visiting a school on inspection, and then return-

---

*I have now solved the mystery. Owing to family commitments he was not able to go to a university. So he joined the Customs as a junior officer and eventually became deputy Director-General of Customs in 1981! This is not surprising because as a schoolboy he got the highest rating of all the TMS schoolboys in intelligence! He is also a Datuk.

ing unexpectedly and catching one unawares. His inspection of the school passed off well, but ten minutes after he left I suddenly saw he had left his hat behind. So I hurriedly warned my staff that he would be returning, which he, of course, did within half an hour, only to find the staff and pupils of the Tuanku Muhammad School hard at work and not in any way celebrating his departure! We all hoped he was duly impressed.

Much of my time at Kuala Pilah was taken up with writing. Many years previously, when I was a teacher of Geography at the Penang Free School, I was asked to set a special geography paper for Malays at the Malay College Kuala Kangsar seeking entry into the Malay Administrative Service. As the Malay College is located within sight of the massive granite Main Range, I set one question asking the candidates to name any geographical feature they knew of, that was made of granite. To my astonishment, they all gave as an answer, not the Main Range which they saw every day, but Dartmoor, England! I discovered the reason why. There was only one book on the geography of Malaya written for Malayans, and that made no mention of the simple geology of Malaya. I therefore decided I had better do something about it. So during my leave in the United Kingdom I came to an agreement with Longman Green the publishers to produce a series of geography books for use in Malayan secondary schools, in collaboration with my old Professor, Dudley Stamp, a famous geographer.

So I started on the books while I was at Kuala Pilah. Fortunately the Department of Education had just published the new geography syllabus, so the kind of geography required had been agreed. For Form 1 the syllabus called for the study of the chief industries of Malaya such as tin mining, rubber planting, padi planting, fishing and so on. I decided I would write from personal experience, and started on a series of lightning visits over the weekends to various plantations (rubber, oil palm, coconut), tin mines and padi fields where I studied the geography of these industries at first hand. Although I had a camera, I took with me a professional Chinese photographer from Kuala Pilah. He seemed to enjoy the experience, and took some excellent photographs for me of Malays ploughing padi fields—he was chased by a buffalo on that occasion!—, Tamils plucking coconuts, Chinese miners mining tin and so on.

Later when I travelled overseas to China, Japan, USA and so on, I carried my own camera, and took thousands of colour photographs which I still have. I eventually wrote over twenty textbooks for Malayan schools alone, and when these were translated into Malay, Chinese and Tamil, the total number of copies sold was surprisingly large. For example, Book I which I wrote at Kuala Pilah eventually sold over half a million copies.

During my stay at Kuala Pilah I therefore travelled a lot in the pursuit of geography, and Lyn usually came with me. On one such trip to study the tin fields of the Kinta valley near Ipoh, Perak, Lyn who was pregnant became unwell as a result of the rough ride, for the roads were in an awful condition with potholes every few metres because of their neglect during the Japanese occupation. When we got back to Kuala Pilah she had a miscarriage, and we lost what should have been our first child. So what I believe was our son is buried in an unmarked grave at the foot of a frangipani tree, on the edge of the jungle on the hill at Kuala Pilah and at a spot frequented by the ghost of *Datuk Gaung*, which is a consolation.

Martin Read, our local Medical Officer, admitted Lyn immediately into the Seremban hospital. The 'ambulance' turned out to be an open lorry with a stretcher supported by two chairs, on it. The nurse was one of the *Yam Tuan*'s wives, and the mother of the present *Yam Tuan*, H.H. Tuanku Ja'affar. On the long and tedious journey to Seremban, and to keep Lyn's mind off her tragic experience, which she did most successfully, she related as one woman to another details of her married life to the *Yam Tuan*.

My final preoccupation at Kuala Pilah was the study of Chinese. Having passed the necessary Malay language examinations in pre-war days in 1941, while I was stationed in Singapore, it seemed the sensible thing to have a working knowledge of the other most widely spoken language in Malaya, that is Chinese, and in particular the national language of China, *Kuo-yu*. My attempts at studying it while I was a prisoner of war had been rudely interrupted. Now at Kuala Pilah I had the desire and the opportunity to pursue my ambition uninterrupted by the Japanese. The only slight embarrassment was the discovery that my Chinese teacher was a dedicated Communist. So my Chinese lessons soon became forty-five minutes of Chinese language study and fifteen minutes of political debate. But my attempts at converting my Communist teacher into a democratically minded Socialist made very little progress, for like most dedicated Communists he was blindly obsessed with dogma and completely unreceptive to logical argument.

When the Japanese were defeated in September 1945, the first troops to appear on the streets of the towns and villages of Malaya were not British or Allied soldiers for they were still on the invasion fleet at sea, but the Communist guerrillas of the Malayan Peoples Anti-Japanese Army (MPAJA) wearing British jungle green uniforms. They boasted they had defeated the Japanese army, and pursued a small scale reign of terror. However, in due course with the arrival of British troops, the MPAJA were persuaded to give up their arms, or at least some of them, and over 6000 of the MPAJA demobilized.

The British Military Administration (BMA) had no choice but to reluctantly recognize the Malayan Communist Party (MCP), and on my arrival at Kuala Pilah the MPAJA were very much in evidence, with their MPAJA ex-Service Comrades Association Headquarters established in the Main Street. I soon made the acquaintance of Tan Fook Loong who had been the Commander of the Negri Sembilan MPAJA; indeed after a while we became quite good friends. We had of course one thing in common, for we had both opposed the Japanese and suffered from the consequences of it.

A glance at the map shows that there is a large lake in central Malaya. This lake which is called Tasek Bera—*Tasek* means lake in Malay—could not be approached by road in the 1940s, for it was surrounded by jungle and swamp. Its very remoteness and inaccessibility made it an object of mystery; moreover, I could not find anybody who had been there or who knew how to get there.

Fortunately, one day I actually met someone who had visited Tasek Bera. He was H. D. Collings, an anthropologist attached to Raffles Museum at Singapore. He told me that the aborigine people called Semelai lived there. I decided that in order to get a balanced view of the people of Malaya for my geography textbook, it would be necessary for me to go there. Collings told me that if I went to the north-east corner of Ladang Geddes rubber estate near Bahau, I would find a jungle track and that if I followed it for several hours, I should with luck eventually get to Tasek Bera.

So one day in April 1948, together with Lyn who never missed the opportunity for a bit of excitement, and two Pakistani policemen who the OCPD asked me to take along with me for my protection against wild animals and also for their edification, we set out for Tasek Bera. First, we called at the Bahau Police Station where Strathairn, the OCPD, had arranged for two aboriginal 'guides' Adang and Lahi to accompany us. But we soon discovered they had no idea how to get to Tasek Bera, so they agreed to come as porters, and carried our *barang*. We then called on the manager of the Ladang Geddes estate, who was slightly apprehensive about our proposed trip, but kindly agreed to take us in his jeep to the north-east corner of his estate where we found the jungle track that was supposed to lead to Tasek Bera.

The path was narrow and damp, and infested with leeches which swayed hopefully from the grass and bushes waiting for a suitable victim to attach themselves to, so that they could suck its blood. After an hour or so we met two Chinese who confirmed that we were on the right track for Tasek Bera. Then a few kilometres further on we came unexpectedly upon some huts in a clearing where there were about twenty Chinese and an aborigine. The Chinese informed us they were collecting jungle produce, and by luck the aborigine was a Semelai. He readily agreed to show us the way to Tasek Bera, so we decided to rest there for the night. Just before nightfall, I was surprised to hear a bugle call, but the Chinese said it was to frighten away the wild pigs. I had no reason to disbelieve what they said, and in any case we all got on very well together, expecially when I produced Kohs Blocks, which is a kind of intelligence test, but which my Chinese friends took to be some kind of gambling game.

That night the Chinese tried to persuade us not to go and warned us that the jungle track was very difficult, and that we would also have to cross about thirty streams. This information proved to be only too correct, for the next day we discovered that the track was littered with tree roots which had to be walked on, tree trunks which had to be climbed over, streams and swamps which had to be waded through and crossed, and leeches which had to be avoided and sometimes removed.

As a protection against leeches we soaked our socks in salt water, and painted a ring of iodine round our bare legs just above the knees, for leeches have an aversion for both salt and iodine. As a final defence I carried an iodine pencil for dealing with individual leeches, but I noticed that the Chinese used lighted cigarettes with equal effectiveness. It was a nightmare of a march. We finally reached our Semelai guide's home among a group of huts in a jungle clearing called Kampong Baape, just before sunset. Lyn's sandals were worn out, Adang my Bahau aborigine was on the point of collapse, and everybody was completely exhausted. So we cooked ourselves some rice and *ikan bilis* (anchovy), and soon fell fast asleep on the bamboo floor of our Semelai guide's house.

The next day as we were too stiff to move, we decided to rest for a couple of days, and made friends with the local Semelai. They were most intrigued with Lyn, for I was told that they had never seen a white woman before, and spent much time touching her, and feeling her in a nice kind of way! They were completely isolated from the rest of the world, but appeared to be quite happy with their lot and for food were growing tapioca, padi, sugar cane and bananas in their jungle clearings, catching fish in the near Tasek Bera, and hunting wild pig and deer which seemed to be quite numerous in the nearby jungle. They also informed me that during the recent war against the Japanese, the MPAJA had a camp of twenty Communists at Kampong Baape. Indeed they showed me a metal container under the house which they said had originally contained medical and other supplies which had been dropped one night from the air by the British for the MPAJA. They also said that on that night two Europeans and two Chinese also parachuted down into Kampong Baape.

One day I was invited to go hunting in the jungle with a couple of Semelai. We did not see or catch anything, so they gave me a yellow fruit to eat; it was about the size of a chicken's egg. I noticed that they swallowed it whole, and I soon discovered why. When I tried to eat mine in a more 'gentlemanly' way by biting into it as if it was a *ciku* or a pear, I suddenly found that its inside consisted of a kind of glue, which sealed my lips so efficiently that I was unable to speak for several minutes, which of course caused hysterical amusement amongst my Semelai friends.

After a couple of days' rest at Kampong Baape we finally reached Tasek Bera, and found not a large lake of clear water as we had expected, but a large reedy swamp. I got into one of the Semelai boats but my modest weight was too much for it; the boat sank and I got wet. After some discussion with the Semelai, they said they could get me a 'big' boat, big enough to carry the seven of us, that is Lyn and myself, the two policemen, and the aborigines, but of course it would take time to get it—a few days in fact. So we returned to Kampong Baape and waited patiently.

The Semelai had a very different attitude to time than ourselves. They measured time not by the hour, for they had no watches or clocks, but by the position of the sun in the sky. So when I asked them how long it would take to get to our next stop, they would indicate by pointing to the position of the sun in the sky. It was a peaceful and relaxed way of living. As far as I know nobody suffered from high blood pressure at Tasek Bera!

After a few days the 'big' boat arrived with a Chinese called Ah Pau and two Semelai paddlers in charge. It was in fact just big enough for all ten of us. I suggested we first went to a remote settlement, further up the lake, and marked on the 1" topographical map as Kampong Datoh. But the suggestion proved unpopular. Even when I suggested that we could walk part of the way did not help. The aborigines made all kinds of excuses. It was difficult to reach, there was nothing there, it would take a long time and so on. So I took the line of least resistance and went downstream towards the Pahang river.

The journey downstream was difficult, for the channel was very narrow running between reeds, and later still narrower running between clumps of thorny *mengkuang*. Occasionally we came across open areas of clear water, but most of the journey was obstructed by fallen trees, *mengkuang* roots and so on. As we paddled along the boatmen sang a rhythmic song in Semelai, occasionally excitedly shouting 'kerbok, kerbok' as bubbles of air from below came to the surface. I later discovered that kerbok was the Semelai word for crocodile, and so learned that Tasek Bera was infested with crocodiles and no place for a swim! After about five hours' paddling we reached a place the Semelai called Chendrong, where there were three attap huts and the friendly Ah Pau had a small 'shop'. I wandered around, and was most surprised to find a large stack of rice bags at the back of his shop. We had a rest, a meal of rice and ikan bilis at Ah Pau's shop, and then continued our journey. After about another hour's paddling we reached a place they called Tanjong Kruin, where there was a hut, a large open space of clear water, and we were informed many kerboks (or crocodiles). We took a fancy to this spot, in spite of the crocodiles, and decided to rest there for a day or two. At sunset the sky became suddenly darkened by thousands upon thousands of what I took to be birds coming home to roost in the jungle around Tasek Bera. Later I discovered they were not birds, but flying foxes, large bat-like animals.

Later that night while the two policemen were sitting outside our hut on the lakeside, they saw a boat-like something moving towards them on the water, and informed me that a Semelai boat was coming to visit us. Then suddenly I heard them rush for their rifles, but when they searched with their torches, they could find nothing. I decided they must have seen a large crocodile floating on the surface in the moonlight, but the Semelai disagreed. They insisted it was a large snake which lived in Tasek Bera, which makan orang or eat people!

The next day, I foolishly decided for some reason that it would be fun to try and catch a crocodile. So I consulted the Semelai and that afternoon an old Semelai and his son arrived to catch one for me, complete with a long piece of rotan and a piece of wood about 15 centimetres long, spiked at both ends, on which the bait would be put. As he strongly advised wild pig or mousedeer as bait, I organized three parties led by Semelais to look for them. We hunted for a couple of hours, but were unsuccessful, although Lyn saw a mousedeer, and there was plenty of evidence of wild pig and deer.

Eventually a wild chicken was used as bait and the trap set. The next morning we all got up early, and got the exciting news that the bait had been taken. Mercifully, however, when the *rotan* was pulled up from a deep pool there was no crocodile at the end of it. The crocodile had swallowed the chicken and the trap, but had wisely disgorged it all, and so avoided capture.

That evening Lyn made an interesting discovery. Wandering into the adjacent jungle where she had seen some brightly coloured wild fowl, she came across a small clearing in the jungle where the turf had been newly dug up and carefully replaced. She wondered who on earth could have wanted to bury or unbury anything in such an isolated place where there was not even one Semelai. I decided not to investigate too closely, bearing in mind that old English saying 'Curiosity killed the cat'.

We left early next morning, and after a couple of hours paddling found ourselves out of the Tasek (lake) and in Sungai (river) Bera. We paddled for a day and a half down the Bera singing the Semelai boat song and occasionally stopping so that the aborigines could pick jungle fruit. The river channel was narrow and sometimes obstructed by fallen trees. There were also many overhanging trees while kingfishers brightened up the scene by flying low along the river. On the way we came to the junction of the Serting with the Sungai Bera. We were surprised to find the Sungai Serting such a small stream considering it was once a famous routeway. Lyn and some of the others had a swim at the small *kuala*, while I kept a look out for crocodiles. Finally, we came to a place called Langu, where there were a few huts and a jungle path leading out to Triang on the railway, and to civilization.

We had our last meal together with Ah Pau and his boatmen at Langu. I paid the boatmen at the rate of $2 per day for ten days, gave Ah Pau $4 for his help, and gave away all our tobacco, rice and fish and wished them a tearful goodbye. I noticed Ah Pau was crying his eyes out. We walked out of the jungle to Triang along a narrow jungle track, which in parts was plagued with leeches. On reaching Triang we continued to walk down the main street, one behind the other as if we were still in the jungle, before adjusting to the urban method. We then caught the daily train at Triang for Bahau, and took a bus back to Kuala Pilah together with Adang and Lahi the two aborigines, as well as a porcupine and a *musang* which we had acquired on the way.

The two aborigines stayed with us for a week and were the centre of attraction for our friends in Kuala Pilah. But the aborigines spent most of their time in the toilet, pulling the chain and marvelling and speculating at the water appearing and disappearing so magically. As one of them commented in Malay to me: '*Ada*' (it's there) and '*t'ada*' (it's not there). The porcupine became a pet and made friends with the dog who would chase him, but could not get close because of the porcupine's sharp quills. The *musang* stayed for a few weeks, and amused himself by nibbling my toes when I shaved in the morning. Then one day he discovered the tall tree in the garden, climbed it and was never seen again.

And so ended a marvellous trip, which unknown to us could easily have ended in disaster. For according to information* now available to us, the Malayan Communist Party had decided to take over Malaya in 1948, and had commenced mobilizing its ex-MPAJA members back into the jungle in March 1948, with the intention of declaring Malaya a Communist Republic in August 1948! Unfortunately for the. Malayan Communist Party, on June 16, 1948, a killer squad of the 5th Regiment of the MPAJA now renamed the Malayan Peoples' Anti-British Army (MPABA) murdered five people at Sungei Siput in Perak, three of them British planters, and in effect started the insurrection prematurely. As this was followed by several more murders, a state of emergency was declared on June 19, 1948 by the Government, while a few days later the MCP was declared illegal.

My innocent expedition into the jungle therefore coincided with the return of over 3000 Communists into the jungle. It is now clear that the twenty Chinese we met on the first day of our expedition towards Tasek Bera were probably an outpost guarding a Communist jungle camp, near Bahau—a

---

*R. Clutterworth: *Conflict and Violence in Singapore and Malaysia 1945–83* (G. Brash).

notorious place for Communists; that the bugle call we
heard probably came from the camp; the obstinate refusal to
allow me to go to the remote Kampong Datoh because there
was probably a MCP camp there; the large stock of rice at Ah
Pau's 'shop' at Tasek Bera probably rice in transit to MCP
jungle camps further up the lake, while the turf which had
been disturbed in the remote jungle clearing and which Lyn
had accidentally discovered near Tanjong Kruin, probably
hid an arms dump! But why did Ah Pau cry so much when we
parted company? I am sure they were not crocodile tears, so
perhaps he had taken a liking to us and thought we would all
be murdered in the coming Communist revolution!

When the state of emergency was declared a month or so
after our return from Tasek Bera, I became very much aware
of my vulnerability, for I did not even have a bow and arrow
for our protection. So the following day I got a gun licence
from the OCPD and rushed off in my car to Kuala Lumpur
to buy a shotgun at the large general store there called
Robinsons. On the way, as I sped through the small Malay
village of Kampong Terachi, which is between Kuala Pilah
and Seremban, I was surprised to pass in a car speeding in
the opposite direction, my old Communist friend Tan Fook
Loong. He waved frantically at me and I responded as he
passed by. But we did not stop, and I never saw him again;
so it would appear that as I was hurrying to Kuala Lumpur to
buy a shotgun, he was scurrying for the jungle to resume his
command of the Negri Sembilan Communists!

The murders of the three British planters, and the declar-
ation of a state of emergency on June 19, 1948, was followed
by more murders and violence in the rural areas, especially
Pahang. Thus on June 29, the police station at Jerantut
(Pahang) was captured and destroyed; on July 12, Malaya's
only coal mine at Batu Arang (Selangor) 42 kilometres from
Kuala Lumpur, was attacked and the police station destroyed; while worst of all, on July 15, Communists guerrillas
liberated the railway town of Gua Musang (Kelantan) and
the nearby Chinese village of Pulai. They held it for four
days, before the police, Malay and Gurkha forces recaptured
it. All this created some excitement but no despondency. In
any case I now had a shotgun and as I was living in a Malay
area, I was not unduly alarmed.

The following month I went on long leave in the United Kingdom, and for the time being, left behind the fears and worries caused by the Communist insurrection. I must admit I had no idea what a serious threat they posed to the independence of Malaya and thought the trouble would soon be over. When I got back to London, I finished my Ph. D. thesis and presented it to the University of London in quintuplet. It was entitled 'A Comparative Study of the Intelligence and Educability of Malays and Chinese in Malaya'.* The viva before several distinguished psychologists passed off without incident, although I was most surprised that I was not called upon to produce some concrete evidence that I had in fact tested the intelligence of the 4500 Malay and Chinese pupils as claimed in my thesis. I had with me all the answer sheets and much other evidence but I was not asked to produce anything. All my figures were taken on trust. I thought this very lax of the examiners, and resolved that if I was ever an examiner for a higher degree, I would take nothing on trust, and make sure that all basic statistics were properly supported with some evidence of their authenticity.

My caution in this matter proved well founded for some years later it was shown that there was reason to believe that even the great Professor Cyril Burt had fudged some of his results to support a preconceived idea!

After several months' leave it was time to return again. I gathered that the Communist insurrection showed no signs of being over; indeed it was getting worse, so I bought a bullet-proof waistcoat from 'Wilkinson, the Sword People' and a long barrelled Luger pistol, especially when I heard that I was being posted to Kuala Lipis, in Pahang, a state which I gathered was a hot bed for Communists.

As I have already indicated, Kuala Lipis was the traditional punishment posting for government officers. My brother Tiny confirmed that H. R. Holgate, the Director of Education, was slightly displeased that I should dabble in education politics, for the conclusions of my Ph. D. had obvious political overtones. So I was being banished to Kuala Lipis

---

*Available in microfiche from the Library, University of Malaya in both Singapore and Kuala Lumpur.

where I could do no harm. But I was not greatly disheartened, for I had read some of Hugh Clifford's books on Pahang. For example, I had read his book entitled *In Court and Kampong* written in 1896, where Hugh Clifford had described the Pahang Malay as follows:

> The Pahang Malay, in his unregenerate state, thinks chiefly in deeds of arms, illicit love intrigues, and the sports his religion holds to be sinful. He is a cock-fighter, a gambler, and a brawler; he has an over-weening opinion of himself, his country and his race; he is at once ignorant, irreligious, and unintellectual and his arrogance has passed into a proverb. *He has many good qualities also, and is above all things manly and reckless ...

and then finished by saying

> but in spite of all their faults and foibles, and ignorance and queer ways I love (them) exceedingly.

Such people sounded on interesting prospect for me, and I wondered whether things had changed very much since those fendal days. Nevertheless I was a bit apprehensive when I learned that Kuala Lipis was located halfway between the notorious Gua Musang and Jerantut!

---

*Kechek anak Melaka, bual anak Menangkabau; tipu anak Rambau; bidaah ana Trengganu; penakut anak Singapura; penjelok anak Kelantan; sombong anak Pahang. (Weedlers are the men of Malacca; boasters the men of Menangkabau; cheats the men of Rambau; liars the men of Trengganu; cowards the men of Singapore; thieves the men of Kelantan and arrogant are the men of

Chapter 8

JUNGLE WAR: PAHANG

Terlepas daripada mulut buaya, masuk ke dalam mulut harimau.
Out of the crocodile's mouth into the tiger's mouth (or out of the frying pan into the fire).

Malay Proverb

I returned to Malaya in March 1949 in considerable comfort, that is first class on the *Oranje*, a luxurious Dutch passenger ship, that sailed between Amsterdam and Jakarta, but called at Southampton and Singapore on the way. Lyn decided to prolong her leave a bit so as to be with her aged mother for a few months, and so did not accompany me.

The *Oranje* was a fast and beautiful ship and the Dutch were very proud of her. But she had one fault: she rolled over on her sides most alarmingly when she was travelling at speed, even in a calm sea. Fortunately the bad company I got into soon found an appropriate solution to the problem, and that was always to put plenty of Bols gin into our orange squash. I consequently had a most enjoyable trip with a small group of Dutch and British passengers.

As we neared Singapore I began to speculate on my future in Pahang. When I reached Malaya I discovered that the country had become a battlefield. In fact during my absence on leave many hundreds of civilians (mainly Chinese) had been murdered by the Communist terrorists (CTs), many police and soldiers had been killed while an equal number of Communist terrorists had been eliminated. There had also been many acts of brutality and terror committed by the Communists, such as cutting peoples' arms off, and burning people alive in their houses; for their objective had been to create terror, especially among the rural Chinese and the isolated plantation workers.

Upon reaching Kuala Lumpur, I stayed the night with my brother Tiny, who was at that time Deputy Director of Education, and then headed for Pahang in my small Ford Prefect car. The first part of the journey was mainly through rubber plantations, so although a bit apprehensive I did not feel frightened. However, when at last I turned eastwards for Pahang at Kuala Kubu Bahru, and saw the huge Main Range with its dense virgin forest which I knew provided cover for the Communist terrorists in front of me, I must admit I was scared, and for a fleeting moment thought of turning back. But as so often in my life before, I decided to face up to whatever unpleasantness lay ahead and accelerated towards the mountains and the jungle.

The road to Pahang winds its way over the Main Range via innumerable hairpin bends, providing suitable ambush points round almost every corner. However, after surviving twenty or thirty such places, I soon settled down to my new environment, and decided not to worry any more especially as like the other infrequent motorists on this road, we were all in the same boat.

When at last I reached the small roadside village of Tras in Pahang, and on the other side of the Main Range, I decided to stop and have a drink at a Chinese coffee shop. As I walked in, instead of the usual welcome from the owner of the shop, I was greeted with silence. There was a small group of Chinese, including a woman, at one end of the shop, and they stopped talking as soon as I entered. They reminded me of a group of schoolboys caught in the act of plotting some schoolboy prank, of which of course I had some expert knowledge. But these were not schoolboys. So I drank my coffee, and departed without appearing to hurry, though I was glad to get away.

When I reached Kuala Lipis I found I would be sharing a house with Mike Day and his wife Jane. Mike was a Special Branch Officer, and when I mentioned my experience to him, he advised me not to stop in Tras in future, for he said it was a hornet's nest of Communists. So bearing in mind the old Malay proverb *Sarang tebuan jangan dijolok* (Don't poke the hornets' nest), I followed his advice. Many years later, I discovered that Chin Peng, Secretary-General of the Malayan Communist Party, had moved his headquarters into the nearby jungle in Pahang in 1949, and that his wife was a member of the Tras Communist District Committee. So perhaps I had unwittingly interrupted a committee meeting!

Kuala Lipis is a small town, built on a number of hills, at the junction of the Sungai Lipis and the much larger Sungai Jelai, and in those days it was approached by one road only. Although it was then the capital of Pahang, it was a dead end in more ways than one. And so I was not surprised when I visited the Pahang Club one evening, and went to the bar for a drink to be met by the remark: 'So what did you do wrong?' So it was true what I had heard that Kuala Lipis was a place reserved for those out of favour.

On reflection, however, I was reassured that the Communist insurrection had obviously changed all that, for the place was full of police and army officers as well as some excellent government officers. Rather I felt here was the cream sent to confront the Communists and save Malaya from Communist rule!

After talking to some of the European officers attached to the Malay and Gurkha Regiments, and hearing how only a few months previously they had been in action against the Communists in the recapture of Gua Musang, I had the stimulating feeling that at Kuala Lipis we were in the front line. Certainly there was plenty of evidence of that, for we were all armed to the teeth, and carried our guns with us all the time. I had two pistols: a short-barrelled Luger which I carried with me all the time and put under my pillow at night, and a long-barrelled Luger which I took with me when I had to go out of Kuala Lipis. The latter was an amazing gun, for although it was a pistol, it could be used like a rifle. One could aim with it, and given time I could hit a target at a distance of over ninety metres. Moreover when I was in my office, I had arranged things so that I always faced the door, and always kept one of my Luger pistols available out of sight, but ready for instant use. Kuala Lipis then was very much a 'wild west' town.

Fortunately, those in charge of affairs were of above average ability and integrity. Both Malays and British co-operated in the job of fighting the Communists in an admirable way. The position of the Chinese was most difficult, for if they were seen to be co-operating with the government they would be marked men and eliminated (i.e. murdered) at the earliest opportunity. Nevertheless there were some very brave Chinese, such as Ong Siong Tek, who whatever the danger, was in the forefront of the war against the Communists.

Some of these exceptional persons who I have referred to above and who were directly involved in the war against the Communists included the following:

Datuk Mahmud bin Mat. He was the *Mentri Besar* (or Chief Minister) of Pahang, a Pahang Malay, who was greatly admired by all who came into close contact with him, including Lyn who later worked for him as a confidential secretary.

W. C. S. Corry, the British Adviser, a senior officer of the Malayan Civil Service, who took much of the worry of fighting the Communists off the shoulders of Datuk Mahmud.

Hume Brett, the Chief Police Officer, who had the responsibility for directing all police operations in Pahang.

Brigadier du Burg Morris, the senior military officer in Pahang, a cool Irishman with a good brain and a sense of humour.

Russell Forsythe, the District Officer of Kuala Lipis who was a personal friend of mine. He was an Australian Rhodes Scholar, with a first class brain, who drew attention to some of our earliest mistakes. Unfortunately, although he was more often right than wrong, he lacked the tact to persuade others, and so did not exert as much influence as he deserved.

Yeop Mahidin, an ex-Anderson School rugby wing three-quarter, who successfully organized the Malays of central Pahang in the fight against the incipient Malay Communist movement led, believe it or not, by his cousin Abdullah C.D. Yeop Mahidin was a modern Hang Tuah, a smiling extrovert who had been the leader of the Wataniah, the Pahang Malay anti-Japanese underground movement, and had collaborated with Force 136, during the war against the Japanese. We became good friends and I greatly admired his courage, for he never hesitated to confront the Communists when they could be found.

Another senior government official, who became a close friend of mine was Datuk Abu Samah, the State Secretary.

His work was concerned mainly with the daily problem of running the state. His office was on the same hill as my school, and he frequently wandered down to my office for a chat. He was a real Malay with a great love for rural areas and rural pursuits. He once told an unbelieving me that coconut trees made good walking sticks! To prove it he presented me with one, made from the hard core of a coconut tree, when a few years later I left the state. I still have it for coshing any intruder who attempts to burgle my house in England. He also had the countryman's unsophisticated artfulness and kept geese at his small government mansion on the hill to guard against Communist infiltration, for he well knew that geese are more alert than Malay policemen, especially in the middle of the night.

Then there was a Malay by the name of Dato Maharaja Perba Jelai (or *To' Raja* for short) who was a local Malay chief who lived at Bukit Betong on the Jelai river just above Kuala Lipis and for whom I had a secret admiration. His family had provided the Malay chiefs for the Jelai river valley from time immemorial. He was a smallish Malay with a jaunty walk and a slightly 'macho' image. Some years before Hugh Clifford came to Pahang, his great grandfather had nearly succeeded in an attempt to seize the throne of Pahang. If he had succeeded *To' Raja* would have been Sultan of Pahang, and no doubt the Sultan's palace would have been at Kuala Lipis, and not at Pekan. As it was, after several attempts a rival to *To' Raja's* ancestor by the name of Che Wan Ahmad eventually captured the throne for himself and for his heirs. Che Wan Ahmad came into Pahang from Dungun, Terengganu via the Tembeling river, and with the assistance of his followers conquered Pahang.

Finally, a few months after my arrival at Kuala Lipis, a young Malay by the name of Abdul Razak reported for duty as an Assistant District Officer. He had recently returned from England where he had studied law and was very keen on the United Nations Organization. In fact he asked me if he could come and speak to my pupils on the subject, which of course I agreed to. I was told that his father Datuk Hussein of Bentong was greatly respected by the British for his honesty and integrity. We became good friends and of course he eventually became the Prime Minister of Malaysia.

He showed great interest in my Ph. D. when he learnt that the subject of my thesis was a comparative study of the intellectual ability of Malays and Chinese. Indeed he was the first Malay to read it. We discussed the matter on a number of occasions and he agreed with me that the Malays were seriously handicapped by their rural environment. When we discussed how best to ameliorate this handicap, I thinking only in educational terms promoted the idea of more hostels, but Razak suggested it would be more effective if the problem was tackled on a wider front, that is by improving the general infrastructure of the rural areas, for example, by building new roads, etc. in the rural areas. And that of course is precisely what he did, when he became Deputy Prime Minister.

Datuk Mahmud was another who was interested in this topic; indeed I had a map drawn for him showing the distribution of Malays in Pahang. It showed that in 1950 most of the Malays lived along the banks of the Pahang river, and especially in the district of Temerloh, whereas most of the secondary schools were located elsewhere. This of course was not the consequence of any deep laid plot to deny the Malays secondary education but the unfortunate result of the fact that previous education officers in Pahang, had gone about their work in motor cars and not in boats.

Clifford School, to which I had been posted as Principal, was of course named after Sir Hugh Clifford, one of the earliest (1892) British administrators in Pahang, a fluent Malay speaker, and the author of many fascinating books on the early days in Pahang, such as *Expedition to Trengganu and Kelantan, In Court and Kampong* and so on. I was slightly disappointed when I first saw it, for the buildings were hardly what I had expected as the premises for the premier school of Pahang. However, the site was excellent, for it was located on the Lipis river, with the river on one side and the *padang* on the other.

The staff as in the case of most schools in Malaya were a dedicated lot, but with a small proportion of malcontents, which I presume was to be expected from a so-called penal station. I felt it was a pity that our J. B. Wilson, better known as Anthony Burgess the author, who was also a member of our Education Department and himself a bit of a dissident, could not have been sent in my place, for he could have had a field day, portraying the various characters at our 'wild west' town of Kuala Lipis.

As it was I had a hard core of excellent teachers, of which the following were the ones that I can now recall most easily:

T. K. Nadarajah, the Senior Assistant who hailed from Jaffna, Sri Lanka was one of them. He was one of those highly intelligent Jaffna Tamils, found in those days throughout our Colonial Empire in the Far East, who could be relied upon to do his work efficiently. He was an ascetic and appeared to lead a life of austerity, for his house was always very clean, with few consumer goods, but always with a book or two lying around.

Supporting him were three more 'of that ilk', that is, they hailed from Ceylon, as it was called in those days, all of them hard-working mature teachers, also with roots I think in Jaffna. They were: S. Somasundram, T. Sinappu and T. C. Chelliah, but all of them with very different personalities.

Somasundram was a philosopher who could see all sides of the question and so drew no conclusions. He was an admirer of Shakespeare and of British institutions, especially the British House of Commons and was a subscriber to Hansard!

T. Sinappu was the quiet, silent type who got on with his job unobtrusively, and with a great love for cricket. He was the kind of teacher much appreciated by headmasters.

T. C. Chelliah had a charming personality, a bit tired to work and waiting eagerly for his retirement. And who could blame him, for he was first posted to the Cinderella state of Pahang about thirty years previously and had lived to tell the tale. He was generous to a fault, and donated a *complete* set of the Oxford English Dictionary to the school library. I last saw him the day he retired, sailing down the Lipis river in a small boat with, I was told, a bottle of toddy as his companion.

Then there were the up and coming ones, especially three intelligent and hard-working young teachers who also had their roots in Jaffna: S. Pathmanathan, K. Purushotham and S. Panchalingam. They too were some of my most loyal and industrious workers.

On the Chinese and Malay side, some of the outstanding teachers were the tall, asthenic and long-serving Lian Ah Shin, and his brother Lian Loy Shin, my perspicacious teacher of geography and Raffles graduate Idris bin Babjee, and the cheerful Othman bin Ngah, the school clerk and scouter who also boasted long and faithful service. Both the latter were made Datuks by a perceptive Sultan of Pahang.

Although I was disappointed with the Clifford School buildings, I sought consolation from the thought that good academic achievements should be the result not of impressive buildings, but of good teaching and a good school library. Unfortunately Clifford School had no library, so I immediately took possession of one of the scarce classrooms and set it aside for a library, and devoted much energy into acquiring suitable books for it, not forgetting a copy of Dicey: *Law of the Constitution* because of what it has to say on democracy and the rule of law. As librarian, I selected the eminently suitable bookworm and subscriber to Hansard, S. Somasundrum.

Life at Kuala Lipis during the next year or so was never dull. On the one hand I was busy doing what I could to improve a school that had obviously suffered from serious neglect in the past, by building up a library and by introducing new activities such as cross-country run and rugby football; and on the other hand, by taking care not to get shot by the Communists. The first cross-country run unearthed a small boy called Balwant Singh, who went on to become a Malayan cross-country champion, while rugby football produced some anxious reactions from some of the older generation Malays brought up on nothing more violent than *sepak raga* (a game played with a kind of rattan ball) and top spinning. One who was alarmed with the arrival of rugby football at Kuala Lipis was my friend Datuk Abu Samah, especially when his son Abdul Razak (now a High Court Judge) became the school Rugby Captain, and no doubt sometimes returned home the worse for wear!

And of course the Communist guerrillas made sure that there was never a dull moment. Thus one day they set fire to the *penghulu*'s house just across the river from my office, while I was at my desk; and on another occasion sent a hail of bullets over my bungalow on the hill while I was having a shower. They even opened fire from the other side of the Jelai river, at the Chinese Club in Jelai Street, while I was being entertained with some others to dinner. Finally, one moonlit night I became aware that there was a man in the garden outside my bungalow, and thinking he must be a Communist terrorist I phoned the Kuala Lipis police station. I told them who I was and said, '*Sila mari sini cepat. Ada orang jahat di luar rumah saya.*' (Please come quickly. There is/are Communists outside my house.) After waiting for half an hour, no police came (no doubt I thought fearing an ambush). So I phoned my neighbour Mike Day of the Police Special Branch. He crept round in the dark. We met at an agreed rendezvous at the back of my bungalow, and together we discovered that our intruder was a mentally unbalanced Chinese who had wandered up our hill to my house in the dark. It later materialized that the police had not come because of my faulty Malay. I should have said '*ada seorang jahat*', not '*ada orang jahat*' for the latter implied that there could have been hundreds!

Then there was a rather sad occasion in August 1949, when I was invited to the mortuary to see the dead body of the notorious Malay bandit Wan Ali. He had terrorized the Malays in the Jerantut–Temerloh area for several months, and had been killed by kampong guards. The Malays firmly believed that he could only be killed with a silver bullet. I felt sad when I saw him, for he was a good-looking Malay, with no doubt a sense of adventure, but unfortunately the wrong cause.

So it is not surprising that the journalist Harry Miller* reported of Pahang during this period as follows:

Pahang became the lonely state. Very few people ventured into it by car from the west, it was too dangerous. Kuala Lipis the capital was rarely visited by casual visitors....

Apart from our local incidents there were of course many incidents in the other parts of Pahang. Thus on September 11, 1949, over three hundred Communists attacked Kuala Krau, located about half way between Jerantut and Temerloh and killed some Malay policemen and two European railway

---

*Harry Miller: *The Jungle War in Malaya*, Chap. 15: The Battle for Pahang.

engineers, while a month later over two hundred Communists raided an isolated estate in Pahang, and burnt down all the buildings including the manager's house. Such attacks continued unabated during the next two years, not only in Pahang, but throughout rural Malaya, with about a hundred people being killed every month.

Travel by road out of Kuala Lipis was of course unavoidable; one just had to take a chance of not running into an ambush. I am aware that I drove through a few unscathed, presumably because my car number was not on the Communist's black list.

Soon after I arrived at Kuala Lipis, and the police became aware of the fact that I had recently visited Tasek Bera, they asked me if I would agree to fly over Tasek Bera and report anything I thought to be of interest. So one clear day I was flown over Tasek Bera in an army plane on a reconnaissance. I could pick out very little of my old route, but I was able to pick out the Semelai boats. They looked like long pencils lying on the lake from the air, and were all huddled at the southern end of the lake. I decided that this meant that the Communists had taken over Tasek Bera, and had forced the Semelai into the upper and more remote part of the lake, that is near Kampong Datok.

Lyn came out in September 1949, and I went to meet her at Singapore. I decided that my small Ford Prefect car had very little chance of getting me through an ambush, so while I was in Kuala Lumpur changed it for a large Ford V8, with a view to putting armour plate around it. I never got around to doing that, but instead always wore my bullet-proof waistcoat, which I had camouflaged a bit to look like a pullover! This gave me some protection against small arms fire, but of course no protection against a Bren gun of which the Communists possessed a number.

It was clear that there was little sign that we were getting on top of the Communist insurrection, rather the reverse. I gathered that there were over 3000 armed, mainly Chinese Communists in the jungle, and that they were organized into ten regiments including one regiment of Malays in the Temerloh area. The Communists had large camps in the deep jungle, where they had parade grounds and lecture halls—I guessed one such camp must be located at or near Kampong Datok, the place I failed to get to on my recent visit to Tasek Bera. They were supported by thousands of mainly unarmed Chinese squatters, organized into the so-called *Min Yuen* (or Peoples' Organization) who kept the armed guerrillas supplied with both food and information, either willingly or under duress.

The object of the Communist terrorists (or CTs) was to get the sympathy of the Chinese squatters, terrorize the waverers, and to paralyse the economy by slashing rubber trees, smashing the machinery on tin mines, ambushing and burning buses and trucks; in fact to create chaos.

Although the police force had been greatly expanded, and there were many battalions of British, Malay and Gurkha soldiers in action, the Communist offensive was increasing in ferocity and hundreds of civilians and soldiers were losing their lives. Consequently, in April 1950, the government appointed General Briggs, a retired British general who had gained much experience in Burma during the war against the Japanese, to be a new Director of Operations. With others, he devised a plan—the Briggs Plan to defeat the Communists. Briefly the plan was to isolate the armed Communists in the jungle from all sources of food, arms and information from outside the jungle, and to protect the people and especially the Chinese squatters from intimidation.

Both Lyn and I were soon directly involved in the operations against the Communists. In March 1950, she started to work as confidential secretary to the British Adviser (in the morning) and as confidential secretary to the *Mentri Besar* (in the afternoon), while two months later I was asked to take charge of psychological warfare in Pahang and appointed the State Emergency Information Officer (SEIO). In this capacity I sat on the Pahang SWEC, which included the Chief Police Officer (Hume Brett), the Brigadier (Brig du Burg Morris), the British Adviser (W. C. S. Corry) and with the *Mentri Besar* (Datuk Mahmud) as Chairman. I now found myself thoroughly involved in the war, but Datuk Mahmud suggested I still continue as Principal of the school, as it would provide me with a cover for my new work, which would undoubtedly make me a target for the Communists if they became aware of it.

Of course I knew nothing about propaganda or psychological warfare and could find nothing to read on the subject.

I did, however, get a copy of Goebbel's Diaries, and thought that as he had been the head of Nazi Germany's propaganda machine during the recent war I might learn something useful. I discovered that Goebbels advocated wholesale lying and believed that if you tell a lie often enough, the people will believe you. Unfortunately, it appeared that Goebbel's lies were found out many times, so that towards the end of the war nobody believed him, even when he spoke the truth.

I therefore decided I wouldn't make the same mistake as Goebbels, and adopted a policy of always making sure that my facts were true. I found that within such parameters, it was still possible to get the anti-Communist message across. There was no need to tell lies and I am convinced that was the correct policy. Thus when the Communist burnt a bus, I reported the matter accurately and pointed out that such actions showed how little consideration the Communists had for the travelling public, by disrupting their travel arrangements in such a way. When the Communists confiscated or destroyed their identity cards, I was again able to show how inconsiderate they were, for such actions meant at least a day's pay lost, while the unfortunate victim went to the nearest Registration Office to get a new identity card.

But one of my propaganda schemes was a disaster. Thinking that many Chinese squatters were at heart Socialists and not Communists, but didn't know the difference, I thought that perhaps I could turn them into democratic Socialists, and abandon the idea of gaining power by force. So I founded my own Kuala Lipis anti-Communist Socialist party. Of course it did not exist in reality, but some of the anti-Communist propaganda strips I had printed purported to emanate from this Chinese democratic Socialist party. So one night my agents plastered Kuala Lipis and nearby Benta with my propaganda strips written in Chinese characters. The result was a disaster, for it now appeared to the local inhabitants that the Communists had even penetrated Kuala Lipis itself. I had overlooked the fact that Malays and Indians don't read Chinese characters, while many Chinese are illiterate. Consequently the majority of the people assumed that the Chinese propaganda that confronted them that morning emanated from the Communists. I dissolved my ghost Socialist party quietly overnight.

But I did have some successful ventures. The most successful one was the issue of safe conduct passes to the
Communists who wanted to surrender. The pass was a piece
of paper, with the Pahang crest on top, and a statement in
English, Malay and Chinese that the bearer should be given
safe conduct to the nearest police station and well treated.
The other side, which was the main feature of the pass,
showed a group photograph of half a dozen recently surrendered Communists, including one leading Pahang Communist. In case it was thought the photograph was in some
way forged, I had the photograph taken with the six
Communists sitting on and standing against one of the latest
police armoured vehicles, smiling and looking well-fed—
which indeed they were. It was convincing proof that they
would be well treated if they surrendered; and also that
some of their friends had already done so. Many tens of
thousands of these passes were dropped over the Pahang
jungle and many surrenders obtained. One of the best
customers was Jock Hindmarsh, the police officer in charge
of the Temerloh district—he ordered a million copies. When
he retired he ended up in the Tower of London; as the
Keeper of the Tower I hasten to add!

Most of the Communists were astonished at the lenient
treatment they received upon surrendering, and in return co-
operated with the police, even to the extent of leading police
and army patrols back into the jungle and co-operating in
seeing their former comrades ambushed and killed.

On one occasion, General Briggs came to Kuala Lipis and
attended one of our top secret SWEC meetings, so as to
acquaint himself with how we did things in Pahang. Half-
way through the meeting we had a short break for coffee.
The coffee was served by two burly Chinese wearing unusual clothing. When General Briggs asked what branch of
the police they were in, he was at first rather surprised and
then amused when he was informed that both were recently
surrendered Communists!

One day in late June 1950, my brother John, who was at
the time Assistant Comptroller of Customs, Selangor, suddenly appeared without warning in Kuala Lipis. He explained
that as nobody knew he was coming, he presumed nobody
would be waiting to ambush him! Nevertheless, he found the

latter part of the journey a bit nerve-racking, for when he entered Pahang he was obliged to check in at every police station on the way to confirm that he had not been ambushed and was still alive—a new experience even for a cool customer like my brother John. He stayed the weekend with us. After spending the evening with Hume Brett, the Chief Police Officer and an old friend of John's, we then took him to the Pahang Club. Here he was quite surprised to see how the members, some of them planters, piled their pistols and stenguns on the bar counter as they entered and ordered a drink, and how we were all armed to the teeth.

As mentioned earlier, Lyn was also involved in the anti-Communist operations, and as confidential secretary, both to the *Mentri Besar* and British Adviser, knew all the top secrets. Indeed all top secret information that had to be sent to Fraser's Hill and Kuala Lumpur by telephone was sent via her. The reason for this will be apparent, from a letter I recently came across from the British Adviser (Corry) addressed to Lyn. It said:

> Please ring Mrs Paramor and tell her in your ancient and venerable language that Colonel Crookshank from Raub and one other officer will occupy the Pahang Bungalow on Saturday–Monday next 10–12 Nov. No rent.

The ancient and venerable language referred to, which it so happened was spoken by both Lyn and Mrs Paramor (née Margaret Evans of Machynlleth) the lady in charge of the bungalows on the holiday hill resort of Fraser's Hill in Pahang, was of course Welsh, a language as far as we knew not known to any potential phone tapping Chinese terrorist.

When I was first appointed SEIO Pahang in May 1950, Alex Josey the journalist was the psychological warfare chief in Kuala Lumpur. I found him a likeable boss. He was a Socialist, but his socialist approach in fighting the Communists did not meet with universal approval. So in September Hugh Carlton Greene, a future Director-General of the BBC was sent in his place. Some time after his appointment he came over to Pahang to see how I was coping.

He arrived with a heavy police escort, and expressed the desire to visit Temerloh. As this meant traversing some of the most dangerous roads in Pahang, especially Raub–Tras–Bentong–Karak road I suggested we travel incognito, alone in my car, and without an escort. After the initial surprise and some hesitation he agreed; so off we went with my faithful Awang in the back of the car armed with my shotgun as my unpaid bodyguard, while Hugh and I sat in the front with our respective Lugers, etc. On the way we stopped at Bentong, and spent the night with Johnny Love the District Officer and his wife. He must have had an uncomfortable night, for Hugh was 6 feet 4 inches tall, but his bed under 6 feet!

We continued our journey and reached Temerloh without incident, so became more courageous and went south along the lonely road to Triang. On the way we passed many strips of propaganda stuck up on the rubber trees, and he complimented me on my work. On the return journey, however, as soon as we were' clear of the propaganda strips, I informed him that the propaganda he had seen belonged to the enemy!

Having the unpleasant feeling that we were now travelling through enemy-dominated territory, and as we were driving along a very lonely part of the road between some tall *lallang*, Awang suddenly spotted something running through the tall grass and shouted, '*Babi, Tuan, babi*' (Wild pig, sir, wild pig). So I jammed on the brakes and both Awang and I opened fire at the hidden wild pig. By this time Hugh (not being a Malay speaker), had thrown himself flat on the road, thinking we were engaging the bandits!

We then continued until we came across some more Communist literature at a lonely spot on the Bentong–Tranum road, stuck on some roadside telephone poles. Hugh wondered whether I could kindly collect some so that he could have them translated at Kuala Lumpur. Of course, I would normally not have stopped to pick up such titbits in case they were a trap for the unwary. But I obliged and took the strips of Communist propaganda off the poles with ease, for the glue was still wet, and so I was able to give him some enemy propaganda 'hot' off the press.

By this time, we were both thoroughly alert, if not scared, and drove rapidly through the notorious village of Tras and then entered a deep cutting, only to our dismay to see that at the end of the cutting there was a rubber tree across the road. The following split second conversation then took place.

Excited Hugh : My God, it's an ambush, it's an ambush!
Unruffled Me : No, I don't think so.
Agitated Hugh : How the hell do you know?
Relieved Me : We'd be dead by now if it was.

And so it turned out to be. It was just a rubber tree that had been blown down by the wind across the road in an ideal ambush position. Poor Hugh had seen enough of Pahang by the time we got back to Kuala Lipis, the courageous Awang had thoroughly enjoyed it, and I thanked my lucky stars that we had got back safely once more.

It was of course not surprising that our trip should have been an exhilarating one, for a month or so previously in September 1950 to be precise, the Communists had abducted Mrs Stutchbury, the Chinese-speaking English wife of the District Officer, Bentong, who had just held the job previous to John Love. Stutchbury had been preparing to set out with a police escort on the Bentong–Kuala Lumpur road. Mrs Stutchbury perhaps rather recklessly, decided to go ahead with a Chinese interpreter and had stopped on the way in a most unfortunate position. It was the very spot where the Communist terrorists had set up an ambush. They therefore had no difficulty in abducting both Mrs Stutchbury and the Chinese interpreter, and then murdered them both in the nearby jungle. She was shown no mercy: she had her throat cut. The news caused great despondency in Kuala Lipis, and it demonstrated to us what would happen if we allowed ourselves to be captured in an ambush.

I had of course considered what I should do if I ever ran into an ambush and found my way blocked. I had decided that I would seek cover as soon as possible in the jungle, firing my Luger to discourage any followers, and then seek the first stream and follow it downhill. And in case I was captured alive, I also had a plan. I carried with me a forged pass signed by my old friend Tan Fook Loong, Commander of the Negri Sembilan Communists, and typed on note paper belonging to the 12th (Malay) Communist regiment, which had come into my possession. The pass said:

Comrade G. E. D. Lewis is a friend of mine and a secret member of the British Communist Party. Please assist his passage to me.

Tan Fook Loong

Of course Tan Fook Loong had not written it or signed it. I had written it, and a Chinese Special Branch Officer had forged his signature in Chinese characters for me. I surmised that if I survived an ambush, and they made an attempt to send me to Tan Fook Loong in his jungle headquarters, I might on the way have an opportunity to escape. Fortunately my plan was never put to the test.

Soon after Mrs Stutchbury's murder, I was posted to Raub as the acting Senior Inspector of Schools. The posting was not unwelcome for it helped to maintain the illusion that my work was only concerned with education and in no way connected with the war against the Communists or the 'Emergency' as it was called.

People have often wondered why this full scale war between the government and the Communists was officially always referred to as the Emergency. The reason was to do with insurance. Apparently if the war had been called a 'civil war' which it most certainly was, then the insurance rates would have been raised and some claims on the insurance companies made by rubber estates and tin mines not met. So for economic reasons we pretended there was no war, even though during the three year period 1949–51, over 2000 Communist guerrillas were killed, while over 1000 police and soldiers lost their lives.

Just before taking up my appointment at Raub, while I was still acting as Principal of the Clifford School, I applied for money from the Senior Inspector of Schools at Raub for three projects at the school which were very dear to me. Then a week or so later, now that I was sitting in the chair of the Senior Inspector of Schools, Raub, the chief clerk of the Education Office, a colourful venerable-looking Sikh with a long white beard, and known to most of us as 'Father Christmas', presented before me this application from the Principal, Clifford School for money for some of his pet schemes. I could see from the look on his face that he relished the occasion and no doubt believed that I would now hatch my cleverly laid plot and would approve all three applications without hesitation. I asked him how much money was available, and then approved only two of the applications. At first he looked very puzzled. Then a sudden large smile appeared out of the beard and he approvingly said: 'Now I know what they mean by British justice.'

If Kuala Lipis was a hot spot, Raub seemed even hotter. The District Officer was a cheerful Malay called Abdullah, and the senior police officer (the OCPD) a famous character by the name of Bill Stafford.

Stafford was a stocky, broad-shouldered, tough Cockney, quite unlike the typical public school type normally recruited to the Malayan Police in Colonial days. His greatest claim to fame was that he and his Chinese detectives had killed the Communist leader Lau Yew in his jungle hideout near Kajang, where Lau Yew was ambitiously planning a full-scale attack on Kajang, soon after the beginning of the Emergency. He had thus deprived the Communists of their one and only outstanding military leader. So when, soon after my arrival at Raub, I found myself having a drink with Stafford on the verandah of the Raub Club watching a cricket match, and I thought looking very much exposed to attack, I said to him, 'What would you do now, Bill, if a CT suddenly appeared in front of us?' In a flash he replied, 'I would do this', and unexpectedly pulled out a pistol from under his left armpit, and then even more unexpectedly another from under his right armpit. No wonder he was called 'Two-gun Stafford'. I was much reassured.

There was also plenty of action in Raub. Thus one morning while quietly working at my files in the Education Office, there was a sudden ear-splitting outburst of gunfire which shook our ancient building to its foundations. A cloud of dust descended on us, and Father Christmas, our venerable Chief Clerk, desperately disentangled cobwebs which had fallen from the ceiling on to his beard. The Royal Hussars who had just arrived at Raub had decided to make their presence felt by opening fire with their fieldguns on to an unknown target in the jungle.

On another occasion while I was having tea, O. W. Walters with whom I was sharing a house, walked in with bruises and scratches on his face and informed me he had just been ambushed near by between Raub and Tras, and had escaped by abandoning his car and rolling down an embankment into some long grass.

Finally, there was an incident in which the local Chinese school was involved. One night the Raub–Bukit Koman road was plastered with Communist propaganda, one Malay policeman was nearly decapitated as he went to investigate by an unseen wire stretched across the road, and a Chinese murdered. Bill Stafford thought the Chinese school was involved, so with my short-barrelled Luger deep in my pocket, I called on the Chinese headmaster for a coffee. He was quite friendly, and even friendlier when I showed off my limited knowledge of Chinese. When I asked him if any children were absent, he said no. But when I started going round the school checking the registers, I found that about one-third of them were absent, and at least another one-third looked bleary-eyed. So it was pretty obvious that the school had had a night out putting up Communist propaganda, though they no doubt had very little choice in the matter.

My Chinese assistant Inspector of Schools was a very likeable young man, but a bit scared, for he was an obvious target for Communist vengeance. So I was not surprised when one day he came and asked me whether it would be possible to have the description of his occupation on his identity card as a Chinese Inspector of Schools changed. I said I thought it would be possible, and when I asked him how he would like to be described, he replied. 'Carpet Salesman'! So a carpet salesman he became, better that than dead!

One day I received from the Director of Education in Kuala Lumpur, a request which I thought was a bit super-fluous, for a return of education officers in Pahang even though I was the only one in the state, by the following categories: Qualified and Underqualified. So when I com-pleted the return, and feeling a little wayward that day, I added a new category for myself, as I was the only London Ph. D. in the Malayan Education Service. And so the Pahang return read:

Qualified Education Officers 0
Underqualified Education Officers 0
Overqualified Education Officers 1

I was not surprised when soon after that I received a letter from the humourless Holgate, the Director of Education, saying that of course I would be acting as Senior Inspector of Schools for only a few weeks. I gathered from my brother (TPM) who was his trusted deputy that he thought I was going round the bend in Pahang, which was far from being the case, for I was enjoying the rather stressful life immensely.

Anyhow as my time was limited, I decided I would visit some of the schools that had not been inspected for many years and was advised that the east coast schools had not seen a Senior Inspector of Schools for ages.

I therefore informed the Malay Inspector of Schools (East Coast) of my proposed visit. He lived in Pekan, the Sultan's place of abode, and had a reputation of being a good organizer and a Malay nationalist. His name was Abdul Rahman Talib. I decided that for a Malay to want self-government was not an unreasonable desire. So when in due course we met and he discovered that I sympathized with his sentiments and that I was Welsh, we became very good friends. I visited his house many times, and together with his attractive wife, occasionally went swimming together in the sea.

Later when he informed me, that he was considering resigning his job and entering politics, I advised him against it, but told him I would give him all the assistance I could if that was his final decision. He eventually did as he threatened, entered politics and became the Minister of Education! So within the space of a few years he became my boss and an even better friend. But alas his attractive wife no longer spoke to me when she became a Minister's wife. As the Malays say, it was a case of 'Belalang telah menjadi helang' (the grasshopper becomes an eagle).

Anyhow Rahman arranged for me to visit a large number of Malay schools, and together we made some changes. For instance, I found that children in the fishing villages on the east coast as part of their lessons in 'handwork' were taught how to make, of all things, waste-paper baskets. I arranged that in future they would be taught how to make fish traps and fishing nets, which I thought would be more useful.

I also made some trips with a nice old gentleman called Sheikh Ahmad. He was busily learning English, and keen to show off his knowledge of it. Unfortunately as so often happens when you learn a new language, he got his 'left' and 'right' mixed up. Consequently his instructions to me of how to get to a Malay school was often a few kilometres off the mark. As a result I saw some of Pahang's exotic wildlife. Thus one day, while walking along a remote beach far to the south of Pekan, looking for one of Sheikh Ahmad's schools I suddenly came across a rare large lizard that looked almost as big as a crocodile, and later a bit inland an even rarer animal, a peacock!

The final trip I made in the capacity as Senior Inspector of Schools, Pahang was to Ulu Tembeling. This is a remote jungle region, at the source of the Sungai Tembeling, which can only be reached, even today, by boat and through many rapids. The Sultan of Pahang had visited it, was charmed by its peaceful rural atmosphere, but surprised to find that it had no school. He had therefore written to the Department of Education drawing our attention to this state of affairs, and wondered whether something could be done about it.

So with such a brief, I was soon on my way to Ulu Tembeling to reconnoitre this remote paradise. I shared a boat with the Protector of Aborigines, Howard Biles, (now Datuk Biles), an Englishman who was also interested in visiting the area, and prayed that it was too remote even for the Communists. The journey to Kuala Tahan was without incident. At Kuala Tahan we were told that there were *seladang* (wild Malayan buffalo) to be found in the jungle, which had the nasty custom of hunting any humans who went in search of them, so we did not stop. Higher up the river we had to overcome several rapids, some short but some, for example Jeram Panjang, quite long. Consequently, we were occasionally required to get out of the boat, while the boatman pulled the boat up the river against the current. Awang bin Sulong, my Malay servant, who had come with me as my bodyguard, was in his element, being a Terengganu Malay. I discovered that we had fortunately chosen the right time of the year to make the trip and had avoided the flood season when it was too dangerous, and the dry season when the water was too low and the river too difficult to traverse.

When we eventually reached the promised land, we found a small, well-established Malay community, more or less completely cut off from the rest of Malaya, and with no hospitals, schools, electricity, telephones, motor cars and so on. Just groups of attap-covered Malay houses and a few bicycles which could be used along the narrow footpaths. There were two places suitable for a school, one at the junction of the Tembeling river with the Sungai Sat, that is Kuala Sat; the other at the junction of the Tembeling and Sungai Sepai, a place called Kampong Bantal. I decided on the latter, as it appeared to be in the most central point.

The *penghulu* was delighted with the news that at last Ulu Tembeling was going to have a school, but when I explained that it would take time, especially to get a teacher, he was disappointed for he realized it would be too late to be of much benefit to his own son Ramli. So I promised to admit him to my old school Clifford School immediately, and took him back with me in our boat to Kuala Lipis. So Ramli became the first Malay from Ulu Tembeling to learn English! I recently had a letter from him—forty years later!

On the way back, I called at Kuala Sat and met the *Ketua Kampong* or Village Headman. He too had a son he would like to send to school. He assured me he was under twelve years of age, the minimum age I felt we could admit him to school. So I asked if I could see this small boy, and in walked a tall, good-looking youth, smoking a long cheroot. I felt disinclined to call the *Ketua Kampong* a liar, so I admitted him too; indeed he later came to the Victoria Institution in Kuala Lumpur. As he had no visible means of support, I provided a sleeping accommodation and meals for him at the back of my house. Awang told me most Malays thought he was my son. He is now a flourishing settler on a Felda estate in Pahang. I had a letter from him too the other day. It started 'Dear Uncle', which I think should settle the matter of his ancestry!

I have therefore come to have a special regard for Ulu Tembeling, especially as I can claim to have brought what we call education to that region, for better or for worse! My daughter Rhiannon recently bravely faced the rapids to visit Ulu Tembeling again for me in 1989. She met an old man who said he remembered two *orang putih* (white men) visiting the place long ago!

At the end of October 1950, I returned to Kuala Lipis. I was quite happy not to have to travel any more on the dangerous Pahang roads. Here I found a letter awaiting me from the Director of Education, requesting me to open a Cambridge School Certificate Centre at Kuantan on the east coast for the forthcoming examination. This meant taking delivery of all the Cambridge papers and getting them to Kuantan, arranging for an examination hall, and of course travelling over 240 kilometres along the bandit-infested road to Kuantan. Fortunately Brigadier du Burg Morris, who I knew from my work as SEIO Pahang offered to fly me to Kuantan in one of his army planes. So one morning, I drove to the nearby Benta rubber estate, where there was a small airstrip, and an Auster Airplane awaiting me.

The army pilot asked me which route I wished to follow. Did I want to follow the road, or would I like to go direct? When I asked him what difference it made, he said: 'If we are forced down, I can land the plane on the road; but if we come down in the jungle we will probably both be killed.' I sensed he was testing me, so said, 'Let's go direct,' so we took the direct route. The plane seemed to be a very fragile machine, with the wires controlling the rudder and flaps fully exposed to any madman with a pair of pliers, I thought. And as this flying matchbox had only one engine, I listened attentively to it as it sometimes gurgled and spluttered a bit. But the flight was full of interest, as we flew over a huge area of what appeared to be unpopulated virgin forest, with occasional majestic limestone cliffs rising out of the sea of jungle.

While at Kuantan I stayed at the Rest House, and was looked after by my friend Abdul Rahman Talib. The Kuantan Rest House was a favourite meeting place, a kind of social centre where many people met to get the latest news. One day while I was having a drink, a British planter by the name of Bill Dobbie walked in, and sat at my table. He was a cheerful rugged character, and on that day looked unusually rugged for one side of his face was badly bruised and scratched. I asked him whether he had just fallen. 'No,' he said, 'just ambushed.' He was the manager of a rubber plantation in the Jabor Valley, just north of Kuantan. Apparently that afternoon as he was driving along the estate road on his way to Kuantan in his jeep, a Chinese Communist terrorist with a shotgun had suddenly stepped out from behind some bushes, and fired at him as he drove by. But the cartridge was a home-made one, and contained not the usual lead pellets but bits of tin, nails and tintacks. One side of his face only was lacerated and bloody, because the other side had been protected by the windscreen. He refused to go to hospital and said a whisky would do him more good!

After a week or so at Kuantan supervising their first ever Cambridge School Certificate Examination Centre, I flew back to Kuala Lipis and resumed my work at Clifford School, and as SEIO Pahang. As far as the school was concerned, my main preoccupation was with the development of new buildings including more hostel accommodation for the rural Malay pupils. The latter had become something of an obsession with me, perhaps because I was once myself a rural boy, but also because I had for so long felt that Malay rural pupils were seriously handicapped in their opportunity for English education because of this. I also felt that we badly needed new buildings for the proper conduct of the work of the school, especially for the teaching of Science. So in collaboration with the government architect, we drew up plans, which at the time were merely castles in the air. Then one day there was an unexpected windfall. The United Kingdom government presented Malaya with a large sum of money for schools. Some of this was made available for Pahang, and so our dreams became true, and in 1951 work started on the construction of our new buildings. The site for the new buildings was carefully chosen. It was well above the highest point reached by the great 1926 flood.

The 1926 flood created havoc in Pahang, and most of Kuala Lipis town was submerged by it. Datuk Mahmud told me that he was an Assistant District Officer at Kuala Lipis in 1926, and had helped the leading Chinese rice dealer carry hundreds of sacks of rice to high ground. What's more, he complained to me that after working all day at this back-breaking work, 'he didn't even give me a cup of coffee.' An oversight, no doubt, in the stress of the moment.

The annual flood time at Kuala Lipis was an annual threat. Indeed all government officers were instructed to buy a month's supply of food in October. The 1926 flood level was clearly marked on the Rest House for all to see and be warned. When it is realized that the Lipis and Jelai rivers drain a huge area to the north of Kuala Lipis, parts of which have a rainfall of over 500 millimetres in the single month of December alone, it is not surprising that Kuala Lipis periodically suffers such terrific floods. Moreover, as timber loggers were also busy cutting down the forest in much of the area, I anticipated that the future floods would get worse, not better. So imagine my dismay when forty years later, I visited Kuala Lipis and the headmaster proudly showed me a beautiful new hostel, built on the *padang* many metres below the 1926 flood level! I consoled myself with the thought that the Malays are good swimmers. Indeed during my tenure of office they had, when necessary, played water polo in place of rugby on the rugby pitch.

Apart from the above I was also actively engaged in running the school, and especially in developing its sporting activities. For we are told that 'all work and no play makes Jack a dull boy'. In this respect we were very fortunate, for in spite of being a small school, with pupils of both sexes and with both primary and secondary levels, we managed to hold our own against the big secondary schools such as the much-acclaimed Victoria Institution and the Malay College.

This was due to a small group of excellent sportsmen, who represented the school in most of our sporting activities. I cannot now recall all of them, but the following are some of them:

Abdul Majid bin Din	M. Ganeswaran
Ahmad Baharuddin	Jamaluddin bin Teh
Ahmad Baba	Lian Kwen Chih
Abdul Wahab bin	Mustapha bin Datuk
Majid	Mahmud
Abdul Razak bin	Osman Sham
Datuk Abu Samah	Sabaruddin bin Sulaiman
K. T. Anandaratnam	Abdul Razak bin Hitam
Chong Tek Yin	Norah Murray
Cyril Marsh	Yuhani binte Shafie

Many of the above also distinguished themselves later. Thus both Abdul Razak bin Datuk Abu Samah (rugby Captain) and Mustapha bin Datuk Mahmud went to Cambridge University where they studied law. The former also became a High Court Judge at Kuala Lumpur, while the latter joined the Foreign Service. Ahmad Baharuddin, who as a schoolboy was noted for his skylarking, settled down and now enforces the rule of law as OCPD at Kuala Lipis, while Abdul Majid bin Din also reached senior rank in the Malaysian Police. As for Sabaruddin bin Sulaiman an outstanding sportsman, and his brother Dahalan bin Sulaiman (now a Datuk) they both distinguished themselves in the Malaysian army, the former as a Lieutenant-Colonel and the latter as a Major-General.

Some also intermarried. Thus Osman Sham (now a Datuk) joined the Malayan Civil Service and married Yuhani Shafie, while Cyril Marsh became a Lieutenant-Colonel in the Malaysian Army and married Norah Murray.

Others who did well include one of our relay runners, the tall Yusof Din who became a Lieutenant-General in the Malaysian army; Abdul Razak bin Hitam one of our best rugby players who is now a Datuk and served on the Pahang State Executive Council; Ahmad Baba who ran like a hare on the wing in our Rugby XV, became a State Agriculture Officer, and then ran off to New Zealand; and the gentle and quietly spoken Jabar bin Abu Bakar who is now a Haji and the head of the Religious Department in Pahang—which is I suppose what one would expect, for all of them were gifted in their various ways, and followed their natural talents.

One who did exceptionally well was Radin Soenarno (now Tan Sri) and formerly Director-General of the Economic Planning Unit in the Prime Minister's Office. As he himself said to me recently, he was fortunate in that I admitted him into Anderson School 'under the punka' (that is unofficially), where he was able to start on his study of economics, and so gain entry into the University of Malaya in Singapore. But of course he well merited his selection, as his future career has shown. But there is no doubt that many of my Pahang pupils suffered from the lack of facilities and the lack of an adequate staff at Kuala Lipis, for entry into a university. Those who did best academically were those who managed to get their higher education outside the Cinderella state of Pahang.

Although the general scene in Pahang throughout 1950 and 1951 was one continued military activity, ambushes and killings, the work at the school continued more or less undisturbed. Thus the pupils attended school as usual and played the normal cycle of football, cricket, rugby and hockey. Special occasions such as Speech Days, Empire Days, and Sports Days were also held and attended by the local dignitaries such as the *Mentri Besar*, the State Secretary, the District Officer and so on.

Our devotion to sport also now began to pay off, so we ventured forth and took on some of the schools in the nearby states and more than held our own. Thus in 1950 we beat High School, Klang at cricket, and both Sultan Idris Training College and Tuanku Muhammad School at hockey. Even at rugby, we only lost by 3–0 against the Victoria Institution, while the match against my old school Tuanku Muhammad School, Kuala Pilah was epoch-making. We started badly and were 15–0 down at half-time, but then after I had given them a pep talk, Clifford School came to life and started to score so that when the whistle went, the score was 15–11. The excitement was such that the father of one of the TMS players Danny Sharman suffered a heart attack and had to be taken to hospital!

In 1951 we continued to improve, for our rugby team was well looked after by Che Halimi our Rugby Master and we now had the benefit of coaching from some of the officers of the local 48th Brigade HQ, while the cricket lovers were coached by the CPO Mr Caldwell. Consequently, next time round on our 1951 tour although we lost again at rugby to my old school TMS at Kuala Pilah, we beat big brother Victoria Institution at rugby 14–11, a sweet victory for us jungle *wallahs*.

Unfortunately I did not witness our famous victory over the Victoria Institution, for I suddenly contracted pneumonia and was admitted into the Kuala Lipis hospital for a couple of weeks, though the result, no doubt, helped me to recover.

There was one sporting event that was much treasured by our schoolboys. It was the almost weekly football match we had with Budu rubber estate. Budu was a French-owned estate, managed by a tall, extrovert young Englishman called Mathews. He was worried about the stress suffered by his mainly Tamil labour force, as a result of the ever present threat posed by the Communist terrorists in the nearby jungle. So he started the Budu football XI made up of the clerks and tappers on the estate as a diversion. The team was a huge success as a morale booster. The first time they played us, they lost 18–0, but they persisted and eventually improved to such an extent that after about a year they were losing by only a few goals, which was of course as good as a victory.

The latter part of 1951 saw a peak in Communist activity, culminating in the ambush and murder of Sir Henry Gurney, on his way up the winding road to our nearby Fraser's Hill on October 6, 1951. Although at the time we all thought that this attack was a result of information the Communists had received of his proposed visit, it was actually a fluke. The ambush which had been laid by thirty-eight guerrillas, some equipped with Bren guns, had actually been intended for a military convoy. But after a day or so of waiting, and as the convoy did not appear, they decided to attack the first suitable alternative to appear. By luck for the Communists, this happened to be an anonymous chauffeur-driven Rolls Royce and an escort, carrying Sir Henry Gurney.

This murder caused great despondency. For if the High Commissioner himself with an escort could be killed so easily, what chance was there for us ordinary people. The ambush marked a low watermark in our morale. All the people in Tras were removed!

My posting to Pahang came to a close soon after Gurney's ambush. And so after three dangerous years and sometimes some excitement, I went on six months' leave in early January 1952. After many farewell parties and a tearful leave of our faithful Malay servants Awang and Timah, we started on our last journey out of Pahang. At one point between Tras and Tranum I thought, indeed, it was going to be our last journey anywhere for high up on a hill above the road as we sped along it, I saw a man waving a bush to another unseen person. It looked very much as if we were passing through an ambush, but the signal presumably meant 'don't shoot'. It would have been rather unfair if we had indeed been shot up on our way out! When I reached Kuala Lumpur, the Director of Education, by now L. W. Whitfield, told me that a batch of Malayan teachers would be going home with me on the same ship, on the way to the Malayan Teachers' Training College at Liverpool, and would I keep an eye on them and report any problems.

Unfortunately as soon as I got on the ship—the P & O *Chusan*, I suffered a relapse from my pneumonia, and was admitted into the ship's maternity ward as there was no room elsewhere. A week or so later, I was joined by one of the Malayan women students who had measles. So I sent my Director a cable: 'All's well, but one woman student admitted ship's maternity ward—with measles.' When Whitfield got my cable, I am told he went to the Minister of Education, Datuk Thuraisingham, and mischievously read my cable out aloud to him, pausing slightly at 'maternity ward'. At this point the learned Datuk was horror-struck and exploded, 'I knew something like that would happen', which shows how unwise it is to jump to conclusions!

Chapter 9

PEACE AT LAST WITH THE COBRAS: IPOH

Bagai anjing dapat pasir

(Like a dog which finds itself on a sandbank or Pleased as Punch)

Malay Proverb

The *Chusan* reached London in mid-winter in a snowstorm! And as I was still suffering from pneumonia, I was taken off the ship on a stretcher and admitted into Guys Hospital where I recovered slowly under expert attention. As soon as I recovered, Lyn came and took me home to our house in London.

My six months' leave was soon over. Lyn stayed on a bit to be with her aged mother, and so I returned to Malaya on the *Wilhelm Ruys,* a sister ship to the *Oranje,* the Dutch ship on which I had travelled several years previously. But this time the trip was a quiet and relaxed one, with plenty of time for sunbathing and reading.

When I got to Singapore, a letter from the Director of Education awaited me, informing me that I was posted as Assistant Director of Education, Kuala Lumpur. Then, when I got to Kuala Lumpur, the Director L. W. Whitfield informed me that he wished me to have some administrative experience as an Assistant Director, before taking over the Victoria Institution, where the Science side had been developed to the disadvantage of the Arts. I was happy with these developments, and enjoyed working under Whitfield, who was a Director with a nice sense of humour for a change. He also withstood the problems and difficulties faced by a Director with equanimity, and when I once commented on this said, 'Well, Lewis, you must remember that in this job you are sometimes under a cloud, but you must also not forget that all clouds eventually pass away.'

As an Assistant Director I was called upon to do a variety of jobs. One of them was to write some speeches for General Templer. In the first speech I wrote for him, I started off, 'We Malayans ....' and so on. When the speech was delivered I noticed he had changed all the 'We Malayans' to 'You Malayans', which I suppose was an example of his integrity.

My 'In' tray was usually piled high with matters referred to me for my attention. So one day I was surprised to find that one of the files was marked 'Confidential. Confidential file of G.E.D. Lewis,' which the busy chief clerk had, I presume, inadvertently put in my 'In' tray. I wasted no time in reading it and discovering a few things about myself. I discovered that in 1940 Professor Margaret Read of the Institute of Education, University of London had asked if I could be seconded to the University for a couple of years to lecture on education. Cheeseman, the then Director, had replied I must first pass my Malay examinations before it could be considered. I also discovered that H. R. Holgate took a far more favourable view of my abilities than I had imagined, and had blocked my application for secondment as Professor of Education at the newly established Department of Education, University of Malaya, Singapore in 1949 because I was indispensable! So I was not unduly disheartened. It appeared that the general view was that I was a good mixer and got on well with my other officers, a good geographer, but potentially dangerous in the field of race psychology, so I should be encouraged to follow my interest in geography, which I suppose is why I wrote so many geography books.

One day the Director L. W. Whitfield instructed me to go to Kuala Pilah and attend the Speech Day at the Tuanku Muhammad School as his representative. I called on the Senior Inspector of Schools, Negri Sembilan at Seremban on the way. He was a Welsh-speaking fellow countryman of mine by the name of Noel Rees, better known as 'Tinggi Rees'. He was a fluent Malay speaker, much loved by the Malays for his friendly, charming character and ready wit. I asked him how he liked the job, and he said: 'I wish people wouldn't throw so many bricks at me,' and then pointed at a small pile on the grass outside his office, as if to prove the point. He also had a Siamese wife, generally known as 'mangosteen'.

When I got to Kuala Pilah I found that the District Officer was W. Foulsham. As I sat on the stage waiting for the proceedings to begin at the Tuanku Muhammad School Speech Day, I found myself sitting next to him. He told me that he had once been at the London School of Economics, and that like myself he had been the Rugby Captain. So feeling very much at ease with him, and seeing a most attractive lady in the audience, I said confidentially to him, 'She looks a nice bit of stuff, doesn't she?'

'Yes,' he replied. 'She's my wife!'

The Headmaster was a genial character by the name of Clark, Nobby Clark to his friends. I spent the night with him, and he told me how during the reign of H. R. Holgate as Director, he had been called upon to explain how it was that he had allowed one of his Indian schoolgirls to become pregnant. He told me that he had replied that he was in no way responsible, that he had investigated the affair and had come to the conclusion that the unfortunate incident was the result of an 'out of school activity'.

About six months after my arrival at Kuala Lumpur, I had to visit Singapore, as one of the Director's representatives at a meeting at the University of Malaya. I was accompanied by our Science expert, a live wire by the name of Arthur Godman, who was also the author of many textbooks. While I was there I took the opportunity of looking up some old friends such as Claude Lyle and John Ewart, my rugby-playing friends of pre-war days. Claude Lyle now held a senior appointment in the Department of Chinese Affairs, while John Ewart was working under Holtum the famous Botanist, at the Botanical Gardens, Singapore.

I also ran into Belle Tudor, the wife of my former War Tax colleague Dudley Tudor. She invited me to accompany her to the races. I had no difficulty in accepting for she was a most attractive and well-named young woman, and also offered to pick me up by car at the Raffles Hotel where I was staying. In due course she arrived to my surprise in a Rolls Royce lent to her, she explained, by a friend, one of the Shaw brothers who apparently had several such vehicles. As we arrived in great style at the Singapore Race Course, I recalled that my last visit there had been as a prisoner of war, and was then suddenly aware of the fact that the Race Course steward checking us in at the entrance was none other than one of my old POW friends. He was a bit surprised to see me installed with a beautiful girl in a Rolls Royce, and then had the great presence of mind to give us both a most perfect 45-degree Japanese bow, to remind me of the old days, I presume.

I had very little experience of betting on horses. But I fortunately soon found myself face to face with Datuk Thuraisingham, my Minister of Education, who was so far away from home, because he was an inveterate race goer. I sought his views. His advice was that a certain horse running at the three o'clock race was certain to win, so I backed it heavily, for I knew that if there was anything our Minister of Education was expert at, it was race horses. The horse led all the way more or less as he had predicted, and then when only about 27 kilometres from the finishing point and about to win, tripped and fell and could not get up. It came last. He was very apologetic and then gave me some more advice: 'Don't bet unless you are prepared to lose.' When I told him I had bet as a preparation for winning, he smiled and promised me more advice so that I could recoup my losses. So I returned to Kuala Lumpur a slightly poorer and wiser man, but a racing confidant of the Datuk.

Unfortunately the opportunity to make good my losses never occurred, for my posting to the Victoria Institution had to be postponed and Whitfield asked me if I would mind going to the Anderson School as Principal for the time being, in view of tragic events which had occurred there. G. P. Dartford the historian who was the Principal at the Anderson School had suffered a tragedy. His baby daughter had been accidentally drowned in her bath, and he wished to leave the scene of his misfortune.

So in April 1953 I moved to Ipoh to take up a new posting as Principal of the Anderson School.

The Anderson School was bigger, better-equipped and much better-staffed than my old school in Pahang. It, too, had primary as well as secondary sections. But it had a total enrolment of over 1500 pupils, a teaching staff of 56, of whom ten were university graduates and seven were Raffles graduates. The staff were a harmonious hard-working team, and many of them were exceptionally able teachers. The following merit some special mention:

Ung Kek Cheow, a Raffles Graduate and the senior mathematics teacher who was well known for his ability and success as a teacher of mathematics and as a rugby enthusiast. His success as a teacher of mathematics was due not only to his innate teaching ability but also to some unique forms of chastisement, which caused no bodily harm, but was effective in persuading his pupils to concentrate on their studies. His interest in rugby was based on practical experience, for he had played as a scrum-half for Perak in the 1930s, but it has to be admitted that his knowledge of rugby was seriously rivalled by that of his wife, who was well known for her comprehensive understanding of the game.

J. R. P. D. de Turville, BA (Cantab), the Senior English master, an eccentric, much loved by the boys for his eccentricity and kindness, was another. In the right job such as directing his own Malay version of Emlyn Williams' play 'Night Must Fall' he was brilliant, but as the master in charge of the Malay Hostel accounts, a disaster. It was also suggested that his name had originally been Joe Bloggs, or something similar, and that he had changed it to his present more attractive one; if that is true, who can blame him?

P. K. Sen Gupta, was a very lovable, highly intelligent gentleman from the Indian sub-continent, who had been denied the opportunity of a university education because there was none available in Malaya in his time. He was also an Anglophile with an excellent knowledge of English literature and an excellent command of the English language. Once on a visit to England he suddenly surprised me by saying, 'You know there are far too many black people in England.'

The Anderson School had a strong international team of science teachers led by a fellow Welshman and rugby enthusiast John Park, B. Sc. (Wales), and supported by Tsang Ah Liat, a Raffles graduate, better known in Ipoh circles as the most eligible bachelor than as a scientist; M. B. Menon, BA (Madras) a softly spoken gentleman from southern India;

D. S. Malla, B. Sc. (Bombay) who hailed from Nepal, and last but not least the gregarious Tiny Norris, BA (Canada) who came from Canada and who helped out with the teaching of science. So our senior scientists consisted of a Welshman, a Chinese, a Tamil, a Gurkha, and a Canadian—a veritable League of Nations.

On the Arts side, apart from the imperturbable R. W. Swales, BA (London), the rugby enthusiast, N. J. Ryan, BA (Bristol) and the Raffles Graduate and modest Neoh Thean Chye who all taught history; there was a supporting cast of excellent teachers such as the two cricket-loving Indians, S. Sabaratnam and C. Krishnan; the smiling trigger-happy and Raffles Graduate Yap Hong Guan who ran the Cadet Corps; the highly efficient hard-working and bearded Mangal Singh who supervised the Middle School; the extrovert Nadarajah who was the jack of all trades; the courteous and respectful Mohd. Yusof who taught Malay; my old schoolboy from the Penang Free School Chin Ah Ngan who taught Commercial subjects, and his assistant, the lively Miss Tang; the enthusiastic and talkative teacher of geography and economics S. Selvamany, BA (Singapore); and the horse-racing enthusiast and Raffles Graduate Ooi Beng Hoi.

Finally, there was a primary section of the school, a busy beehive efficiently administered by our English lady expert on such matters Miss Turley, and her staff of lady teachers. And, of course, I cannot possibly forget our diligent school clerk P. Masalimany and his assistant, the charming young Malay girl Izan.

As my posting to the Anderson School stretched into a two-year stay, there were some additions and amendments. Thus we acquired what the Chinese might describe as a 'red-headed devil' by the name of J. A. McCumskey, BA (Cantab), an eccentric like de Turville, but a red-headed eccentric of Polish extraction rather than an English one. He had previously acquired some notoriety at Kuala Pilah for flying the Union Jack on Empire Day after *Merdeka*, but all was forgiven when he introduced for the first time Malay sports such as *sepak raga* and kite flying on Sports Day and flew the Federation flag.

Others who joined the staff in 1954 and 1955 were Mrs Betty Brett, BA (Dublin), the wife of the Chief Police

Officer, Perak, and the artistic Mrs Hutton Williams, wife of the SEIO Perak, who taught Art. There must have been many others, but they were all part of a most marvellous and harmonious team that made the Anderson School second to none in both academic attainment and in the sporting field.

I recall one year, I think it was 1954, when the Anderson School produced six Malay boys with Grade 1 School Certificates, when at the same time the Malay College was not able to produce one. Some of our Malay boys were much amused that the Eton of Malaya could do no better. Moreover, in 1954 we proceeded to enter sixteen students for the full Cambridge Higher School Certificate for the first time in the history of the school, of whom ten passed. They were: Abdul Rahim bin Jalaluddin; Ahmad Sabki; Bachan Singh s/o Melagar Singh; Chan Soo Har; Cheah Bee Lee; Chin Tuck Chuen; Jaffar bin Mohd. Wazir; Lai Wah Seng; Mohd. Khair bin Mohd. Said and Khair Yang Amri bin Kamaruddin. They were the pick of the bunch, and they all went to universities. Indeed in 1955 we sent over twenty-eight students to the University of Malaya. One of them was Radin Soenarno, one of my old students from Pahang, who later had a most successful career in the Malayan Civil Service, as mentioned earlier in this book.

There were also others who achieved even greater distinction by winning various scholarships for study overseas. Thus the following went to the United Kingdom in 1954: Ng Siew Kee the School Captain and the Captain of rugby and soccer, who studied Agriculture at Durham University and Rothamstead where he obtained a doctorate; Raja Abdul Aziz Addruse who studied law at Lincoln's Inn, London; Mohd. Annuar bin Aziz who studied Forestry; Talha bin Hashim who studied Engineering and Shahrum bin Yub who did Anthropology. Others included Hamzah bin Mahmood who did Architecture and Sivaloganathan also a School Captain who did Medicine at Singapore. And, of course, there were many I have overlooked.

These successes were due not only to the intelligence and industry on the part of the boys themselves, but to the diligence and teaching ability of the school staff and to our facilities consisting of a modern science block and to a new library which I had established soon after my arrival. In retrospect I have often wondered how many other potential geniuses have rotted away in remote kampongs, using their talent for playing truant instead of putting their ability to better use.

Some twenty-five years later, in 1990 to be precise, wondering what these bright boys had achieved in later life I made inquiries, and as expected find that most of them have done exceptionally well. Thus Dr Ng Siew Kee is a consultant and a world authority on the oil palm; Raja Abdul Aziz Addruse is a lawyer and past Chairman of the Malaysian Bar Council; Talha bin Hashim (now a Datuk) and Director of the Public Works Department; Shahrum bin Yub (now a Datuk), and Director-General of the famous Muzium Negara at Kuala Lumpur; Sivaloganathan (now a doctor) and a plastic surgeon; Ahmad Sabki (now a Datuk) and Chief Executive of the Malaysian Rubber Licensing Board; Cheah Bee Lee, manager of the Chartered Bank; Lai Wah Seng until recently a senior executive of Shell Co.; while Khair Yang Amri bin Kamaruddin is Deputy Secretary-General of the Malayan Civil Service. And there were several others such as Salehuddin bin Mohamed (now Tan Sri) who became Chief Secretary to the Government, Mohd. Khalil bin Hussein (now Datuk Seri) who became Secretary-General to the Ministry of Agriculture, and so on, not forgetting the elusive Zainal Abidin bin Mokhtar (now a Datuk) who became the Deputy High Commissioner in London where I met him and where we had dinner together many times; Lourdesamy (now a Ph. D.) who heads the Petaling Jaya Community College and Syed Mohamed (Tarzan of school days) who is now a medical practitioner somewhere in Cairo. And, of course, there must be many others.

It is this kind of success which is so gratifying to those of us concerned with education, especially when such success is not tainted with bribery and corruption.

Corruption of course is like cancer. Once it starts it is almost impossible to stop, which is why the rules for government officers in my time were so strict. The rule was that a government officer was not permitted to accept any unsolicited gift no matter how small; but if the receiving of such a gift was unavoidable, then the officer was obliged to pay into the Treasury the value of the gift.

When I was at Kuala Lipis I once received such an unsolicited gift. A Chinese, who was completely unknown to me, thrust a live turkey into my lap while I was in my car and ran away. He gave no name but I presumed he would one day reveal himself as the generous donour of the gift and want a generous favour. So I rang the sub-Treasurer at the Kuala Lipis Treasury, who was a Tamil gentleman and had the following conversation with him:

Me:	Dr Lewis here. I have an unsolicited gift which I wish to hand into the Treasury. When would it be convenient for me to see you?
Sub-Treasurer Mr Ramasamy: (Not his real name)	Any time in office hours will do, sir.
Me:	Can you manage a live turkey, Mr Ramasamy?
Sub-Treasurer:	Oh goodness gracious me, please do not be bringing live turkeys to the Treasury, sir.
Me:	So what shall I do?
Sub-Treasurer:	Please take it to Cheam See Loo (the local grocery), sir. Ask them to value it, and pay the money into the Treasury. Thank you, sir.

So that is what I did and Mr Ramasamy gave me an official receipt for it. No doubt the news of the incident was the gossip of the town for a day or two, and that an attempt at minor corruption had been thwarted!

Although there must have been some corruption in my time, we were proud of the fact that the government service was, generally speaking, free of it. That is why I was so delighted, when many years later, after *Merdeka*, on a visit to Perak, I went to a police station in Bagan Serai to make a telephone call, gave the elderly *mata mata* (policeman) fifty cents for the call and he gave me a receipt for it. I complimented him on his honesty and he smiled and said, '*Saya ikut regulations, Tuan*,' (I am following the rules, sir). God bless him.

The Anderson School had extensive and attractive grounds, which provided some security problems. So when the aged Sikh *jaga* (or watchman) retired, I decided that the new watchman should be an active rather than a passive one. I advertised for a new watchman and got eight applicants, mainly Sikhs. I then took them out on to the rugby pitch, and lined them up on the goal-line, and informed them that the first one to reach me at the other end of the pitch when I blew a whistle would get the job. As most of the contestants were over 70, it proved a walkover for one young Sikh, who of course got the job. He proved a great success and chased out a number of intruders. In fact he was much feared by trespassers, because he always carried a hockey stick!

My sojourn at Ipoh was a holiday as compared with my stay at Kuala Lipis. Apart from examining some teachers at practical teaching in rural schools, with a nice Yorkshire girl called Sylvia Dickinson, which involved some travelling, I had little occasion to go along isolated country roads. In any case the security forces were now beginning to get the better of the Communists, for the tide began to turn when General Templer arrived on the scene and took charge of things. In fact my fears at Ipoh arose not so much from Communist terrorists as from a most unlikely source—cobras. My house was located in the school grounds and near a slightly swampy part of the Kinta river. As a result there were cobras in my garden. As a bite from a cobra can have serious consequences, I had to take care especially when walking through long grass, and endeavoured to get the school gardeners to keep all grass well cut.

One of my predecessors at the Anderson School, Sandy Hunter had a narrow escape. He returned home rather late one night from the Ipoh Club, having wined and dined rather well, and saw what he thought was his black cat sitting in the semi-darkness on the stone steps leading up to his front door awaiting to greet him. So he bent down to stroke its head, but instead of being greeted with a friendly 'mi-yao' he suddenly heard a loud hissing noise rather like a puncture in his tyre. It took him a few seconds to realize that his 'cat' was a cobra coiled up on his stone steps enjoying the cool air.

I also had one or two exciting experiences myself. One day, Awang my faithful Malay servant who had followed me from Pahang, dashed into the bungalow and announced excitedly that there was a cobra in the garden and could he borrow my shotgun. After a few minutes' search he found the cobra again and shot it in the middle, cutting it in half. When I saw it, I was amazed at its size or rather its thickness. Although it was only about 1.8 metres long, it was as thick as a man's leg in the middle.

Then on another occasion the *kebun* (or gardener) rushed in to say that he had just seen a cobra go into my garage, where I kept a number of empty tea chests and empty crates. Awang organized a search with the help of the school gardeners, and examined each crate carefully, but could find nothing. So we decided that the cobra had escaped. Lyn then got Timah to serve orange drinks to all those who had taken part in the search. While we all relaxed, with Awang sitting on one of the tea chests, I suddenly saw the head of the cobra emerge slowly from the tea chest upon which Awang was sitting, and behind his back! When I gave Awang the unwelcome news, he jumped up so quickly that the cobra was tipped out of its hiding place, resulting in absolute bedlam as everybody scattered. But the cobra was surrounded and the gardeners quickly recovered and killed it.

After these unpleasant experiences, and finding yet another cobra having a siesta under our house, I made inquiries about cobras and was told by an old Malay that cobras liked clumps of bamboo, and that if I had one in my garden to get rid of it. So as I had such a beautiful clump, I had it removed and never saw another cobra!

I have already mentioned that the academic achievements of the Anderson School were second to none. We also had an excellent record on the sporting field with the sole exception that I don't think we ever beat King Edward VII School at rugby during my reign. Of course my brother T. P. M. (or Tiny) Lewis was very pleased to hear that, because he had been a history teacher at King Edward in the early 1930's, in the days before the Iskander bridge had been built over the Perak river at Kuala Kangsar, and had expanded the playing of rugby at King Edward to five teams—one per house!

We had many outstanding sportsmen, and many of them also did well academically. At athletics, our stars were W. Ranatunga, Ahmad Sabki, Osman Hogan Shaidali, Yau Seng Yoon, and Sharkawi bin Bahauddin; at football,

Sulaiman Hashim, Sabaruddin, Lai Wah Seng, Chai Hon Yoong, Ranatunga, Hassan and Ahmad Sabki; at cricket, S. Sundralingam, Darshan Singh, Sivaloganathan, Oi Yak Han, S. Sachithanandran, Patrick Ayathurai, Chin Chin Tet, and Jagit Singh; at hockey, Ng Hock Onn, Hamzah Ishak, Osman Hogan Shaidali, Ahmad Sabki, Darshan Singh, Balwant Singh, Sulaiman, Yang Amri and Mohd. Annuar; and at badminton, Cheak Fook Sen. As for rugby, there were many cooks stirring the broth, and we had an excellent team, the stars being Lai Wah Seng, Ng Siew Kee, Darshan Singh, Yau Seng Yoon, Hassan bin Ahmad, Osman Hogan Shaisali, Lourdesamy, Syed Muntaz, Sharkawi, Fadzil and others.

Of course many of my friends and acquaintances thought I was obsessed with rugby. But although I have the average Welshman's love of the game, I had special reasons for looking upon rugby as a game eminently suitable for a school; it provided violent exercise for the maximum number of boys. Whereas cricket and football teams consist of only eleven players, a rugby team has fifteen players.

We had six houses at the Anderson School, so I introduced rugby at four levels, thus creating twenty-four rugby teams, which meant that 360 boys (24 x 15) played rugby. But as we had over 2000 pupils one can see the difficulty of providing adequate recreation for such a huge school. I suppose the only answer would have been to have a cross-country run once a week.

Anyhow it explains why so many schools have problems with the behaviour of their pupils. According to Dr Desmond Morris the well-known biologist, because of our animal origins, man is naturally aggressive. So it is natural for young healthy boys to be aggressive. Moreover, if they are not provided with a suitable outlet for their aggression they will find less desirable ways themselves. I found rugby an excellent outlet for healthy pupils to let off steam, and especially the second row of the scrum for the more aggressive ones!

In 1953 the Anderson School did not have space for a quarter mile running track, so we extended the playing field in front of the school by filling up and levelling some rough ground adjacent to it. This operation involved transporting many tonnes of sand, which we removed without permission from some old tin-mining land just outside Ipoh. As we could not afford to hire a contractor to do the job, we cajoled and bullied all manner of people to bring in sacks of sand in the boots of their cars; but I thought that perhaps we were going a bit too far when I discovered that the local ambulance had been pressed into the work! Anyhow in due course the low land was filled, but only just in time, for a week before we completed the work, I got a letter from some government department instructing me to stop this removal of sand from state land, and threatening me with prosecution for the illegal removal of government property!

Another operation which took up a lot of my time was the setting up of a proper library suitable for post School Certificate work. I arranged for a large room to be set aside for this and semi-air conditioned it—the first school library in Malaya to be air conditioned. We then collected thousands of dollars for the purchase of books, and had the library officially declared open by the *Mentri Besar*, Perak who was himself an Old Boy of the school. I then put the book-loving Sen Gupta in charge of the library, for he was not only a lover of books, but had himself done a little writing. For I discovered that during the Japanese occupation he had endeavoured to earn an honest penny by writing romantic novels, but of course he did not now wish to be reminded of this activity. Nevertheless, some mis-chievious schoolboy had discovered this, and had infiltrated several copies of the said works into the school library and of course without the permission of the librarian!

Some time in mid-1954 we had a fleeting visit from General Templer—the Tiger of Malaya. This was his farewell visit to Perak on his return to England, after having successfully turned the tide against the Communist insur-rection by resolute military action and a sympathetic under-standing of the problem. Of course we were all very much on our toes about his visit, for he was a man of action and did not suffer fools gladly. It had been agreed that the whole school, that is all our 2000 boys and girls, should welcome him by lining the road which ran through the school grounds, and along which it was planned he would drive on his way from the Ipoh railway station to the airport, but the precise time of his arrival, perhaps for reasons of security, was not known.

I decided that notwithstanding the fact that he expected all such arrangements to work like clockwork, it would be unfair to keep my 2000 pupils standing out in the hot tropical midday sun for perhaps half an hour or more. I knew from previous dress rehearsals for fire alarms and so on, that I could get everybody out on parade within two minutes, so set up three warnings points on his route to monitor his progress: one at the railway station, the second at the half way point and the third at the hospital just outside the school gates. I waited for ages for the first warning telephone call but none came. Then after much delay the telephone rang to say, 'General Templer has just passed the Hospital, sir.' He was literally within 180 metres of the school, my monitoring system had broken down, and my 2000 were still at their desks in their classrooms. I pressed the alarm bells immediately, the well-trained Anderson School pupils were out in their correct positions within two minutes, and as I reached the porch of the school, the General and his guard of Royal Hussars armoured cars drove into our grounds. He stopped and walked briskly to meet me and said apologetically, 'I hope I haven't kept your boys out in the hot sun too long.' I was lost for words.

Then when he saw so many schoolboys: 'How the hell do you keep so many under control?'

And then I found my tongue and said, 'Templer methods, sir.' He looked surprised, then obviously liked the idea, smiled and gave the school a half holiday for such a fresh and smart turnout.

As I was not directly involved any more in the prosecution of the war against the Communists, I had more time for textbook writing, in particular a series that I was now engaged upon for use in primary schools, called the *Junior Malayan Geographies*. The series was planned to consist of four books so as to cover the requirements of Standards 3 – 6. I had already managed to write a book for Standard 3 while I was at Kuala Lipis. For Standard 4, the syllabus called for the study of the geography of Malaya in simple terms, through the study of the occupations of a selection of typical Malayans. Most of those I described were real people though I changed some of their names, but I have no doubt that some of them must have been surprised when their children brought home textbooks featuring themselves under new names. Some of them became well-known characters especially Awang the Fisherman at Beserah, Abdullah the Padi Farmer at Kuala Pilah, Ah Kow and Ah Mooi the Tin Miners from Taiping and so on.

I called the book the *Peoples of Malaya*, and it was highly successful in its English and Malay versions, for over the years more than half a million copies were sold. Technically, I think it was the best book I ever wrote, for apart from being a study of the chief occupations of people in Malaya. (later Malaysia), the book also introduced pupils to the main routes linking up the chief towns of Malaya, and to some simple map-reading as well.

I first of all tried the book out at the Anderson School Primary Department in cyclostyled form, and as a result made many changes to the original draft. This was because I discovered that pupils at this level cannot read continuous text for longer than ten or fifteen minutes, so I broke the text up into suitable instalments. I also noticed that there is a very great range of ability between the brightest and the most backward pupil in the average class, so devised exercises that could be attempted by the whole range of ability. Finally, I found out that one of the greatest problems faced by a young teacher facing forty or so exuberant youngsters is discipline. I realized that the best way of coping with this difficulty is to give them something to do. So the book had a large number of exercises to keep the brats busy. In any case, it became clear after a while, that pupils learn best by doing things, and so I provided a lot for them to do. Indeed at a later stage I introduced a workbook which consisted of more things to do. Anyone who intends to write textbooks, whether for the young or for the older student, would do well to take notice of the above observations.

I normally visited the primary department once a week to try out the cyclostyled chapters of my proposed book. It was an experience I thoroughly enjoyed. There is nothing more rewarding than to teach a class of Chinese, Malay and Indian ten-year-olds, with their expectant and attentive faces. When you have something interesting to say they are like sponges soaking it all up, but when you have nothing worthwhile to say, the class soon deteriorates into chaos, like the buzzing of bees in a hive.

I was also amazed how quickly such children learnt to speak and even to write English, as the following essay by a eight-year-old Chinese boy after only a few weeks at school shows:

My house god one cat. My mother take me go to town and I see a dog cross the road the dog bark the boy.

Lee Hoon Kuan

But sometimes there were surprises in store for one, as when I once decided to try my hand at teaching English to a mixed class of Malay, Chinese and Indian eight-year-olds at the Clifford School, Pahang, and my teaching was suddenly interrupted by a charming little Chinese girl who suddenly put her hand up as if in a hurry. So when I said, 'What is it you want, Lucy?' (not her real name), she replied, 'Please, sir, I want to shit, sir.'

One day on the Sultan of Perak's birthday, Lyn and I were invited to tea at the Sultan's Palace at Kuala Kangsar. There were quite a number there in their best suits and feeling very hot. I found myself sitting opposite Drake Brockman of the Malayan Civil Service, and formerly District Officer, Kuantan where he had been generally known by the Malays as *Tuan Mandor*, because of the personal attention he gave to the matter of clean drains and town hygiene at Kuantan, a matter normally delegated to the Tamil Mandor in charge of such matters.

At the end of 1954, Lyn discovered she was pregnant, but as she had a slight complication with her blood (Rhesus-negative) the doctor suggested it would be advisable for her to have the baby at Queen Charlotte's Hospital in London if possible. So I saw her off at Penang together with my daughter Megan, where she got on the P & O *Chusan* (her favourite ship) once more, and returned to London while I soldiered on till the end of the term when I was due to go on leave.

As I now found that I would be going home alone, I decided to take advantage of the situation and travel back to the United Kingdom via Hong Kong, Japan and the USA and so get some firsthand information for the remaining two books of my Junior Series, which I now decided to call *Our*

Neighbours Near and Far, that is the people of Indonesia, Thailand, the Philippines, China, Australia and so on; and the *Peoples of Far Away Lands*, that is the people of North America, South America, Europe and Africa. My objective was to describe some of the people and their occupations in these lands from personal experience as far as possible, as I had been able to do with *Peoples of Malaya*. Such an ambition was expensive, and it took me to places I would never otherwise have visited, and having bizarre experiences such as nearly falling off a cliff into Lake Baikal and losing my hat in that remote Siberian lake.

I travelled to Hong Kong by boat and some of my fellow passengers were obviously Chinese Communists retreating from Malaya to a more secure base in the land of their fathers. At Hong Kong I had booked a passage on a Norwegian cargo boat, as there were no passenger ships available, and spent a few days in Japan where I found my knowledge of *Nippon-Go* very useful. I then had a long trip across the Pacific to San Francisco. While crossing the Pacific, I had plenty of time to ponder how best to write my remaining Junior geography books, and how to select the peoples to be described. I eventually came to a conclusion. I would select the people to be described not randomly but from carefully selected environments that were typical of the different climatic regions of the world. Thus I would describe a padi farmer from Central Thailand where the climate was Tropical Monsoon, a wheat grower on the Canadian Prairies where the climate was of the Temperate Grassland type and so on. So when I arrived in California I made a study of the fruit farmers of sunny California, visited a famous raisin factory at Fresno, and fell in love with California so much that I had some difficulty in tearing myself away from such an agreeable Mediterranean type of climate.

Eventually after a long train journey across the USA and a rough crossing of the Atlantic, I reached London once more, where I was greeted by Lyn and another daughter, Rhiannon. Rhiannon eventually grew up to be an expert on family law, and a partner in a firm of solicitors in Lincoln's Inn, London.

Chapter 10

MURDER, SECRET SOCIETIES, AND *MERDEKA:* KUALA LUMPUR

Democracy consists of choosing your dictators.

Anonymous British humorist

I returned to Malaya after six months' leave in the United Kingdom, and as had been promised took up my appointment as Headmaster of the Victoria Institution, Kuala Lumpur on January 9, 1956. The Victoria Institution was generally considered to be the premier school in the country, and the post as its Headmaster a much sought after appointment. The school has an interesting history; in fact its foundation might almost be described as an accident of history.

The Golden Jubilee of the reign of Queen Victoria which took place in 1887 was celebrated in great style in the growing mainly Chinese tin-mining town of Kuala Lumpur. A fund was formed, mainly with money contributed by the citizens of Kuala Lumpur for the purpose of building a permanent memorial to Queen Victoria, but when this had been done, and a statue erected in a corner of the *padang*, there was still a lot of money left over. So the community leaders who had helped raise the Jubilee Fund, *Towkay* Loke Yew, *Towkay* Yap Kwan Seng and Mr Thamboosamy Pillai met the British Resident Mr W. H. Treacher, and between them they decided to utilize the funds left over to establish an educational institution in Kuala Lumpur on the lines of Raffles Institution in Singapore.

The government agreed to provide financial support, the foundation stone was laid by Mrs Treacher on August 14,

1893, and His Excellency the High Commissioner (Sir Cecil Clementi) and His Highness the Sultan of Selangor (Sir Abdul Samad) consented to become patrons of the school. His Highness also promised a donation of $1000 for the school fund. The site for the new school and the headmaster's quarters was opposite the High Street police station, quite near to the Klang river, and the total cost about $11,500!

The school opened in July 1894, the medium of instruction was English, and the first Headmaster Mr Bennett Eyre Shaw, MA (Oxon). He was headmaster for 28 years, a record! The school expanded rapidly under his able guidance. In 1923 it moved to its present majestic buildings on Petaling Hill; while in 1929 the primary classes were transferred to a newly built school in Batu Road (Jalan Tuanku Abdul Rahman), the Batu Road School.

The Victoria Institution had many headmasters, but until my arrival none of them had stayed longer than three years and some of them much less than that, only a few months. Bennett Eyre Shaw was the notable exception. As already mentioned he was headmaster for 28 years and so it is not surprising that the road past the school was for many years named after him, and was known as Shaw Road.

During the long reign of Shaw as headmaster, and while he was on leave in 1911, there was a most unfortunate incident. The wife of the acting Headmaster, Mr W. Proudlock, was had up for murder; indeed in June 1911, Mrs Ethel Proudlock was found guilty of murder and sentenced to death. The memory of this skeleton in the V.I. cupboard has since been almost totally lost in the mist of time. The details* of the tragedy were, however, published in the current issues of the *Straits Times* and *Malay Mail*, while the unfortunate event was of course a sensation and universal gossip throughout the length and breadth of the Malay Peninsula. The *Malay Mail* spoke of a 'tragedy which created a profound sensation in Kuala Lumpur' and reported that on April 23, 1911, Mrs Ethel Proudlock, wife of the acting Headmaster of

---

*There now seems no point in suppressing the details for they have been widely published. The version I give is a summary of the incident as relatively recently published in the London newspaper, *The Sunday Observer, Observer Magazine*, February 22, 1976.

the Victoria Institution, shot on the verandah of her home a Mr William Crozier Steward, the manager of a local tin mine. According to Mrs Proudlock while her husband was having dinner at the house of another teacher, a Mr Ambler, she was visited by an acquaintance, Mr William Crozier Steward. Steward arrived by rickshaw soon after she had dined alone dressed in a tea gown, and had instructed the rickshaw puller to wait about twenty paces from the verandah. Mrs Proudlock and Mr Steward talked about the weather and the nearby flooded river Klang; she got up to get a book from her bedroom, and then Mr Steward followed her, put out the light and tried to rape her. She stretched out her hand to switch on the light, but instead her hand came into contact with a revolver which she kept for her protection, and then she added, 'I think I must have fired twice'. But Steward was actually shot six times.

There is, however, reason to believe that Steward was Mrs Proudlock's lover, or one of her lovers, and that the meeting that evening was not a casual social call but a pre-arranged meeting. So why did a quiet woman shoot her lover six times? Of course nobody will ever know, but it has been suggested that it was not a case of attempted rape but a case of jealousy, and that Mrs Proudlock may have discovered that Steward also kept a Chinese mistress back in the mine. If that was so, it would account for the frenzied attack on Steward.

In any case, the poor Mrs Proudlock was charged with murder and sentenced on June 14, 1911, to death by hanging by Mr Justice Sercombe Smith in the High Court, Kuala Lumpur. Public opinion was of course sympathetic to Mrs Proudlock, and petitions organized for her amnesty sent to the Secretary of State for the Colonies, and to Queen Mary in London, and to the Sultan of Selangor. But the critical petition was the one organized on June 29 to the Sultan of Selangor and signed not only by the staff and pupils of the V.I. but by 'several hundreds of the leading Chinese gentlemen of Kuala Lumpur', praying for a free pardon. As a result, shortly afterwards the following announcement was made: 'His Highness, the Sultan of Selangor has been pleased to grant Mrs Proudlock a free pardon.' And so she sailed for England soon afterwards a free woman.

But that is not the end of this intriguing, but sad story. For in 1956 while I was Headmaster of the Victoria Institution, and I first learnt of the tragedy from an elderly but eminent lawyer in Kuala Lumpur, who had himself been a pupil at the V.I. at the time of the murder, he informed me that in his opinion Mr Steward was not shot by Mrs Proudlock, but by a jealous rival, which would account for so many shots being fired. Mrs Proudlock had then attempted to protect the unknown rival (possibly her favourite lover) by making up the story of the attempted rape and her alleged part in the shooting. The evidence to support this theory according to my legal friend was a Sikh *jaga* (or watchman) who, it was reported, saw a European swim across the Klang river, near the scene of the incident, a most unusual thing for a European to do with his clothes on, especially as on that day in 1911, the Klang river at Kuala Lumpur was not only full of flood water but full of crocodiles! Was the mystery swimmer across the crocodile-infested Klang river, the unknown rival? We shall never know.

One final consequence of this incident, which may be of interest to those who have read some of Somerset Maughan's short stories is that it is generally believed that this tragedy which took place in 1911 at the V.I. Headmaster's house was the inspiration for his story 'The Letter'. Somerset Maugham visited Malaya and the Far East in 1922–25 and based many of his short stories on real events and skeletons in people's cupboards.

There have been many other noteworthy (but not so tragic) events in the history of the V.I. and some Old Boys still alive who can bear witness to them. Thus Mr Lee Kuan Yew (not the Prime Minister of Singapore) a member of the V.I. Board of Governors, told me of his school days when the V.I. was still located in the High Street, and how the Headmaster Major Richard Sidney would review the school Cadet Corps on horseback, and also of the 1926 flood when the Headmaster Mr G. C. Davies and his family had to be rescued from the swirling waters of the Klang river by means of a sampan, much to the delight of the schoolboys. He also remembered the great move of the V.I. from its premises in High Street to its present elevated location, in 1929, and how the boys carried their chairs with them as they marched along High Street and Birch Road* to their new buildings.

I also had pleasure in meeting that fine old gentleman R. Thambipillay. He was born in 1879, joined the V.I. as a pupil in 1895 and became a teacher at the V.I. in 1898. When I showed him round the school in 1957, he was delighted with the experience, and when he saw a boy at the back of a class sprawled all over it like a jelly fish, said to him, 'Sit up properly, boy, this is not the MBS,'; the MBS of course being our nearby Methodist Boys School who claimed to be our rivals.

The Japanese invasion and the occupation of Malaya had a devastating effect on the school, and its books and equipment were all destroyed. Among those who took a leading part in the rehabilitation of the school was its post-war Headmaster between 1946 and 1949, F. Daniel, the author of the well-known science course *General Science for Malaysians*. His love of the V.I. amounted almost to an obsession, for he had spent most of his life in Malaya as its Senior Science Master. During his headmastership he lived on the job. He converted one of the classrooms into a flat, the classroom was in the science wing, of course!

Another who had a great love for the V.I. was E. M. F. Payne. He followed Daniel as Headmaster for the period 1949–52, but had wider interests, for Payne was not only a scientist but a Malay scholar as well and the author of *Basic Syntactic Structures in Standard Malay* (Ph. D. Thesis). And of course as I soon discovered to my cost, those who served at the V.I. soon fell under its spell, and so I too soon became very attached to it. Loyalty to the school was catching.

---

*Now renamed *Jalan Maharaja Lela* by someone with a sense of humour as well as a sense of history. In case the reader does not know his history of Malaya, perhaps I should explain that Birch was the first British Resident of Perak and that he was murdered in 1875 by Maharaja Lela a Malay chief. Birch was apparently a well meaning but tactless hot-tempered man, with a short fuse, who wanted to introduce British ideas of good government such as the abolition of some feudal customs then prevalent in Perak, in a hurry. He could not speak Malay and did not realize that Malays like to do things politely and slowly, or perhaps not at all, and so an explosion was inevitable. To perpetuate his name as a street name was a bit insensitive and tactless.

I played a small part in the rehabilitation of the school. I managed to recover the original brass plate, which covered the foundation stone of the V.I. and had it cleaned and put back. One day an elderly Chinese gentleman came to my office and said that there was a brass plate covered in dirt amongst some junk in his backyard which had the words 'Victoria Institution' on it. I went off immediately in my car to his place, and as soon as I saw it realized its value. I gave him twice its scrap value for it as a reward. He was very happy and the V.I. recovered a bit of its history.

I also bought one of the last rickshaws in Kuala Lumpur. I was told that a certain Chinese in Petaling Street (now Jalan Petaling) was using one of the few rickshaws left in Kuala Lumpur for carrying charcoal. I got Richard Pavee our school secretary to buy it from him for $100 out of school funds, and had it placed on a pedestal in one of the school corridors for posterity!

As for the history of the V.I., it was fortunate that in 1962 I was able to persuade one of our recently qualified history graduates, who was also an Old Boy, to write a history* of the school, which I then made compulsory reading for all new admissions.

I also engaged in writing when I could find time, being mainly occupied on a more advanced book on the geography of Asia while I was at the V.I. While doing some field work for the book, which eventually sold over half a million copies, I visited Negri Sembilan one weekend in an attempt to find the exact location of the ancient portage which I knew existed somewhere between the rivers Serting and Muar, near Bahau. As I searched for the exact spot in the *belukar*, I unexpectedly came face to face with Tuanku Abdul Rahman, who had been the *Yam Tuan* or the ruler of Negri Sembilan while I was stationed at Kuala Pilah in 1946. He was now the *Agong* (or King) of Malaysia—indeed its first *Agong*. He was wearing a sarong. It was of course a surprise for both of us. I explained what I was up to, and he told me that he had a secluded rural bungalow near by. So he took me to his rural retreat, where he gave me a drink and I took

*Suntharalingam: *A History of the Victoria Institution* (published by the Victoria Institution).

his photograph. In due course I sent him a copy of the photograph and asked him to kindly autograph it for me. After a short while the photograph came back duly signed as requested. I was informed by his ADC that it was his last official act before he died in 1960.

The Victoria Institution was Malaya's first secondary school. After 1929, entry into the school was by a competitive examination only. At first it took the cream of its feeder schools the Batu Road School and the Pasar Road School; later it also creamed off the best from some of the girls' schools for its sixth forms. So those who gained entry were naturally very proud of their achievement and very proud of their school.

When I arrived at the Victoria Institution in 1956, it had the best science laboratories in the country and a well-deserved reputation as the leading science school in Malaya. This was due to the excellent work done by a series of head-masters, with scientific backgrounds, and all of them successful authors of scientific textbooks. They were F. Daniel, E. M. F. Payne and Arthur Atkinson. There were also several teachers who also excelled as authors of science textbooks, in particular my friend Arthur Godman. It is therefore not surprising that in 1955, of the ten V.I. candidates who passed the full Cambridge Higher School Certificate, all of them were Science students. There was not a single Arts student.

I was informed by the Director that I was being posted to the V.I. to boost the teaching of the Arts a bit, though I was determined that the teaching of Science should not suffer as a consequence of my appearance. Although the existing library was in many ways satisfactory, it was not adequate for sixth form work, especially for the Arts students. So I modernized and expanded it and air conditioned it as well; indeed on completion it was probably the best school library in South-East Asia! I felt confident, given the calibre of our Arts students, that if they were provided with the books they would deliver the goods. And so it turned out for the results were dramatic. Within a few years we began producing large numbers of students with full Cambridge Higher School Certificates in the Arts as well as in the Sciences. And as it turned out it was eventually the Arts students who appear to have achieved the most. Thus in

1955 the score for the full Cambridge Higher School Certificate
was Science 10, Arts 0; but in 1960 it was Science 26, Arts 37,
and in 1961 Science 48, Arts 49, thus making a total of 97
students with the full Cambridge Higher School Certificates.

These commendable results were not just the consequence
of first class science laboratories and an excellent library.
They were of course due to our outstanding students and to
the excellent teaching at all levels. We were fortunate in
having some excellent teachers. Thus on the Science side we
had Chong Yuen Shak (Physics), Sim Wong Kooi (Chemistry),
Yeong Siew Mun, Yeoh Oon Chye and Miss Floyd, as well as
several old and experienced Raffles graduates such as Lim
Eng Thye, Toh Boon Hua and the Indian graduate
S. C. Ayyar. On the Arts side we also had some good and
dedicated teachers such as John Doraisamy (Economics),
Dr Jones and Saw Chu Tong (History) and Lam Kok Hon
(Geography). Finally, we had some lady teachers such as the
lively minded Yvonne Stanley and the highly intelligent Mrs
J. Devadeson, and the expatriates, T. A. M. Bennett and Alec
Milne who set high standards in the teaching of English. It is
interesting to note that when on one occasion I had a visit
from one of the UK's most experienced inspector of schools,
he remarked that Chong Yuen Shak was the best teacher of
physics he had even seen! It was most unfortunate that this
gifted teacher should die at an early age.

But of course all this would not have been possible unless
the foundations of the pyramid had not been properly built.
And again we were fortunate in having excellent teachers
and I will mention a few of them, especially some of whom I
have fond memories.

C. R. Ananta Krishnan, BA (Hons) Madras was one of them.
He was a gentle, dedicated teacher of mathematics, who was
known to cry when his pupils failed a test. He was a veritable
Mr Chips—an Indian Mr Chips.

T. Ramachandran was another. He, too, was a dedicated
teacher, who specialized in teaching the small boys on their
first entry into the V.I., and instilled into them an understanding of the difference between right and wrong, and in a
pride in their new school. He was also a keen golfer and
attempted without success to improve my golf by presenting
me with his driver.

Then there was a group of old hands such as Harry Lau; T. J. Appadurai; Chew Ah Kong who looked after the rugby players; Ganga Singh who had spent most of his life at the V.I. and especially Richard Pavee, the highly efficient and long-serving school secretary. There were also birds of passage such as Gorbex Singh, MBE, best known for his sporting and courageous anti-Japanese activities during the war, and a bunch of up-and-coming young teachers, many of them with their roots in the Indian sub-continent such as S. T. Abraham, E. J. Lawrence now a well-known lawyer in Kuala Lumpur, Valentine Manuel, S. G. Durairaj and Ayadurai. Some of them were hard-working, but all of them were loyal colleagues. And there were three more, our hockey expert Yap Chai Seng and the hard-working and reliable Chan Bing Fai and Ho Sai Hoong.

Later many other enthusiastic and hard-working young teachers arrived on the scene such as Patrick Ng, a gifted artist; T. Rajaratnam and S. Peethamparan both all round sportsmen; Che Hasanuddin who ran our Cadet Corps with efficiency; Lim Heng Chek, an Olympic swimmer who taught our boys swimming and Che Othman bin Haji Mohd. Ali, a young dedicated teacher and a future Mr Chips. We also acquired a whole bevy of graduate lady teachers such as Miss Wong Yook Lin, Mrs Creedy, Che Fatimah Hashimah, Che Zahirah, Mrs Yiap Khin Yin, Mrs Eee, Mrs Tan Soo Hai, Mrs Teh Khoon Heng, Mrs Swallow and Miss Fay Siebel. Finally, but by no means least we had a welcome addition to our office staff in the highly efficient Anna Yap, who joined our loyal and hard-working Richard Pavee not only in preparing the school salary sheet, but also later in wedlock.

The V.I. then was most fortunate in the quality of its staff. It ensured that we stayed in front not only academically but on the field of sport. The influx of lady teachers did us no harm, for although they could not teach our boys rugby or cricket, they were more assiduous at marking essays than the men. So what we lost on the swings we made up on the roundabouts.

But we did have one letdown. One day a number of missing school library books were found in the library peon's house—a case as the Malays would say of *Pagar makan padi* (the fence eats the padi). But as the English would say, 'It is the exception that proves the rule.'

It is clear from what I have said so far that the V.I. had many exceptionally gifted and brilliant students. And with over two hundred boys in the sixth forms alone, it meant that to be a prefect was an exceptional achievement. Consequently, to be the Head Perfect, or School Captain as he was known at the V.I., was like being managing director of a multinational global company; it was in itself a sign of an exceptional personality. The School Captains during my headmastership were as follows:

Zain Azraai (the first task I performed when I arrived at the V.I. was to sign his leaving certificate), Lee Chong Keet, Phang Kow Weng, Mustafa bin Mohd. Ali, R. Krishna, Choo Min Hsiung, Chung Choeng Hoy, and Lim Chooi Tee. To be a Vice-Captain was also a distinction and some of those I remember are Isher Singh Sekhon, Khoo Choong Keow, Kok Wee Kiat, Chong Sun Yeh and especially Gan Kong Eng. Most of them have distinguished themselves since leaving school, while some have reached high office.

Thus Zain Azraai, now Tan Sri, is Secretary-General of the Ministry of Finance; Mustafa Mohd. Ali, now a Datuk is a director of Malaysia's largest multinational corporation—Sime Darby; Lee Chong Keat and Phang Kow Weng, medical practitioners in Sydney and Kuala Lumpur respectively while Lim Chooi Tee heads a highly successful firm of accountants.

During my seven-year reign, literally hundreds (over a hundred per year) of V.I. boys and some girls gained admission to universities, some of them in the United Kingdom, Australia, New Zealand and the USA but most of them to the University of Malaya in Singapore and Kuala Lumpur. Of these, several hundreds had passed the full Cambridge Higher School Certificate, an examination conducted of course in the English language.

Some of these students achieved astonishing academic results. Thus in 1956 one boy Ooi Boon Seng was awarded distinction in all eight of the subjects he took in the Cambridge School Certificate, while in 1958 two boys, Soo Suk Suet and Indran Devadeson also got distinctions in all the eight subjects they sat. An even more astonishing result was achieved by Foo Yeow Khean in 1961, for he was awarded distinctions in all the five subjects he sat at the full Cambridge Higher School Certificate examination.

There were also many who achieved excellence at school as sportsmen and in other ways. Thus some of our outstanding players at football were Amiruddin bin Liin, Mustafa Mohd. Ali, Thiruchelvam, Zamri bin Yahaya and Gan Kong Eng; at rugby Jaafar bin Sidek, Lee Heng, Koh Ah Guan, Choo Min Hsiung, and Lim Chooi Tee; at hockey Surjit Singh, Kirpal Singh, N. Sivaneethan, A. Ambikapathy, Khalid Haji Ismail; at cricket R. Sundralingam, R. Tharmalingam, S. Tharmaratnam, C. Thavaneswaram, Poon Yew Chin, Anandrajah and M. Rajasingam; at swimming Tan Lin Fook, Dickie May, Ho Wing, Lam Ah Lek and How Wan Hong; at badminton Martin Lee, Choo Min Hsuing, Chan Chor Keen, and Lim Boon Kuan and finally at athletics Krishna Rajaratnam, Chan Yew Kee, Wong Yin Fook, and Gan Kong Eng. It will be noted that most of our leading performers at cricket and hockey have Indian names!

As was to be expected, the V.I. did well on the games field. Our football, hockey and cricket teams, generally speaking, got the better of the opposition. We also had good rugby teams, but found it difficult to beat the Malay College; in fact I cannot ever remember beating them at rugby, for the Malays make good rugby players, just as the Indians are good at cricket and hockey.

If we excelled at anything it was probably on the running track. I introduced a cross-country run for the whole school soon after I arrived, and a system of standards for the different distances, which all boys were encouraged to achieve. Consequently, we had some good relay teams.

Of course school relay teams always conjured up some hero worship, and the V.I. relay teams were no exception. Some of our best results were achieved between 1958 and 1961. Thus in 1958 the school relay team consisting of Wong Yin Fook, Lee Yuen Hon, Kok Lit Yoong and P. Nathan broke the Malayan Schools record for 4 × 100 metres. One of the most exciting was the relay race in 1960 against the Federation Military College which we looked like winning, until our Athletics Captain Chan Yew Kee dropped the baton! But possibly our best relay team was the one consisting of Eddy Lee, Syed Nor, Ghazali Yusof and Kenny Siebel. They broke the Combined Schools Federation Record for 4 × 400 metres in 1961 at the Merdeka Stadium.

Finally, there were those who distinguished themselves in other ways, for we had a wide range of activities, including over forty clubs and societies, such as a Cadet Corps, a Society of Drama, a Chess Club, an Aeromodelling Club, a Debating Society, a Geographical Society and so on. If a boy had a talent, we made every effort to develop it. Thus the following revealed themselves as gifted actors: Alladin bin Hashim, Maureen Siebel, Kok Wee Kiat, Fuziah binte Datuk Ahmad, Krishen Jit, Shirley Loo, G. Jeyanathan and the following as debaters: Kok Wee Kiat, Baljit Singh, Ooi Boon Seng, Seto Kuan Mun, Foo Yeow Khean, Sheila Sodhy and many others.

A welcome development in 1957 was the construction of a hostel for Sixth Form students, especially for those from Pahang, Terengganu and Kelantan where facilities for post school certificate studies did not exist. It was unique for it was a hostel for boys of all races. As the hostel was located within a hundred metres from of my house, I got to know the boys very well. Some of the first inmates were Mustafa Mohd. Ali, Kok Wee Kiat (Selangor) and Koh Ah Guan and his brother Koh Ah Siong (from Pahang). Then later came Zamri bin Yahya, Zainuddin bin Awang Ngah (Pahang); Mohd. Zaman Khan, Foo Say Ghee and Tengku Halim (Kelantan) and of course many others whose names I cannot now remember.

I had some experience of hostels, and found that they could be a hot bed for discontent, the trouble being usually over the quality of the food. So I delegated the running of the V.I. hostel to the boys. It was an experiment in democracy and it worked very well. I noticed with interest that the committee in charge of food was frequently voted out of power!

One evening just before dusk I received an urgent message from the hostel. One of the hostel boys had seen a man lurking in the bushes within the hostel compound and near my house; they suspected he was a burglar. So I made my way cautiously to the scene armed with my Luger pistol, and suddenly found myself face to face with a Chinese. As soon as he saw my Luger, he suddenly produced a pistol, but as he made no move to use it, I did likewise. When I said, 'Who are you?', to my surprise he replied, 'I am a CID Officer.' And then when I asked him what he was doing in our compound, he explained apologetically that he was waiting to ambush some members of a Chinese Secret Society who were about to commit a robbery.

After this incident I decided that the hostel boys also ought to be in a position to protect themselves against any such robbers or gangsters that might present themselves. I could not arm them with shotguns, so each boy kept a long piece of wood under his bed. Zaman Khan, the hostel Captain, was in charge, and I also instructed him that if I blew my police whistle at night, he should come to my rescue with his platoon of hostel boys. Unfortunately, much to their disappointment, they were never to see action. Some of those hostel boys were and still are after thirty years my best friends. But of course today they have more serious things to attend to. For example, Zaman Khan is now the Head of the CID and a Datuk!

With so many talented boys at the Victoria Institution, it is not surprising that large numbers of them have had very distinguished careers. I have already mentioned two former school captains Tan Sri Zain Azraai and Datuk Mustafa Mohd. Ali, but there were many others who have had similarly distinguished careers, so I will mention a few that I know of. Among them are Ooi Boon Teck and Tan Hong Siang respectively Professor of Engineering at the University of Montreal, Canada and the University of Malaya, Kuala Lumpur; Ooi Boon Seng, Professor of Medicine at the University of Washington, USA; Alladin Hashim, now a Datuk and formerly Director-General of FELDA; Kok Wee Kiat, now a Datuk and former Deputy Minister of Trade and Industry; Khalid Haji Ismail, Secretary-General, Ministry of Culture and Tourism and Ahmad Shamsudin, Director of the Mines Department, Kuala Lumpur.

Then there are scores who have been successful in business such as T. Teow Yong, Managing Director of Cycle and Carriage, Kuala Lumpur; Darwis bin Daek, Managing Director of Malayan Industrial Development and Finance; Foo Yeow Khean with IBM Australia; Nik Ibrahim Nik Kamil, Chief Executive of the *New Straits Times*; Gan Kong Eng, General Manager of Food Co. Singapore; Chan Yew Kee with ICI Malaya; Shirley Loo, Company Secretary, Development Bank of Singapore; Azlan Hashim, Deputy

Chairman of Arab-Malaysian Bank; Benny Yeo, Managing Director of Caldbeck McGregor; Aziz Mohamed, a Director of Boustead and so on; while others, many others, have distinguished themselves in the professions such as Koh Ah Guan, Deputy Director of the Weather Bureau; Krishen Jit, Assistant Professor of History at the University of Malaya, Kuala Lumpur; Kamal Din and Hajiedean Majid as architects; innumerable doctors and lawyers as well as members of the armed forces including General Tan Sri Hashim bin Mohd. Ali, Chief of the Armed Forces in Malaya.

We also had at the V.I. a few boys who were admitted by special entry. They were special cases such as the sons of expatriate European government officers, sons of ambassadors and so on. They were admitted provided they passed my intelligence tests, and they all did very well. Thus Richard Forsyth, whose father had been the District Officer, Kuala Lipis during my time there and in the hectic days of the early 1950s, and John Carbonell whose father was the Commissioner of Police spent some time at the V.I., and both played cricket for our first XI. Then came Amirol Razif and his brother whose father was the Indonesian Ambassador, and Likit Hongladorum whose father was the Thai Ambassador. Likit knew next to no English when he was admitted, but he was a very popular boy and soon became fluent in English and even gained entry later on into Trinity College, Cambridge—his father's old college. I called unexpectedly to see him at Cambridge while I was on leave, and found him entertaining a pretty Swedish girl—'teaching her English,' he explained.

But our most celebrated special entry was Hassanal Bolkiah, the eldest son of the Sultan of Brunei, and his younger brother Mohamed. I had a friendly introductory meeting with Sultan Haji Omar at his palace in Kuala Lumpur. He explained that although he had himself been a pupil at the Malay College at Kuala Kangsar, he wished his sons to go to a school where the boys were of all races, and to the Victoria Institution because it was the most famous school in Malaya! The Sultan was a fairly small man but obviously a highly intelligent and diplomatic Malay, as his complimentary remarks about the Victoria Institution would suggest. He also added that he had heard that I was a famous author

of geography books, and said that he too had written some
books, and took me to a cupboard in the palace, where there
were several piles of them; he gave me one as a gift.

The conversation was entirely in Malay, but as we were
seated at a royal distance from one another, and the Sultan
spoke very softly, and I was slightly deaf as the result of
many Japanese *bintoks* which I had acquired during the
Japanese war, I had some difficulty in hearing what he had
to say. Fortunately the Sultan had arranged for a mutual
friend, Osman bin Talib, a former MCS officer who I knew
well from my Ipoh days, to be present. Osman explained that
the Sultan was also worried about the personal safety of his
boys, for he had read in the newspapers that there were
secret society gangs at the V.I. He was worried that his boys
might be kidnapped and held to ransom, so would I please
agree to his sons having bodyguards while they attended
school, in the classroom! Although this was a most unusual
request, I readily agreed but suggested it would be better if
the bodyguards' presence was discreet, and not in the classroom, and promised to make the necessary arrangements. I
also said I would make some additional arrangements of my
own to protect the two boys.

I decided that the most important thing to do was not to
draw undue attention to them in any way, and to treat them
like the other boys. I persuaded the two Brunei Malay bodyguards to hang about in the shaded car park near the boys'
classrooms and pretend they were car drivers waiting for their
owners to return. I paid no obvious public attention to the
two boys, but took a number of discreet precautions, for
example, entry and exit from the school compound was
normally by one gate only, where a Sikh *jaga* lived permanently. I also gave the *jaga* instructions that if he heard my
police whistle being blown at any time, he was to close the
gate immediately. I also formed my own highly mobile force
of schoolboys for use in an emergency, created in the first
place for other reasons, but eminently suitable as a strike
force against any thugs who might enter our compound and
also more mobile than the Sultan's bodyguards! It was
called Club 21, and consisted mainly of our top sportsmen.

I also got assistance from some of our Old Boys, who I
allowed to use part of our grounds once a week for athletics

training, such as sprinting and throwing the javelin. One afternoon a gang of youths entered the school compound on bicycles on an intimidating patrol and looking for trouble. I blew my police whistle, the old *jaga* went to shut the gates at the main entrance, and an Old Boy with a javelin threw and narrowly missed penetrating one of the hurriedly retreating gangster trespassers! These precautions had the desired effect. We had very few undesirable intruders, for they knew that although they might be able to get in quite easily, it might not be so easy to get out!

Meanwhile the Brunei boys, as they were generally referred to, settled down to school life. Hassanal, the future Sultan of Brunei was a shy, friendly and popular boy, who endeared himself to me by becoming a promising rugby player and indeed played for the Under-15 School XV at a later date. Mohamed was an intelligent boy notable for his invisibility, which helped with the matter of his security.

Because Hassanal was a bit bigger than most of the other boys in his class, some of his detractors have suggested that he was in some way immature. This was far from being the case. His early education had been partly at the hands of a private tutor, and so he had not benefited from the discipline of a regular primary education. In the circumstances he did quite well, and together with his brother, held his own in spite of our high academic standards. Apart from rugby, Hassanal's main interest was the Cadet Corps, so I was not surprised when he later opted to go to the Royal Military College, Sandhurst. But I have two regrets. One is that because of the calls of duty in Brunei he was not able to go on to a university such as Cambridge, and the other is that circumstances have prevented him becoming a constitutional monarch like the Malaysian Sultans.

Finally, last but not least the V.I. had as sixth form pupils about fifty or sixty girls. Far from causing problems, the girls made the school a more lively and cheerful place. They caused no dilemmas, they were hard-working and co-operative. They were almost too good to be true. Some of the outstanding ones that I can now recall were Leong Siew Mun, now Chief Librarian at the University of Malaya, Loo Ngai Seong, Fuziah binte Datuk Ahmad and Aloyah binte Rahmen, all Head Girls with brains and attractive personalities. But there were many others who obviously had bright futures ahead of them. One of them was Rafidah Aziz, now Datuk Seri, and the Minister for Trade and Industry.

There was one notable development in 1956 and 1957—the enormous Merdeka Stadium was built close by and at the back of the school. A huge hole was dug in the ground in order to create a giant sunken ampitheatre, by monster earth-moving machines which made monster-like noises. In fact the noise was so terrifying that many teachers removed their classes on to the *padang*. I visited the scene of this activity almost every day and got to know the ingenious chief architect in charge, S. E. Jewkes, very well. We were very tolerant of the disturbance and he very appreciative of our co-operation, and so we consequently benefited, for he built a new car park for us free of charge from some of the excavated earth, and also levelled much rough ground that had previously been unusable!

The Malays have a saying *Bunga yang harum ada juga durinya* (The sweet-smelling flower also has its thorns). And so it was with the Victoria Institution, for although most of our pupils were admirable in all ways, we did in fact have a few bad eggs. For soon after my arrival, I discovered that we had a few boys who belonged to gangs associated with Chinese secret societies. Such gangs were not innocent groups of boys, but gangs with criminal activities.

Lawlessness and violence have been caused by Chinese secret societies in Malaya for over a hundred and fifty years. Consequently, when soon after my arrival at the Victoria Institution in 1956, I discovered that some of our boys were members of these gangs and extorting money from fellow schoolboys, that some teachers were aware of it but had not brought the matter to my attention because they were frightened of the consequences, I decided that strong measures were called for.

My investigations also revealed that the position was more serious than I had first anticipated. Some of my gangsters belonged to Gang 21, an offshoot of the *Ang Bin Hoey* Triad Secret Society. So recalling the old English saying 'From small acorns mighty oaks grow', I decided to nip matters in the bud and caned six boys who we discovered were members of Gang 21, though the punishment meted out did not merit the extravagant newspaper headlines which appeared the following day in the *Straits Times* as follows: 'Screams ring out at Gang boys' caning'.

The Chinese Inspector in charge of the Secret Societies branch of the CID Kuala Lumpur also enlightened me on the position in Selangor. There were he said two main secret societies in Selangor: *Ang Bin Hoey* and *Wah Kei.*

The *Ang Bin Hoey* was a Triad society with of course a long history of criminal activities such as gang robbery, murder, intimidation and the extraction of protection money from unfortunate Chinese shopkeepers, rickshaw pullers, stallkeepers and so on. In Kuala Lumpur most of its members were Hokkiens.

It also appeared that the lawless *Ang Bin Hoey* had several criminal gangs associated with it. They were (i) the 08 or 108 Gang (ii) the 21 Brothers (or Gang 21) consisting mainly of Chinese, Indian and sometimes Malay youths and (iii) the 360 Gang.

The *Wah Kei* was mainly a Cantonese secret society, different from the Triad *Ang Bin Hoey* and normally in conflict with it, as each society attempted to gain ascendancy over the other. However, the *Wah Kei* had a less criminal record, and their clubs were frequently purely social and always anti-Communist.

Thus enlightened, I was more than ever determined to rid the V.I. of its gangster hooligans. The impending celebrations to mark the Independence of Malaya in August 1957 resulted in a police crackdown on secret societies and all the known secret society gangsters were arrested. But this relatively peaceful state of affairs did not last long, for 1958 and 1959 saw a revival of secret society activity, so much so that in February 1959, Tunku Abdul Rahman, the Prime Minister, spoke at length and warned the country against the growing menace of secret societies. This coincided with a fresh outbreak of gangs at the V.I., but I had by now gained some experience of dealing with them and had formed my own gang – Club 21.* Membership of Club 21 was reserved for our best athletes and achievers; it was for exceptional merit. I discovered that our juvenile gangsters belonged almost entirely to Gang 21 and the 08 Gang, so by playing one off against the other I gained much useful information. The procedure I used was the one my own housemaster successfully used when I was at school, and that was to isolate the culprits in a separate room, persuade them to confess, and suggest that one was informing on the other. But in my case I made sure that they all confessed in writing and so could not retract at a later date. I soon found that members of Gang 21 were eager to tell me which of our schoolboys were members of the 08 Gang and of their evil deeds, and vice versa!

So in due course I was able to discover the names of most of our boys who were in gangs. This time round I netted about twelve juvenile gangsters, about equally divided between Gang 21 and the 08 Gang. Most of them had been monthly subscribing members paying varying amounts of money to the head gangster, and indulging in various kinds of misbehaviour as well as the intimidation of their fellow schoolboys and relieving them of fountain pens, pocket money and so on. A few indulged in more serious crimes. One for example went to Bentong on a special mission to attack and beat up a member of the *Wah Kei* Society for a fee of fifty dollars. Favourite habitats of our boy gangsters were Imbi Road, Campbell Road, Pudu and so on. I was loath to expel such boys, but endeavoured to change their ways by the liberal administration of the old-fashioned remedy always kept in a Headmaster's office.

---

*Membership of Club 21 was for those who had enhanced the good name of the school by any kind of exceptional meritorious achievement. The following were its members between 1958–62: Kok Lit Yoong, Chan Yew Kee, N. Sivaneetham, Cheong Yong Kuay, Goh Chin Leng, Bobby Lee, A. Krishen Jit, Billy Tan, M. Shanmughalingham, Chua Lai Hock, Shariful bin Azman, D. Hector, Leong Ming Tuck, Fan Yew Seng, S. Thiruchelvam, C. Thavaneswaren, Lim Chooi Tee, Sha Kam Choy, Chew Meng Ian, Thiruchandran, Ho Wing, Cheong Yong Young, Raja Zaini Ismail, Gan Kong Eng, Kenny Siebel, Arumugam, Zamri Yahya, Bakhtiar Tamin, Indran Devadeson, Felix Gabriel, Lam Ah Lek, Tengku Halim, Roslan Thiruchandran, Foo Yeow Khean, Thanabalan, Ghazali Yusof, Yaacob, Eddy Lee, Ghazali Mahyuddin, V. Manikavisagam, Koh Tong Chiu, Lee Yat Loong and Kamal Din.

Of course many claimed that they had been forced to join through fear, so I decided that the only solution was to create a greater fear, and rather rashly warned that in future anybody found to be a member of Gang 21 would be caned 21 times, 08 Gang 8 times and so on. It must have had some effect for the only one caught thereafter was a member of the 08 Gang. He was a rather small Chinese boy, and when I confronted him with his inevitable punishment, he admitted he was a member of a gang, but explained that the number of his gang was not 08 but .08! I was intrigued by the argument but not convinced. There were three canes in the office, for use on juvenile gangsters: a thick one, a medium thick one and a thin one. I allowed him to choose his cane so that there should be no animosity between us. Unfortunately he chose the thin one, that is, for him it was the worst choice.

Lyn was very much against corporal punishment, and I also found the practice of it distasteful. However, I knew I would be failing in my duty, not only to the parents but to the errant boys themselves, if I did not prescribe the necessary medicine. Fortunately, it had the desired results, for although secret societies continued to flourish in Kuala Lumpur, I had no more cases of our boys joining their gangs. Other schools were not so fortunate.

Of course there was some risk involved in taking a strong line against such gangs, and I received many threats. For example, one evening I had a telephone call and had a short conversation with an adult voice as follows:

Voice: You assaulted some of our members yesterday. We are going to come and get you.

Me: Why don't you come tonight?

Voice: Why tonight?

Me: Because I shall be waiting for you with my Luger pistol!

Such conversations were not conducive to sleep. So I took precautions. During the periods when I thought I must be unpopular with the gangs, I slept with my Luger pistol under my pillow; Awang my faithful Malay servant, who was always longing for a fight, slept with a loaded shotgun near his bed; the dog was left loose at night to run around the house; and the old Sikh night watchman was encouraged to stay awake.

Nothing happened until one night, when the Sikh watchman woke me up at about 2 a.m., and explained in Malay that he had caught two *orang jahat* (or dangerous persons), a man and a woman, in the school car park in the dark and had brought them to me. When I asked them, out of my bedroom window, to explain their presence in the school grounds so late at night, the man (a Chinese) answered out of the darkness in perfect English, 'I am an Old Boy, sir. I am very proud of my old school and I wanted to show it to my girlfriend!'

Malaya achieved its independence or *Merdeka* on August 31, 1957. It was achieved in a very civilized way. Everybody took part in the celebrations. There were no riots and nobody was hurt. It was achieved without a bloody conflict because the friendly and amiable Tunku Abdul Rahman charmed the British Government in London. They found the requests of this polite and reasonable Malay difficult to resist. I had a special mug made for the V.I. to celebrate the occasion, as I thought it would be useful for holding cold drinks in a hot country. But most of the boys used it for holding water during their art lessons.

Many of the expatriate colonial officers were required to retire, but some were invited to stay. I was interviewed on the subject by the Minister of Education, Rahman Talib, who was of course an old friend, and had once worked under me as an Inspector of Malay Schools in Pahang. During the interview, he invited me to stay. I then mentioned that I had expected him to say that regretfully he wished me to retire. So when I asked him why, he replied, 'Better the devil you know, Lewis, than the one you don't!' That seemed a good reason, so I stayed another six years.

In many ways the next few years were the most interesting during my sojourn in Malaysia. Many embassies were built in Kuala Lumpur, and each embassy had at least one social function every year. So Lyn and I found ourselves invited to at least one reception a fortnight. One of them was at the invitation of the High Commissioner for New Zealand, the Maori Colonel Bennett, to meet the Prime Minister of New Zealand, Mr Nash.

There was a very long queue of distinguished foreign Ambassadors, High Commissioners, Ministers, Heads of Departments and so on, waiting to meet the Prime Minister of New Zealand. When Lyn and I reached Mr Nash, Colonel Bennett introduced me and added, 'Dr Lewis is a Welshman.' The tired octogenerian Mr Nash suddenly came to life and said, 'So I suppose you think it was a try.' He was referring to a try Wales scored against New Zealand in 1911 and which had been in dispute ever since! He then went on to tell me a long story of how he had been a member of the Commonwealth War Cabinet in 1916, and how he had visited Cardiff and was met at the railway station by the Lady Mayor of Cardiff, and how he had also greeted her in the same way. The reply he said was most unexpected, for she said, 'Mr Nash, it was a try and my husband scored it.' Of course it took quite a long time to tell the story, and those in the queue behind were exhausted from waiting. Among them were the British High Commissioner Sir G. Tory and Datuk Razak, the Deputy Prime Minister as he then was, and both of whom I knew well. They were both most inquisitive to know what we had in common, but I did not let on especially as I knew Datuk Razak's interest was hockey!

My years at the V.I. were therefore full of interest, what with a thousand or so of Malaya's best young brains to take care of, the odd juvenile gangster to deal with, the occasional threat over the telephone and the socially pleasant interludes at one of the innumerable receptions, and cocktail parties then prevalent in Kuala Lumpur, which some found a bore, but I found a pleasant change.

Of course we had a circle of friends that we visited from time to time. One of them whose company I always enjoyed was Captain Salleh bin Haji Sulaiman, formerly State Secretary and for a while *Mentri Besar* of Negri Sembilan, but now in retirement acting as a magistrate in Klang. He was a charming popular Malay, a good friend of mine, and a perfect host. He spoke perfect English, and had a great sense of humour. In the entrance hall of his house in Klang, he displayed an English bowler hat and a rolled up umbrella ready, he explained, in case he had to go to London!

Lyn and I were well aware that a first trip overseas could be a traumatic experience for young Malayan students, especially if they came from a rural background. So she often invited the occasional boy or girl on their first visit to England to dinner where she would introduce them to the mysteries of knives and forks, so that they would not be embarrassed when first confronted by an invitation to a formal European dinner party. Her advice was when in doubt, wait and see what the others do. In any case the natural good manners of most Asians and especially the Malays was always one of their greatest assets when they went overseas.

Lyn would also warn them about the peculiar habits of the English, and explain that the Englishman's reserve should not be confused with unfriendliness. She would tell them about my former schoolboy from Kuala Pilah, Noordin bin Keling, and how when he was a student in England, he once travelled for many hours from the north of England to London by train, sitting opposite a well-dressed Englishman, who said nothing all the way, but on reaching Kings Cross (in London) got up and shook Noordin warmly by the hand, commented on what a nice journey it had been, and wished him goodbye!

In 1960 my daughter Megan surprised me by passing the entrance examination for entry into St. Paul's Girls' School, London. It was rather like a boy passing the entrance examination into Form 1 at the V.I., that is, it was no small achievement. Megan had been brought up at Kuala Lipis, Pahang, and her first language was Malay (not Welsh); indeed on one occasion, I found Datuk Razak speaking to her in Malay and being highly amused about something. So when I asked him the cause for his amusement, he said she spoke very good Malay, and then with a smile, very good Pahang Malay!* As Lyn had also been to St. Paul's Girls' School, we decided that it would not be right to deny her the benefits of an education at one of England's top girls' schools, so when I went on leave in 1961, we decided to leave her behind. But we soon found this a rather distressing experience, and so I decided to retire in 1962.

At about this time it became clear that in future the Victoria Institution would have to finance some of its development out of its own resources. So in 1961 I established the V.I. *Endowment Fund* which I hoped would in due course

---

*Megan eventually went to the School of Oriental Studies, London where she obtained an M. A. in South-East Asian Studies including Malay.

provide the school with a steady income. I anticipated that it would prove to be a popular way for wealthy former pupils to help their old school financially, for all donations to the fund are free of Malaysian Income Tax. I visited one of our Chinese millionaire Old Boys and he promised in due course to make a substantial contribution. Unfortunately soon after, he was killed in an air crash. When I retired, the fund held about $10,000 but that was nearly thirty years ago; today I am told by the Headmaster it is $133,000!

My last Speech Day took place in April 1962. It was attended by many distinguished guests and visitors. The distinguished guests included: Tun Razak, the Deputy Prime Minister and Sir Alexander Oppenheim, the Vice-Chancellor of the University of Malaya. The distinguished visitors, who were mainly parents of boys and girls at the school, included several Ambassadors and Ministers. It was a very successful occasion. It was also a memorable occasion for me, for during his address, my old friend Tun Razak gave me what might be described as my unexpected testimonial, as follows:

> I understand this is the last Speech Day for the Headmaster, Dr Lewis. I have known Dr Lewis for many years since I was in Pahang and then I saw a lot of his work when I was Minister of Education. He is one of the last expatriate Education Officers to remain in this country. His interest in education and the services that he has rendered to this country in this field over many years will long be remembered not only by the many old boys that he has taught throughout this country but by parents and well-wishers.
>
> I would like on behalf of the Government to wish him good fortune in his well-earned retirement and to say that he will always be welcomed to see us in this country whenever he can find the time to do so.

I have visited Malaysia several times since I retired, and on one occasion met Tun Razak as his own retirement was drawing near. So I asked him what he intended to do after his retirement. His reply, probably in jest, was, 'I hope to become the manager of the Jengka Triangle.' This of course was the huge oil palm estate developed in central Pahang for the benefit of landless Malays, like my former protégé from Ulu Tembeling

Mohd. Nazar, which was a huge success, and was the brainchild of Tun Razak. But he unfortunately died before his time, though I am told he managed to see his favourite English football club Arsenal play a few days before he died. My last few months in Malaysia were spent in innumerable farewell tea parties, Chinese dinners, speeches and most dangerous of all many *Yam Sengs*. It was also spent in more formal farewells, for example, a farewell with the *Agong*, His Majesty Syed Putra, formally the Raja of Perlis and also formerly my schoolboy at the Penang Free School in 1938–39 (see Chapter 3). It was arranged that Lyn, my daughters Megan and Rhiannon and myself should all meet him at the *Agong*'s *Istana*, and he invited us to tea. I had not seen him for 23 years, when he called me 'Sir', and I called him Syed Putra, so I wondered how our meeting would go. But I needn't have worried, for as soon as we met he said, 'Let's dispense with formalities, Lewis,' and so there was no embarrassment, just typical Malay politeness.

Another most memorable farewell was when we took leave of everybody at the railway station, Kuala Lumpur on September 4, 1962. There must have been a couple of thousand friends, many of them my old staff and pupils to see us off. The platform ticket machines ran out of tickets, but as the Indian station master had a son at the Victoria Institution, he opened the floodgates and so all and sundry poured on to the departure platform for Singapore free of charge, for as he well said, 'What to do, man.'

The School Cadet Corps had provided a smart Guard of Honour to see us off, and as I went round to inspect it, I spied Private Hassanal Bolkiah. As I knew he would one day be the Sultan of Brunei, and he was showing interest in my favourite game rugby, I had a word with him and gave him some suitable advice about working hard at school and not wasting his pocket money. It was only some years later that I discovered that he had done that and had become the wealthiest man in the world while I had been moving in the opposite direction.

The departure from Kuala Lumpur was a traumatic experience, for I was leaving behind not only hundreds indeed thousands of friends, and a country which had become home to me for about a quarter of a century, but also so many other things which had become part of my life such as *'Bangun, Tuan'* (Get up, sir) from my Malay servant every morning, Sunday curries, cool misty mornings, torrential thunderstorms, house lizards and so on. But what I think I missed most of all were the ordinary unsophisticated people especially the polite Malays in their colourful sarongs, the industrious Chinese and their so-called 'sundry goods' shops, the garrulous Indians in their *dhotis* and last but not least the bee-like buzzing of a thousand schoolboys. And of course, I had left behind a part of myself, I mean of course, a probable son, on the slopes of that small hill in Kuala Pilah, in the care of the legendary *'Datuk Gaung'*.

GLOSSARY

agong (M), the King of Malaysia
bach (Welsh), a term of endearment
barang (M), things, luggage
belukar (M), secondary jungle
bin (M), son of
binte (M), daughter of
baju (M), a kind of shirt
bintok (Japanese), face slap or punch
cangkul (M), a hoe
dato or datuk, (M) Honorary Malay title
gambo (Welsh), a kind of horsedrawn cart
gaji (M), wages
haj (M), pilgrimage to Mecca
haji (M), title for Malays who have performed the
    pilgrimage
imam (M), leader of a mosque community
istana (M), palace used by Malay royalty
Jawi (M), the Malay (modified Arabic) script
kampong, (M), Malay village
kerbok (Semelai), crocodile
mata mata, (M) policeman
mandor (M), head labourer
munshi (M), language teacher
mukim (M), administrative sub-division of a district
penghulu (M), headman, usually of a group of mukims
punkah (M), a large cloth overhanging a dining-table
    which keeps the diners cool when the punkah is
    activated
persatuan (M), association or society
padang (M), field or park
P.J.K. (Pingat Jasa Kebaktian), a Malaysian State
    award for long and distinguished service

Rumi (M), Latin script (as opposed to Malay Arabic script)

sarong (M), a cloth worn by Malays round the middle and tucked in round the waist

songkok (M), Malay hat

sungai (M), river or stream

syce (M), driver

Sikh jaga (M), Sikh watchman

S. W. E. C. State War Executive committee

Tan Sri (M), very high honorary title

tukang kebun (M), gardener

tukang air (M), water carrier

tukang masak (M), cook

Tun (M), very high honorary title

ugama (M), religion

yam seng (Chinese), empty your glasses

zakat (M), a religious tax

(M) = Malay

INDEX